Sentence Dynamics

Sentence Dynamics

An English Skills Workbook

SIXTH EDITION

Constance Immel

West Los Angeles College, Emeritus

Florence Sacks

West Los Angeles College, Emeritus

PEARSON
Longman

New York Boston San Francisco
London Toronto Sydney Tokyo Singapore Madrid
Mexico City Munich Paris Cape Town Hong Kong Montreal

Senior Vice President and Publisher: Joseph Opiela
Senior Acquisitions Editor: Susan Kunchandy
Senior Supplements Editor: Donna Campion
Senior Marketing Manager: Melanie Craig
Production Manager: Ellen MacElree
Project Coordination, Text Design, and Electronic Page Makeup: Nesbitt Graphics, Inc.
Cover Design Manager: John Callahan
Cover Designer: Jo DePinho
Senior Manufacturing Buyer: Al Dorsey
Printer and Binder: Courier
Cover Printer: Phoenix Color Corporation

Please visit us at http://www.ablongman.com

ISBN 0-321-14559-3

1 2 3 4 5 6 7 8 9 10—CRK—07 06 05 04

To community college students
who have shown that they can
achieve academic excellence given
encouragement and opportunity.

Brief Contents

Detailed Contents

Preface

The sixth edition of *Sentence Dynamics* retains many features of the previous edition. We have successfully used the material in the first five editions of *Sentence Dynamics* in our own writing classes, and we believe that the clearly worded definitions and examples, together with the variety of exercises, can help students in developmental writing courses, in English-as-a-second-language classes, and in writing laboratories and tutor-assisted classes.

To help students write clear, error-free sentences, the sixth edition of *Sentence Dynamics* features:

- **Thorough coverage** of key areas of grammar.
- **Clear explanations** with a minimum of grammatical terms.
- **Definitions** at the beginning of each chapter to serve as a reference guide.
- An **abundant variety of exercises**—multiple choice, sentence completion, sentence expansion, and original sentence generation.
- **Chapter reviews, lesson reviews, practice tests, summaries,** and **sentence combining** based on the skill presented in each chapter.
- A comprehensive **Instructor's Manual** with **answers to all text exercises,** a **test bank,** and **additional writing assignments.**
- **Group Activities** that encourage students to consult with one another as they work through some of the writing assignments.

New to This Edition

The changes we have made to the sixth edition of *Sentence Dynamics* are in keeping with our philosophy that students at this level learn best when they are actively engaged in the learning process. Therefore, we keep the explanatory material short, but we provide extensive examples and exercises that demonstrate the principle. Thus, the students are never faced with long, complicated explanations that are difficult to understand.

In Chapter 2, Verbs, we added new material on irregular verbs and moved the list of irregular verbs from the back of the text to the chapter on verbs. We also added instruction, examples, and exercises on the verbs *lie* and *lay* and *sit* and *set.*

In Chapter 3, Understanding the Parts of the Sentence, we moved the lesson on prepositions to earlier in the chapter to emphasize the importance of recognizing the prepositional phrase as an aid in identifying the subject and verb. We also added a second list of prepositions.

In Chapter 4, Adjectives and Adverbs, we emphasized the differences between adjectives and adverbs. We inserted additional practice exercises on choosing between adjectives and adverbs, which are commonly misused.

In Chapter 9, we moved the section on usage to the beginning of the chapter to provide students with needed practice in discriminating between words that sound or look alike. We deleted the sections on the hyphen, the dash, italics, and abbreviations to decrease the number of less frequently used topics.

Chapter 10, Writing a Paragraph, has been revised so as to follow the natural development from sentence to paragraph to longer writing assignments. It still includes a section on the writer's voice as well as a section on keeping a journal. We have expanded the coverage on the search for ideas, major and minor support, outlines, the topic sentence, methods used to develop paragraphs, unity, coherence, and the need to proofread and revise a draft before submitting an assignment. Furthermore, we have referred the student to the material in this chapter in the Writing Assignments' specific **step-by-step procedures** throughout the first nine chapters.

Grammar Tip boxes, Spelling Tip boxes, and **Writing Tip boxes** have been added in each chapter to help students focus on important information.

Editing Practices have been added throughout the chapters and at the end of each chapter Practice Test, as well as in the Appendixes.

Group Activities were inserted to enable students to complete projects together as well as check their work with each other.

Combining Sentence Exercises were added as lessons in each chapter, and we provided additional instruction on the relevance to the information given in each chapter.

Writing Assignments were changed to support the material taught in each chapter, and we added references to the instruction in **Chapter 10** to clarify methods of paragraph organization.

In the **Appendixes,** we replaced the Readings with additional editing practices on sentences and paragraphs.

A **Progress Chart** has been provided on the inside cover to help the student become more independent and to see areas of improvement or areas to work on during the semester.

Most of the exercises are in paragraph form or contain sentences all on one topic. They cover a wide range of subjects. The new topics we have supplied for writing assignments in each chapter should interest students, who then should be able to express opinions about them, based upon their own reading and observation. As in earlier editions of *Sentence Dynamics,* we have chosen expository topics rather than narrative or descriptive assignments. These topics include material on **public issues, popular culture,** and **matters of scientific interest.** We believe that students at this level should be learning how to write with the objectivity they must demonstrate in their college classes and in their careers.

Instructor Supplements

The **Instructor's Manual and Test Book** (ISBN 0-321-14561-5) contains material for the classroom in an easy-to-photocopy format. It includes teaching suggestions and an answer key to all exercises, Group Activities, Editing Practices, and tests. We have provided three different chapter tests for each of Chapters 1 through 9, a midterm exam, a final exam, and additional suggested writing assignments.

Printed Test Bank for Developmental Writing.   Features more than 5,000 questions in all areas of writing, from grammar to paragraphing through essay writing, research, and documentation (0-321-08486-1).

Electronic Test Bank for Developmental Writing.   Instructors simply choose questions from the electronic test bank, then print out the completed test for distribution OR offer the test online (0-321-08117-X).

Diagnostic and Editing Tests, Sixth Edition.   This collection of diagnostic tests helps instructors assess students' competence in standard written English to determine placement or to gauge progress. (Paper: 0-321-19647-3. CD: 0-321-19645-7).

Competency Profile Test Bank, Seventh Edition.   This series of objective tests cover 10 general areas of English competency, including fragments; comma splices and run-ons; pronouns; commas; and capitalization. Each test is available in remedial, standard, and advanced versions (0-321-02224-6).

CLAST Test Package, Fourth Edition.   These two, 40-item objective tests evaluate students' readiness for the Florida CLAST exams. Strategies for teaching CLAST preparedness are included (0-321-01950-4).

The Longman Instructor's Planner.   This planner includes weekly and monthly calendars, student attendance and grading rosters, space for contact information, Web references, an almanac, and blank pages for notes (0-321-09247-3).

Student Supplements

My Skills Lab (www.ablongman/myskillslab).   This website houses all media tools for developmental English (reading, writing, and study skills) in one place: Avoiding Plagiarism, Exercise Zone, Research Navigator, Longman Writer's Warehouse, Reading Roadtrip, Longman Vocabulary Website, and Longman Study Skills Website (0-321-26323-5).

Research Navigator Guide for English, by H. Eric Branscomb & Linda R. Barr.   Designed to teach students how to conduct high-quality online research and to document it properly, Research Navigator guides provide discipline-specific academic resources; in addition to helpful tips on the writing process, online research, and finding and citing valid sources. Free when packaged with any Longman text, Research Navigator guides include an access code to Research Navigator™—providing access to thousands of academic journals and periodicals, the NY Times Search by Subject Archive, Link Library, Library Guides, and more (0-321-20277-5).

The New American Webster Handy College Dictionary.   A paperback reference text with more than 100,000 entries (0-451-18166-2).

Merriam-Webster Collegiate Dictionary.   This hardcover comprehensive dictionary is available at a significant discount when packaged with any Longman text (0-321-10494-3).

The Longman Writer's Portfolio.   This unique supplement provides students with a space to plan, think about, and present their work. The portfolio includes an assessing/organizing area (including a grammar diagnostic test, a spelling quiz, and project planning worksheets), a before and during writing area (including peer review sheets, editing checklists, writing self-evaluations, and a personal editing profile), an an after-writing area (including a progress chart, a final table of contents, and a final assessment). Also includes 10 Practices of Highly Effective Students (0-321-163565-6).

The Longman Writer's Journal, by **Mimi Markus.**   Provides students with their own personal space for writing and contains helpful journal writing strategies, sample journal entries by other students, and many writing prompts and topics to get students writing (0-321-08639-2).

A Guide for Peer Response, **Second Edition.**   This guide offers students forms for peer critiques, general guidelines, and specific forms for different stages in the writing process and for various types of papers (0-321-01948-2).

Learning Together.   This brief guide to the fundamentals of collaborative learning teaches students how to work effectively in groups (0-673-46848-8).

Newsweek **Discount Subscription Coupon (12 weeks).**   *Newsweek* gets students reading, writing, and thinking about what's going on in the world around them. The price of the subscription is added to the cost of the book. Instructors receive weekly lesson plans, quizzes, and curriculum guides as well as a complimentary *Newsweek* subscription. The price of the subscription is .59 cents per issue (a total of $7.08 for the subscription) (0-321-08895-6).

Interactive Guide to *Newsweek.*   Available with the 12-week subscription to *Newsweek,* this guide serves as a workbook for students who are using the magazine (0-321-05528-4).

Acknowledgments

We greatly appreciate the assistance and understanding of Susan Kunchandy, our editor at Longman and her assistant editor, Meegan Thompson.

We would also like to thank the following instructors for reviewing this new edition of *Sentence Dynamics:* Wayne Wooten, Catawba Valley Community College; Robert S. Caim, W. Virginia University; Stephanie G. Hall, Pitt Community College; Lealer R. King, Craven Community College; Jayne Williams, Texarkana College; Viola Olsen, Rogue Community College; Joe Allen, Dutchess Community College; Susan Hardebeck, Kaskaskia College; and Rebecca Caraway, Western Piedmont Community College.

Finally, thanks to all those reviewers who reviewed previous editions of this text: Cynthia S. Becerra, Humphreys College, Jessica Carroll, Miami-Dade Community College; Alice Cleveland, College of Marin; Mary Likely, Nassau Community College; Cecilia Lim, Arizona Western College; Kristina R. Michaluk, Community College of Beaver County; Linda Scholer, College of San Mateo; Gary D. Turner, Central Texas College; Alfred J. Zucker, Los Angeles Valley College; Patrick M. Haas, Glendale Community College; Helen M. Lewis, Western Iowa Tech Community College; Marcus C. Lopez, Solano Community College; Maria C. Villar-Smith, Miami-Dade Community College; Elizabeth Winkler, Columbus State University; and Holly Young, Arkansas State University at Beebe.

Constance Immel
Florence Sacks

Sentence Dynamics

Nouns and Pronouns

In Chapter 1 you will learn about parts of speech called **nouns** and **pronouns**.

Definitions of Terms

A **proper noun** names a specific person, place, thing, idea, or activity.

A **noun** names a person, place, thing, idea, or activity.

A **common noun** names people, places, things, ideas, or activities in general.

A **noun marker** is an adjective (an, this, your) that points to the noun that follows it.

A **possessive noun** is a noun that changes spelling to indicate a belonging-to relationship.

A **pronoun** is used to take the place of a noun or to refer to a noun. A **personal pronoun** shows person, number, and gender.

Person indicates the person speaking, the person spoken to, or the person or thing spoken about.

Number Pronouns have singular and plural forms. **Singular** means one person or thing. **Plural** means more than one person or thing.

Gender Third-person pronouns have masculine, feminine, or neuter gender.

LESSON 1   Introduction to the Sentence

When you write a letter applying for a job or a term paper for your psychology class, you must communicate as clearly as possible. You can improve your ability to write by learning as much as you can about the English language. Working through the chapters in this book will help you understand the dynamics of the sentence by learning how sentences are put together.

A sentence has two basic parts: a subject and a verb. The **subject** of a sentence is the person or thing the verb is asking or telling about. The subject may be a **noun** or a **pronoun.** A **verb** tells what the subject does, did, or will do, or it links the subject to another word in the sentence (a **completer**).

GRAMMAR TIP

1. A sentence contains at least one subject and its verb.

2. It begins with a capital letter.

3. It ends with appropriate punctuation.

4. It expresses a complete thought.

EXERCISE 1A

In the following paragraph, identify the subjects by writing "S" above the subject. The verbs are underlined. The first sentence is completed as an example.

     S
Jugglers <u>meet</u> once a year at an international convention. They <u>come</u> from all age groups and many occupations. Each performer <u>gives</u> a demonstration of a specialty. Everyone <u>makes</u> a unique presentation. These artists <u>throw</u> just about everything from cigar boxes to bean bags up in the air. Some people <u>ride</u> unicycles during their performances. One man even <u>eats</u> parts of an apple and a cucumber in his act. The experts <u>have</u> their names in the *Guinness Book of World Records.* An Italian man <u>holds</u> one of the first such records: ten balls or eight plates in motion at once. Jugglers, amateur or professional, <u>keep</u> things on the move.

In Lesson 2 you will continue your study of the sentence by learning about nouns and pronouns.

LESSON 2

Identifying Nouns

If you were asked to give some examples of nouns, you probably would respond with words such as astronaut, Mars, or spaceship. You would be right, of course, because a noun does name a person, a place, or a thing, but a noun can also refer to an idea such as knowledge or an activity such as orbiting. A **noun,** then, names a person, a place, a thing, an idea, or an activity. With this definition in mind, complete the exercise that follows.

EXERCISE 2A

Write one word on each line, according to the instructions printed beneath each line.

EXAMPLE:　Did the <u>defendant</u> tell the <u>truth</u>?
　　　　　　　　　　(person)　　　　　　(idea)

1. A ——————— sat on the ———————.
　　(person)　　　　　　　　(thing)

2. I pledge ——————— to the flag of the ——————— ——————— of
　　　　　(idea)　　　　　　　　　　　　　　　　(place)

———————.
　(place)

3. ——————— is one city that ——————— would like to visit again.
　(place)　　　　　　　　　(person)

4. ——————— is my favorite hobby.
　(activity)

5. ——————— bought those ——————— at a ———————.
　(person)　　　　　　(things)　　　　　(place)

GRAMMAR TIP

Remember this test for a noun:

To determine whether a word is a noun, place a noun marker such as <u>a</u>, <u>an</u>, or <u>the</u> before the word.

EXAMPLES:　<u>a</u> routine, <u>an</u> honor, <u>the</u> Washington Monument, <u>the</u> city

These noun markers (a, an, the) are called **articles.**

EXERCISE 2B

Using the information in the Grammar Tip above, identify the underlined words.

A. If the word is a noun, write "N" above the word.
B. If it is not a noun, write "X" above the word.

                N   X

EXAMPLE: The <u>clouds</u> gathered <u>before</u> the storm.

1. The traffic <u>on</u> the <u>highway</u> stopped.

2. <u>Rain</u> fell <u>last</u> night.

3. Some <u>drivers</u> were <u>cautious</u>.

4. The <u>surface</u> of the <u>road</u> was slick.

5. John's <u>Buick</u> had good <u>brakes</u>.

6. <u>John</u> <u>tried</u> to stop suddenly.

7. His <u>foot</u> slipped <u>off</u> the pedal.

8. John's <u>car</u> skidded <u>across</u> the road.

9. The right <u>fender</u> hit the <u>bumper</u> of another car.

10. <u>Both</u> cars had to be towed <u>away</u>.

Common and Proper Nouns

All of the examples in the Grammar Tip following Exercise 2A <u>except</u> the Washington Monument are **common nouns.** When we use common nouns, we refer to people, places, things, ideas, or activities in general terms. Notice that common nouns are usually not capitalized except at the beginning of a sentence.

However, when we refer to the name of a specific person, place, or thing, we use **proper nouns.** These nouns begin with capital letters. In general, we do not capitalize the names of ideas or activities. Using "the" as a noun test will not always help you identify proper nouns, but remembering that they are capitalized will help you pick them out.

Common Nouns	Proper Nouns
bridge	Golden Gate Bridge
woman	Eleanor Roosevelt
street	Main Street
college	Fairfax Community College

Complete the following sentences by supplying common or proper noun subjects.

1. _____ bought bagels and tortillas at the market.
   proper noun

2. The two _____ tasted delicious, but the _____ was too salty.
   common noun   common noun

3. _____ traveled to Kansas by bus.
   proper noun

4. Her _____ left one hour ago.
   common noun

5. _____ requires skill and concentration.
   common noun

6. _____ often practices as early as 5 A.M.
   proper noun

7. _____ saw a thrilling movie last week.
   proper noun

8. The _____ included a number of famous actors.
   common noun

9. _____ waved and smiled at the crowds lining the street.
   proper noun

10. _____ came back after a month in a spaceship circling the earth.
    proper noun

LESSON 3   Singular and Plural Nouns

Use a **singular noun** when you are referring to only one person, place, thing, idea, or activity, and a **plural noun** when you are referring to more than one.

	Singular Means One	Plural Means More Than One
Person	the astronaut	the astronauts
Place	a planet	planets
Thing	the rocket	the rockets
Activity	a flight	flights
Idea	achievement	achievements

Noun Markers for the Singular

These words indicate that a singular noun usually follows:

one	each
a	every
an	a single

Note: The noun marker **a** is followed by a word beginning with a consonant, and the noun marker **an** is followed by a word beginning with a vowel or a silent **h**.

EXAMPLES: a shoe   a home   an orange   an honor

EXERCISE 3A

A. Write a singular noun after each of these noun markers.

1. every_____   4. one _____

2. each _____   5. a single _____

3. an _____

B. Write five sentences using the noun markers and nouns that you have written above.

1. _____

2. _____

3. _____

4. _____

5. _____

Plural nouns present a special problem. Writing the singular form instead of the plural can change the meaning of your sentence. Study these basic rules for spelling the plural forms of nouns.

EXERCISE 3B

Most nouns form the plural by adding the letter **s.**

> bed, beds   pen, pens   pipe, pipes

Write the plural forms of these nouns.

1. dog _____   4.   test _____

2. date _____   5.   sale _____

3. trick _____

EXERCISE 3C

Words that end in **y,** preceded by a vowel **(a, e, i, o, u)** usually add **-s** to form the plural. Words that end in **y,** preceded by a consonant, form the plural by changing the **y** to **i** and adding **-es.**

> city, cities   duty, duties   But note: bay, bays

Write the plural forms of the nouns on lines 1–5. Can you think of five more nouns like these? Write them on lines 6–10.

1. sky _____   6. _____

2. day _____   7. _____

3. lady _____   8. _____

4. turkey _____   9. _____

5. county _____   10. _____

EXERCISE 3D

Words that end in **sh, s, ch, x,** and **z** form the plural by adding **-es.**

> wish, wishes   church, churches,   buzz, buzzes

Write the plural forms of the nouns on lines 1–5. Can you think of five more nouns like these? Write them on lines 6–10.

1. brush _____   6. _____

2. watch _____   7. _____

3. bus _____   8. _____

4. waltz _____   9. _____

5. tax _____   10. _____

EXERCISE 3E

Nouns that end in **f, ff,** or **fe** usually add **-s.** Certain nouns change the ending to **ve** and then add **-s.** Consult your dictionary to be sure because some words may have two spellings.

knife, knives   loaf, loaves   calf, calves
thief, thieves   roof, roofs   belief, beliefs
proof, proofs   cliff, cliffs   staff, staffs

Write the plural forms of the following nouns.

1. belief _____   4. shelf _____

2. half _____   5. wife _____

3. hoof _____

EXERCISE 3F

Most nouns ending in **o** form the plural by adding **-s.** However, here are six commonly used words that are exceptions: echo, hero, potato, tomato, torpedo, and veto. To these words, add **-es.**

echo, echoes   hero, heroes   potato, potatoes

Write the plural forms of the following nouns.

1. soprano _____   4. tornado _____

2. veto _____   5. piano _____

3. tomato _____

Some nouns do not add **-s** or **-es** to form the plural. These nouns change their spelling.

woman, women	foot, feet	tooth, teeth
goose, geese	child, children	mouse, mice

Fill in each blank with the plural form of the noun in parentheses.

1. The classroom had cages for three _____ (mouse) and two guinea pigs.

2. We should have our _____ (tooth) examined twice a year.

3. Many _____ (woman) watch Monday-night football on television.

4. All of the _____ (child) in Eric's family have gone to college.

5. There are five _____ (man) on the basketball court.

Noun Markers for the Plural

These words indicate that a plural noun usually follows:

all	two (or more)	many	several	one of (the)
a lot of (the)	most	both	few	some
each of (the)				

Write a plural noun after each of these noun markers.

1. two _____   4. all _____

2. both _____   5. many _____

3. several _____

Fill in the blanks with the correct form of the noun in parentheses.

1. Many (tutor) _____ were working in the computer lab when the power went out. 2. One of the (student) _____ had stepped on the cord and disconnected one of the (plug) _____ from the outlet, but nobody realized that at first. 3. Some (student) _____ lost their information because they had not saved all of the (page) _____ they had typed before the power failed. 4. Several (student) _____ were lucky. 5. They had remembered to save their data after five (minute) _____ of typing. 6. Each of the (tutor) _____ tried to figure out what was wrong. 7. Finally, one of the (instructor) _____ decided to check all three (out- let) _____ in the room. 8. Then, several (tutor) _____ crawled around on their hands and knees in the dark until one of the (student) _____ heard a loud "Aha!" 9. Many (student) _____ were huddled in a corner of the darkened room until the computer screens were lighted again. 10. Both of the (instructor) _____ laughed when they saw the anxious faces of the baffled students.

SPELLING TIP

When the instructor returns your composition, correct any words you have misspelled and write the words in a small notebook. Study the list at least ten minutes each day and watch your spelling improve.

Review of Plurals

To review the information in Lessons 2 and 3, complete the following exercise and check your answers with the instructor. If you have any incorrect answers, go back over the material in the lessons. Be sure you correct any mistakes before going on to the next lesson.

Correct the following sentences by writing the correct plural form of each of the underlined nouns on the lines at the right. Check your dictionary for the spelling of irregular plurals.

1. One of the <u>boy</u> bought new <u>shoe</u>.   _____ _____

2. He built more <u>shelf</u> for the new <u>dish</u>.   _____ _____

3. Emergency <u>supply</u> were sent to several <u>country</u>.   _____ _____

4. Many of the <u>model</u> wore <u>bikini</u>.   _____ _____

5. This list includes the <u>address</u> of ten <u>church</u>.   _____ _____

6. All <u>applicant</u> must take a series of <u>test</u>.   _____ _____

7. Answer <u>key</u> are often included in language <u>book</u>.   _____ _____

8. Those <u>box</u> contain old <u>photo</u>.   _____ _____

9. Some of the <u>tomato</u> aren't ripe.   _____ _____

10. Both of the <u>secretary</u> were assigned new <u>duty</u>.   _____ _____

LESSON 4 — Possessives

Since **possessive nouns** often end in **s,** they are sometimes mistaken for **plurals.** Lesson 4 will help you recognize possessive nouns.

Writing Possessive Nouns

1. Add an apostrophe and an **-s** to nouns that do **not** end in **s.**

the girl	the men	Linda
the girl's scarf	the men's coats	Linda's pen

2. Add an apostrophe and an **-s** to singular nouns that end in **s.**

Mr. Harris	my boss	the hostess
Mr. Harris's house	my boss's computer	the hostess's invitation

3. Add *only* an apostrophe to plural nouns that end in **s.**

    the Joneses   the students
    the Joneses' vacation   the students' papers

4. Add an apostrophe and an **-s** to the final word in a compound noun.

    my father-in-law's business   somebody else's mistake

5. Add an apostrophe and an **-s** to the second noun when two nouns are used to show common ownership.

    John and Gina's mother   Smith and Lopez's market

6. When you have more than one noun, add an apostrophe and an **-s** to each noun if each noun possesses a separate thing.

    Amalia's and Claire's husbands are both police officers.

Note: Some writers add only an apostrophe to words ending in **-s** whether singular or plural.

    Lois' decision   the Williams' plans

EXERCISE 4A

Rewrite the underlined words in the possessive form.

EXAMPLE: The claws of the cats are sharp. the cats' claws

1. The names of the cats are Ginny and Max.

    _____

2. They listen to the commands of their owners.

    _____

3. They like to sleep in the bed of Christy.

    _____

4. The mother of Christy chases them out of the bed.

    _____

5. Sometimes Max tries to eat the food that belongs to Ginny.

    _____

EXERCISE 4B

A. Rewrite each of the groups of words so that the underlined word is in the possessive form.

B. Use the possessive form in a sentence.

EXAMPLE: bicycles that belong to <u>children</u>

A. Change to: <u>children's bicycles</u>

B. Your sentence: <u>The children's bicycles</u> were parked in the driveway.

1. the shoes that belong to the <u>ladies</u> _____

   Your sentence: _____

2. the new car that belongs to <u>Juan</u> _____

   Your sentence: _____

3. the jokes that belong to the <u>comedian</u> _____

   Your sentence: _____

4. the wing of the <u>bird</u> _____

   Your sentence: _____

5. the medals of the <u>heroes</u> _____

   Your sentence: _____

Possessive Pronouns and Possessive Nouns

Pronouns are words that substitute for nouns and noun phrases. Pronouns can change their forms as nouns do to show possession. Possessive pronouns can be divided into the following two groups.

Group 1 **Possessive Pronouns Used Without Nouns: <u>mine</u>, <u>ours</u>, <u>yours</u>, <u>hers</u>, <u>his</u>, <u>theirs</u>**

This form of the possessive pronoun is a single word that substitutes for a noun. We use it when the sentence follows another in which the noun is clearly stated.

EXAMPLE: I washed my car. You didn't wash <u>yours</u>.

In these sentences, the reader should have no trouble understanding that <u>yours</u> stands for <u>your car</u> because the noun <u>car</u> is stated in the previous sentence.

Group 2 Possessive Pronouns Used with Nouns: <u>my</u>, <u>our</u>, <u>your</u>, <u>her</u>, <u>his</u>, <u>its</u>, <u>their</u>

These possessive forms of nouns and pronouns that describe and qualify nouns are defined as adjectives.

EXAMPLE: When <u>Gene's</u> car was in the repair shop, he rode his bicycle to work.

An **-s** is added to the noun <u>Gene</u> to modify <u>car</u>, but no change is made in the pronoun <u>his</u> that modifies <u>bicycle</u>.

GRAMMAR TIP

Never add apostrophes to possessive pronouns.

EXERCISE 4C

Bracket all possessive pronouns and possessive nouns.

EXAMPLE: The bike [riders'] protests were loud when they heard that [their] lanes of traffic would be closed.

1. New York City's chief engineer is responsible for maintaining its highways and bridges.

2. His main job is to keep the city's bridges from decaying and collapsing.

3. Today's larger trucks have ruined many of America's roads and bridges.

4. In addition, although salt is used successfully to melt snow, the salt's acidity has destroyed our highways.

5. The chief engineer's judgments about repairs affect many people's lives.

6. But even though drivers' safety may be at risk, many of these motorists complain when their lanes of traffic are closed.

7. Also the politicians' budget cuts have limited his inspection staff.

8. The chief engineer's plan to save a bridge might involve selling rotten wire for $50 a bundle.

9. Many of New York City's citizens agree that the engineer's job is difficult.

10. Their opinion is based on their knowledge that New York's roads are their most valuable asset.

Editing Practice

To improve your ability to proofread your own papers, underline and revise the mistakes in the possessive forms of the nouns in the following paragraph. Write the revised forms on the lines provided at the end of the paragraph.

My new job selling womens clothes in a small shop in the mall offers me a number of benefits. First, the companys policy on vacations is generous. After one years work, I will be given two weeks vacation with pay. Furthermore, I will be paid for all holidays and time and a half for overtime. In addition, I will receive a raise after the first six months work. Another one of the advantages is the 15 percent discount on any of the stores merchandise I wish to buy. Overall, I find the employers attitude very considerate.

1. _____   5. _____

2. _____   6. _____

3. _____   7. _____

4. _____

Special Forms of the Possessive

Relationships other than possession are also shown by using the apostrophe and the letter **s.** Here are some examples:

time:	today's class	yesterday's visit
amount:	money's worth	two dollars' worth

EXERCISE 4D

Put the apostrophe in each underlined noun to make it a possessive form.

1. Rain caused a cancellation of <u>Saturdays</u> game.

2. Tanisha will be paid for one <u>weeks</u> vacation.

3. That <u>countrys</u> flag is red, green, and white.

4. His beard was the result of one <u>months</u> growth.

5. The <u>planes</u> cargo bay will have fire detectors.

Plurals and Possessives

Not every word ending in **s** requires an apostrophe. Most words ending in **s** are not possessive; many of them are noun plurals. The following exercise will give you practice using the plural and possessive forms of nouns. If necessary, review the information given in this chapter on forming noun plurals and possessives.

EXERCISE 4E

Add apostrophes to the possessive forms of the nouns in the following sentences. Some of the nouns are plural but not possessive and do not require apostrophes.

1. I returned the students books to them.

2. Many customers were dissatisfied with the product.

3. Did the company refund the customers money?

4. My parents season tickets are on the 50-yard line.

5. Many parents of the athletes buy season tickets.

Complete the following sentences using the singular possessive or the plural possessive form of the noun in parentheses.

EXAMPLE:　(passenger) This _____ connecting flight has left without him.
You write: This <u>passenger's</u> connecting flight has left without him.

1. (traveler) A _____ arrival at the terminal of a large international airport can be a confusing experience.

2. (passenger) Fortunately, many airports have volunteers who have been trained to assist with these _____ problems.

3. (visitor) Foreign _____ lack of fluency in English, for example, can add to their confusion.

4. (aide) With an _____ help, these travelers can talk to telephone operators who speak to them in their own languages.

5. (volunteer) The _____ training also teaches them what to do in a medical emergency.

6. (worker) On the other hand, an airport _____ pleasant answer to a question simply may make the traveler feel welcome.

7. (tourist) And they can earn a _____ gratitude by recommending local places to visit during a layover.

8. (family) Or a volunteer may relieve a stranded _____ worries by booking a hotel room and another flight.

9. (motorist) They sometimes even find _____ cars when the tired vacationers can't remember where they are parked.

10. (Doris) But these troubleshooters really seem like heroes when they locate your Aunt _____ missing luggage after a long flight.

Add apostrophes to the possessive forms of the nouns in the following paragraph.

My daughters boyfriend, Larry, drives a bright red Honda. On most weekends, Larrys Honda is parked in front of my house. One morning, I noticed the Hondas hubcaps were missing. Someone had stolen the hubcaps from Larrys car during the night. Larry telephoned his insurance agent to report the theft. The agents secretary mailed him two claim forms to fill out. The claim forms arrived in the next days mail. Larry mailed both forms back to the insurance company and waited. After a few days, the insurance company paid Larry for his stolen hubcaps. Within two weeks time, Larrys Honda had new hubcaps.

Noun Markers

You learned in Lesson 3 how useful noun markers can be in identifying singular and plural nouns. Study the noun markers below and use them to help you identify nouns. Remember that the noun does not always directly follow the noun marker. Adjectives (A) may come between the noun marker (NM) and the noun (N).

NM   A   N   NM   A   N

EXAMPLE: She had gained some firsthand experience at her previous job.

Noun Markers

Articles: a   an   the
Demonstrative Pronouns: this   that   these   those
Indefinite Pronouns: some   all   any   both   each   either   every   few   many   more   most   much   neither
Numerals: four   twenty   sixth   eighteen
Possessive Nouns: Mr. King's   woman's   students'   Lucy's   uncle's
Possessive Pronouns: my   your   her   their   our   his

┌─ **GRAMMAR** TIP ───┐

Do not be confused by other words in addition to the noun marker that may be in front of the noun. These words that describe or limit the noun are also called **adjectives** (discussed in Chapter 4, Lesson 1). For example:

Noun Marker	Adjective	Noun	Noun Marker	Adjective	Noun
the	largest	package	a	new	computer

Adjectives answer questions such as <u>which</u> or <u>how many</u> in reference to a noun.

                                                                     Adjective Noun

EXAMPLE: the largest package   Which package?   The <u>largest</u> package.

└──┘

EXERCISE 4H

Referring to the noun markers in the box, identify all the nouns in these sentences. The proper nouns are not preceded by a noun marker. Bracket each noun.

EXAMPLE: Many [students] work during the [summer] to gain some firsthand [experience].

Lori, a junior at Central College, is among those students who work every summer. This spring she found three listings in the local newspaper that matched her qualifications. Most companies were not advertising for an applicant who could only work a few weeks. Lori's first choice was a small company looking for a temporary bookkeeper. Wanting to make a good impression, she wore her favorite green dress and borrowed her roommate's new earrings. The manager who interviewed her seemed impressed by Lori's educational background and her previous experience. At the end of a successful interview, Lori accepted the manager's offer of a job for ten weeks.

Group ACTIVITY

A. Review the information in Lesson 4 by completing the following exercise. Check your answers with your classmates and your instructor. If you have any incorrect answers, go back over the material in the lesson. Be sure you correct any mistakes before going on to the next lesson.

B. Rewrite each of the groups of words so that the underlined word is in the possessive form. Then, working together, write sentences for each group of words.

EXAMPLE: the tools that belong to the carpenter   the carpenter's tools

1. the pay of a month _____

2. the pouch of the kangaroo _____

3. the briefcase that belongs to Mr. Atlas _____

4. a candidate of the people _____

5. the mother of the twins _____

6. the light of the dawn _____

7. the surfboard that belongs to my brother-in-law _____

8. the voices of the sopranos _____

9. the pickup trucks of Timothy and Kelly _____

10. the telephone number of Juan and Selena Martinez _____

LESSON 5   Personal Pronouns

Pronouns are words that substitute for nouns and noun phrases. **Subject** and **object pronouns** act as the subjects or objects of verbs just as nouns do. The use of pronouns avoids the unnecessary repetition of nouns. Although pronouns perform the same functions in sentences as nouns do, you do not make the same changes in their forms. Do not add -s for the plural, and do not add an apostrophe in the possessive.

Person, Number, and Gender

Person

Personal pronouns show person, number, and gender. **Person** indicates the person speaking, the person spoken to, or the person or thing spoken about. **First person** shows the person speaking.

> I mailed the letter.
> We walked to the store.

Second person shows the person spoken to.

> Did you mail the letter?
> You are both invited to the party.

Third person shows the person or thing spoken about.

> She shopped all day.
> He wrapped and mailed the package.
> It should arrive soon.
> They enjoyed the play.

Avoiding Shifts in Person

Try to avoid unnecessary shifts from one person to another. These can confuse the reader. When writing about a person, choose one pronoun and stay with that pronoun.

The most common shift is to the pronoun you.

> **Incorrect:** Most students can pass the tests my geology teacher gives if you study.
> **Correct:** Most students can pass the tests my geology teacher gives if they study.

The noun "students" is in the third person; therefore, write they (third person) instead of you (second person). The pronoun should be in the same person as the noun it stands for.

Remember: Unless you are giving instructions to a specific person when you are writing, avoid using you. Write you when you means the reader.

> **EXAMPLE:**   If you plan to camp in a national park this summer, make your reservations soon.

In this example, the writer is speaking directly to the reader, so the pronoun you is the appropriate choice.

Editing Practice

Some of the following sentences contain shifts in person. Identify each error by drawing a line under the pronoun; then write the correct form above the word. You may have to change the form of the verb.

> They
> **EXAMPLE:**   Many commuters listen to tapes while driving. <u>You</u> can hear stories or even learn a language.

1. I enjoy eating out instead of cooking at home. Living in Seattle, you have a choice of many different kinds of restaurants. My favorite restaurant is a Japanese one near my home. It is small and very popular, so you usually have to wait for a table.

2. When drivers approach a yellow traffic light at the intersection, they should be prepared to stop. You should not try to "beat" the red light by increasing your speed. You hope to save a few minutes, but you also may be risking an accident.

3. During the past year or two, most shoppers have found that the price of food has risen sharply. Every time you go to the market, you can see increases in several items. Not so long ago, twenty dollars bought quite a few bags of groceries, but now you can carry twenty dollars' worth of food home in one bag.

4. I received a camera for a graduation present last year. It worked fine at first, but after a few months, you could tell that something was wrong with it. The pictures were so blurry that you couldn't recognize the people in them. The repairman at the camera shop wanted so much money to repair it that I decided to buy a new one. You would be wasting your money to repair that camera.

Number

Pronouns have singular and plural forms. Singular means one person or thing. Plural means more than one person or thing. Pronouns do not add **s** or **es** to form the plural. **Singular forms** are used to refer to one person, thing, or idea.

> I live in an apartment.
> Don, have you met Carole?
> She sent it to her mother.

Plural forms are used to refer to more than one person, thing, or idea.

> Don't lose them again.
> Three of you are tied for first place.
> We have never met their son.

Gender

Third-person pronouns have masculine, feminine, or neuter gender.

Third-Person Pronouns (Used as Subjects)

Gender	Singular	Plural
Masculine	he	they
Feminine	she	they
Neuter	it	they

Study the pronouns in the neuter gender carefully. Notice that only the singular form of this gender differs from those of the masculine and feminine.

The Pronoun Who

When used as the object of a verb or a preposition, the pronoun who has a special form—whom.

EXAMPLES: Whom do they recommend?
For whom did the city council vote?

Informal English accepts who rather than whom, except after a preposition. In conversation, most people would say, "Who do they recommend?" Also, remember the possessive form whose is used before a noun. Do not confuse it with the contraction who's, which replaces who is. For example: "Who's coming to the party?" But "Whose party did you go to?"

Contractions

In conversation and informal writing, the pronoun is often joined together with the verb that follows it. This is called a **contraction.** The two words are joined together with an apostrophe that takes the place of any missing letters.

> **EXAMPLE:**   I am = I'm   you are = you're   it is = it's

---

GRAMMAR TIP

Do not confuse the spelling of the possessive pronoun your with the contraction you're, or its with the contraction it's.

EXAMPLES: You're (you are) the winner of a pair of tickets for the Giants game. You may pick up your tickets at the box office.
It's (it is) the final game of the season. The team has won its first championship.

EXERCISE 5A

Correct the spelling errors in the underlined pronoun forms.

1. Your moving to Oregon in a new van.   _____

2. Their parked in a no-parking zone.   _____

3. Whose going to the restaurant with us?   _____

4. Its too late to register for this class.   _____

5. Their playing my favorite song on the radio.   _____

6. Joanne gave Marsha her house key because Marsha lost her's.   _____

7. Michelle's friends have many CDs. They offer to lend her theirs'.   _____

8. My dog has learned to give me it's paw when I say, "Give me you're paw."   _____

9. Who's dictionary may I borrow?   _____

10. Your going to pass this test on the first try.   _____

LESSON 6 · Reflexive Pronouns

Pronouns that end in **-self** and **-selves** are called **reflexive pronouns**.

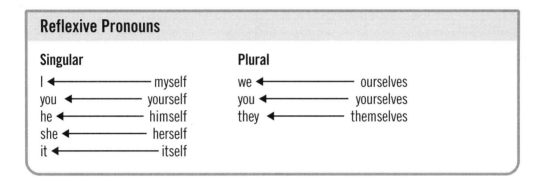

Reflexive Pronouns

Singular	Plural
I ⟷ myself	we ⟷ ourselves
you ⟷ yourself	you ⟷ yourselves
he ⟷ himself	they ⟷ themselves
she ⟷ herself	
it ⟷ itself	

The reflexive pronoun is used in two ways:

a. I cut <u>myself</u>.

In sentence a, <u>myself</u> is used to refer back to <u>I</u>.

b. The president <u>himself</u> shook my hand.

In sentence b, <u>himself</u> is used to emphasize the person named, the president.

c. It is not standard English to use personal pronouns this way: Bill and <u>myself</u> distributed campaign leaflets Saturday.

You would never write: <u>Myself</u> distributed campaign leaflets Saturday. Use the subject form of the pronoun, <u>I</u>: Bill and <u>I</u> distributed campaign leaflets Saturday.

d. The precinct leader introduced the candidate to Bill and <u>myself</u>.

Instead, write: The precinct leader introduced the candidate to <u>me</u>, not <u>myself</u>. Use the object form of the pronoun, <u>me</u>: The precinct leader introduced the candidate to Bill and me. You can avoid making this mistake by using a reflexive pronoun only when it refers to another word in the sentence. <u>Myself</u> does not refer back to any words in sentences c and d.

EXERCISE 6A

Write six sentences using reflexive pronouns.

1. (myself) _____

   _____

2. (yourself) _____

   _____

3. (himself, herself, or itself) _____

   _____

4. (ourselves) _____

   _____

5. (yourselves) _____

   _____

6. (themselves) _____

   _____

Reference Chart of Pronouns

Below is a chart of the pronouns you have studied in this chapter. Refer to it to help you remember the different kinds of pronouns we use in sentences.

Subject Pronouns	Object Pronouns	Possessive Pronouns (with Nouns)	-s Form Possessive Pronouns (Without Nouns)	Reflexive Pronouns
I	me	my	mine	myself
we	us	our	ours	ourselves
you(sing.)	you	your	yours	yourself
you(pl.)	you	your	yours	yourselves
he	him	his	his	himself
she	her	her	hers	herself
it	it	its	—	itself
they	them	their	theirs	themselves

LESSON 7
Sentence Combining

Chapters 1 to 9 of this book include sentence-combining lessons that ask you to rearrange short sentences into one clearly written sentence. As you proceed through the book, these lessons should increase your writing fluency, add variety to your sentences, and give you practice in applying some of the grammatical principles you have been learning.

EXAMPLE: Each of the following four sentences contains information about the writer's brother. When they are read one after the other, the sentences sound choppy and wordy, but when they are combined into a single sentence, the result is a direct, clear statement of the writer's ideas.

1. My brother was a pitcher once.
2. Tim was in high school then.
3. He was on the baseball team at the high school.
4. Tim was the best pitcher there.

Combined Sentence: During high school, my brother Tim was the best pitcher on the baseball team.

This model sentence is not the only way of combining these ideas. You will find that there is often more than one way of combining a group of sentences. Here are some sentences for you to try.

A. Combine these four sentences into one sentence.

1. Scott read the instructions.
2. He read them carefully.
3. They were detailed.
4. They were complicated.

B. Combine these four sentences into one sentence.

1. There was a windstorm last night.
2. It was powerful.
3. It knocked down several trees.
4. They were in our neighborhood.

C. Combine these four sentences into one sentence.

1. Sumi rescued a nine-year-old boy.
2. He was drowning.
3. It happened last summer.
4. She was at Camp Arrowhead.

D. Combine these four sentences into one sentence.

1. The woman was tall.
2. She wore a blouse.

3. Her blouse was red striped.
4. She wore a black cotton skirt.

E. Combine these four sentences into one sentence.

1. I have always wanted to be an athlete.
2. I wanted to be like Jackie Robinson.
3. I wanted to be like Reggie Jackson.
4. I wanted to make a million dollars.

Group ACTIVITY

Combine several sentences from your own writing into one sentence. Bring the original sentences and the revised sentence to class for a group discussion. Decide in each case whether the revised sentence is an improvement. Is the meaning clearer now? Does the new version "sound" better when it is read aloud? Is there a second way to make the revision?

Chapter 1 Summary

common nouns	proper nouns	possessive	gender	number

Complete these sentences by supplying the appropriate word selected from the box.

1. _____ refer to people, places, things, ideas, or activities in general terms.

2. _____ refer to specific people, places, or things.

3. Add an apostrophe when the noun is in the _____ form.

4. Personal pronouns and the definitions of person, _____, and _____ were explained in Lesson 5.

Writing Assignment

Topic

Write a paragraph about an important event that happened during the past five years of your life. This experience should be so important to you that you want to write it down for your grandchildren to read some day. Describe the event and try to explain why it was of such importance.

Step 1. Write down a few key words that come to mind about the event. Ask yourself questions to develop your list of words. (If you prefer, instead of making a list, begin by freewriting or by making a cluster, following the instructions in Chapter 10.)

WHAT?   What was the event?
WHO?   Who was involved?
WHEN?   When did it occur?
WHERE?   Where did the event occur?
HOW?   How did you find out about it? How did it occur?
WHY?   Why was it important to you? Why, many years later, would your grandchildren be interested in reading about it?

Step 2. By the time you have tried to answer each of these questions, you should have several lines of notes. Reading them over, decide which of these ideas to develop in your paragraph. Don't feel that you must include every item on your list in your paragraph.

Step 3. If time permits, after you have written your composition, lay it aside for a few days. Then read it aloud and try to imagine your grandchildren reading it many years from today. If everything you have written seems clear and orderly, you are ready to proofread it. Using your dictionary, check the spelling of any words you are uncertain about. Does each sentence have a subject and a verb, begin with a capital letter, and end with appropriate punctuation? Check any apostrophes, plurals, or possessives you may have used. Then copy it over carefully and submit it to your instructor.

Alternative Writing Assignment

Topic

Interview a person of your grandparents' (or parents') generation about an important event from the past that he or she remembers clearly.

Step 1. Be prepared to take notes during the interview; do not rely on your memory. Ask the following questions, encouraging the person you are interviewing to describe the event using specific details rather than in general terms.

WHAT?	What was the event?
WHO?	Was anyone else involved?
WHEN?	When did the event occur?
WHERE?	Where did the event occur?
HOW?	How did it occur? How did the person find out about it?
WHY?	Why was it important to the person? Why, many years later, does it remain a memorable experience?

Step 2. By the time you have the answers to each of these questions and any other ones you may have asked, you should have enough material for at least a paragraph. Read your notes over carefully, deciding which of these ideas to develop in your paragraph. Don't feel that you must include every item in your notes. Remember to focus on why the event was so important even though you begin by "setting the scene" with descriptive details.

Step 3. If time permits, after you have written your composition, lay it aside for a day or so. If it is possible, read it aloud to check for clarity and accuracy. If everything you have written seems clear and orderly, you are ready to proofread it. Using your dictionary, check the spelling of any words you are uncertain about. Does each sentence have a subject and a verb, begin with a capital letter, and end with appropriate punctuation? Check any apostrophes, plurals, or possessives you may have used. Then copy it over carefully and submit it to your instructor.

CHAPTER 1
PRACTICE TEST: Nouns and Pronouns

Take this practice test to see how well you understand the forms of nouns and pronouns.

Name _____

Date _____ Class Time _____

Instructor _____

I. Using the noun test and your dictionary, identify each word as a noun or some other part of a sentence.

    a. If the word is a noun, place a check under the column headed Noun.

    b. If it is not a noun, place a check under the column headed Other.

	Noun	Other			Noun	Other
1. avenue	_____	_____	6. and		_____	_____
2. if	_____	_____	7. briefcase		_____	_____
3. what	_____	_____	8. dynamic		_____	_____
4. tigers	_____	_____	9. week		_____	_____
5. opened	_____	_____	10. Atlanta		_____	_____

II. Using the noun test and your dictionary, identify the nouns in the following sentences. Write "N" above each noun.

    1. Mrs. Tracy bought a bus ticket to Kansas City.

    2. The doctor's nurse canceled his appointments for the day.

    3. At the end of eight innings, we led by one run.

    4. Before class many students study in the college library.

    5. The wet poodle shook water on the sunbathers.

CHAPTER 1 PRACTICE TEST (Cont.)

III. **Each of the following sentences contains one error in the possessive form of a noun. Underline each error. Write the correct form of the possessive noun on the line at the right.**

1. The striking workers lost a weeks pay.   _____

2. Where will Chris and Terrys bookstore be located?   _____

3. The coachs jacket was on the bench.   _____

4. They waved to attract the bus drivers attention.   _____

5. The audiences response to the concert was
    enthusiastic.   _____

IV. **Write the possessive form of the underlined nouns on the lines at the right.**

1. the speeches of the <u>debaters</u>   _____

2. the desks of the <u>senators</u>   _____

3. the backpacks that belong to my <u>children</u>   _____

4. the rights of the <u>consumers</u>   _____

5. the collars that belong to the two <u>puppies</u>   _____

V. **The following sentences contain shifts in person.**
   a. Identify each error by drawing a line under the incorrect pronoun.
   b. Write the correct pronoun form on the line at the right.

1. Maya doesn't mind waiting in line because you
    can read a book or talk to people.   _____

2. When a person diets, they should not skip
    breakfast.   _____

3. A television newscaster is usually not a journalist.
    Their job is to present the news to the audience.   _____

4. I want to own a restaurant some day. Being in
    business for yourself will be a challenge.   _____

5. Motorcycles are economical to ride, but it can
   have disadvantages.　　　　　　　　　　　　　　_____

VI. Correct the spelling errors in the underlined pronoun forms.

1. They brought their tickets, but we forgot <u>ours'</u>.　　_____

2. <u>Who's</u> car is blocking the driveway entrance?　　_____

3. How do you like <u>you're</u> new job?　　　　　　_____

4. Although classes began last week, they haven't
   attended any of <u>theirs'</u>.　　　　　　　　　　_____

5. The cat sharpened <u>it's</u> claws on the tree.　　　_____

**VII. Write two sentences using the possessive forms of singular nouns.
Write three sentences using the possessive forms of plural nouns.**

1. _____

2. _____

3. _____

4. _____

5. _____

VIII. Write the plural forms of the following nouns on the lines at the right.

1. match_____　　　　4. silver _____

2. test_____　　　　　5. boss _____

3. knife _____

**IX. If the use of the underlined pronoun is correct, write "C" on the line. If
the use of the pronoun is incorrect, write the correct pronoun on the line.**

1. She asked <u>herself</u> why the teacher had
   chosen her.　　　　　　　　　　　　　　　　_____

CHAPTER 1 PRACTICE TEST (Cont.)

2. Logan likes to look at <u>hisself</u> in the mirror.   _____

3. My husband and <u>myself</u> enjoy bowling.   _____

4. Senator Boxer <u>herself</u> spoke at our graduation.   _____

5. We serve <u>ourselfs</u> from the salad bar in the cafeteria. _____

Editing Practice

Some of the following sentences contain shifts in person. Identify each error by drawing a line under the pronoun; then write the correct pronoun form above the word. You may also have to change the form of the verb.

My brother likes his job as a lifeguard at the beach. You don't have to wear a coat and tie to work, and you are out in the fresh air all day. During the summer, Julio conducts water-safety classes for elementary school children. You have to be patient to work with little kids. Lifeguards have an important job. You are responsible for the lives of all the people who come to enjoy the ocean.

2

Verbs

In Chapter 2 you will learn about parts of speech called **verbs.**

Definitions of Terms

An **action verb** tells what the subject does, did, or will do.

A **linking verb** shows a relationship between the subject and a completer.

A **regular verb** adds **-d** or **-ed** to form the past tense.

An **irregular verb** does not follow any spelling rules to form the past tense.

An **auxiliary verb** is a helping verb used with the main verb to form a verb phrase.

The **base form** of the verb is the present form of the verb with no **-s** at the end.

The **past participle** is formed by adding **-d** or **-ed** to the base form of a regular verb.

The **present participle** is formed by adding **-ing** to the base form of the verb.

A **completer** follows the **linking verb** to describe or rename the subject.

Tense is the change of verb form to indicate when the action occurred.

A **verb phrase** is the combination of an auxiliary verb and one of the participial forms of the verb. It is used as the verb of the sentence.

 LESSON 1

Present and Past Tenses: Regular Verbs

Every sentence must have a verb. Let's review three characteristics of verbs that help to identify them.

35

1. The verb tells what the subject does, did, or will do (action), is, was, or will be (linking).

    EXAMPLE: Reggie caught the fly ball.
    What did Reggie do?
    He caught. Therefore, caught is the verb.

2. The verb changes its form to show time (tense).

    EXAMPLE: Reggie catches the fly ball. (The time is the present.)
    Reggie caught the fly ball. (The time is the past.)
    Reggie will catch the fly ball. (The time is the future.)

3. The verb changes its form in the third-person singular, present tense to agree with the subject.

    EXAMPLE: I catch the fly ball. (first person)
    She/He catches the fly ball. (third person)

In Chapter 2 we will discuss two kinds of verbs: action verbs and linking verbs.

Action Verbs

Most verbs tell what the subject (someone or something) does, did, or will do. These are **action verbs** that are usually easy to identify, especially when the action is a familiar one, such as swim, talk, buy, chew, study, or explode.

Linking Verbs

You may find linking verbs more difficult to identify than the action verbs above. **Linking verbs** show a relationship between the subject and a completer. The **completer** describes or renames the subject, and the linking verb links the subject to this completer.

Subject	Linking Verb	Completer
Mr. Lopez	is	my Spanish teacher. (renames the subject)
The exam	seemed	easy. (describes the subject)

The linking verb used most frequently is some form of the verb be (am, is, are, was, were). Some other linking verbs are seem, grow, look, sound, taste, and appear. Linking verbs will be discussed in greater detail in Chapter 3.

Write five sentences, using the verbs in the parentheses.

EXAMPLE: (sell) Mr. Rico <u>sells</u> real estate in Philadelphia.

1. (visit) _____

2. (drink) _____

3. (seem) _____

4. (appear) _____

5. (break) _____

In the following sentences, underline the verbs and write them on the lines at the right.

1. The train stops for only a few moments at Oakhurst.   _____

   The train stopped for only a few moments at Oakhurst.   _____

2. Gene hurries to get on the train already in motion.   _____

   Gene hurried to get on the train already in motion.   _____

3. He trips over a woman's suitcase in the aisle.   _____

   He tripped over a woman's suitcase in the aisle.   _____

4. Gene and the woman glare at each other.   _____

   Gene and the woman glared at each other.   _____

5. In his seat at last, he watches the dawn through the smeary windows of the train.   _____

   In his seat at last, he watched the dawn through the smeary windows of the train.   _____

The verbs in Exercise 1B form the past tense by adding **-d** or **-ed** to the base form. Most verbs follow this pattern. These are called **regular verbs.** Verbs change their forms to indicate the time the action takes place. We call this sign of time

tense. The **present tense** is used in commands and suggestions and to indicate habitual action or continuing ability.

EXAMPLES: **Command:** Deliver this message immediately.
Suggestion: Discourage them from coming if you can.
Habitual action: He paints beautifully.

The **past tense** is used in sentences about an action that happened before the present time. Say "yesterday" at the beginning of the sentence to remind you to use the past tense.

EXAMPLE: Yesterday he sliced the potatoes for tonight's dinner.

Here is a chart showing the pattern of the regular verbs in the present and the past tenses.

Model Verb–Walk					
Present Tense			**Past Tense**		
Person	**Singular**	**Plural**	**Person**	**Singular**	**Plural**
First	I walk	we walk	First	I walked	we walked
Second	you walk	you walk	Second	you walked	you walked
Third	he walks	they walk	Third	he walked	they walked
	she walks	they walk		she walked	they walked
	it walks	they walk		it walked	they walked

Answer these questions by looking at the model verb <u>walk</u> in the chart.

1. What letter do you add to the base form of the verb
   for the third-person singular, present tense?   _____

If you answered **-s,** you are correct. Notice that the singular adds an **s** to the base form of the verb, but the plural has no **-s.**

2. What letters do you add to the base form of the verb
   to form the past tense?   _____

If you answered **-ed,** you are correct. Notice that both singular and plural add **-ed** to form the past tense.

Write five sentences, using regular verbs in the present tense.

1. (place) _____

2. (watch) _____

3. (hope) _____

4. (enjoy) _____

5. (decide) _____

Underline the verb in the sentences you have just written. Rewrite the sentence and change the verb to the past tense.

1. _____

2. _____

3. _____

4. _____

5. _____

All of the verbs in the following sentences are past tense forms of regular verbs. Underline the verbs. Write the present tense forms of the verbs on the lines at the right.

1. Momoko planned a ski vacation in the mountains. _____

2. She worked extra hours in the evenings and on weekends. _____

3. She saved half of her paycheck every week. _____

4. Momoko opened a special bank account. _____

5. Her money increased very slowly. _____

6. She waited for the first heavy snowfall. _____

7. She listened to the weather forecast every day. _____

8. Finally, the weather changed. _____

9. It snowed for three days and nights.   _____

10. She anticipated her ski trip.   _____

LESSON 2   Present and Past Tenses: Irregular Verbs

Most verbs are regular verbs, which means we add **-d** or **-ed** to them to form the past tense. Verbs that do not add **-d** or **-ed** to form the past tense are called **irregular verbs.** Use your dictionary to find the past tense of irregular verbs or consult the chart of irregular verbs.

EXERCISE 2A

All of the verbs in the following sentences are past tense forms of irregular verbs. Underline the verbs. Write the present tense forms of the verbs on the lines at the right.

EXAMPLE: Ricardo and his father <u>rose</u> early.   ___rise___

1. Ricardo and his father drove to the lake cabin together.   _____

2. The next morning they saw a bright frost on the grass.   _____

3. The sweet smell of coffee came from the kitchen.   _____

4. After a breakfast of fruit and pancakes, they took a boat out on the lake.   _____

5. Ricardo held tightly to the fishing pole.   _____

6. He threw the line far out into the water.   _____

7. Suddenly the rod bent in his hands.   _____

8. A large trout hung on his hook.   _____

9. He brought the large trout into the boat.   _____

10. Ricardo and his father caught several fish that day.   _____

Principal Forms of Irregular Verbs

Present (Base Form) Use with I, you, we, they, and plural nouns.	Present + -s (-es) Use with he, she, it, and singular nouns.	Past Use with all pronouns and nouns.	Past Participle Use with auxiliary verbs (has, had, have).	Present Participle Use with auxiliary verbs (is, am, are, was, were).
am, are	is	was, were	been	being
beat	beats	beat	beaten	beating
begin	begins	began	begun	beginning
bite	bites	bit	bitten	biting
blow	blows	blew	blown	blowing
break	breaks	broke	broken	breaking
bring	brings	brought	brought	bringing
build	builds	built	built	building
burst	bursts	burst	burst	bursting
buy	buys	bought	bought	buying
catch	catches	caught	caught	catching
choose	chooses	chose	chosen	choosing
cling	clings	clung	clung	clinging
come	comes	came	come	coming
cost	costs	cost	cost	costing
dig	digs	dug	dug	digging
do	does	did	done	doing
draw	draws	drew	drawn	drawing
drink	drinks	drank	drunk	drinking
drive	drives	drove	driven	driving
eat	eats	ate	eaten	eating
fall	falls	fell	fallen	falling
fight	fights	fought	fought	fighting
find	finds	found	found	finding
fly	flies	flew	flown	flying
forget	forgets	forgot	forgotten	forgetting
freeze	freezes	froze	frozen	freezing
give	gives	gave	given	giving
go	goes	went	gone	going
grow	grows	grew	grown	growing
hang	hangs	hung	hung	hanging
have	has	had	had	having
hear	hears	heard	heard	hearing
hide	hides	hid	hidden	hiding
hold	holds	held	held	holding
know	knows	knew	known	knowing
lay	lays	laid	laid	laying
lead	leads	led	led	leading

(continued)

Principal Forms of Irregular Verbs (*continued*)

Present (Base Form) Use with I, you, we, they, and plural nouns.	Present + -s (-es) Use with he, she, it, and singular nouns.	Past Use with all pronouns and nouns.	Past Participle Use with auxiliary verbs (has, had, have).	Present Participle Use with auxiliary verbs (is, am, are, was, were).
leave	leaves	left	left	leaving
lie	lies	lay	lain	lying
lose	loses	lost	lost	losing
make	makes	made	made	making
read	reads	read	read	reading
ride	rides	rode	ridden	riding
ring	rings	rang	rung	ringing
rise	rises	rose	risen	rising
run	runs	ran	run	running
say	says	said	said	saying
see	sees	saw	seen	seeing
sell	sells	sold	sold	selling
set	sets	set	set	setting
shake	shakes	shook	shaken	shaking
shine	shines	shone	shone	shining
sing	sings	sang	sung	singing
sink	sinks	sank	sunk	sinking
sit	sits	sat	sat	sitting
sleep	sleeps	slept	slept	sleeping
slide	slides	slid	slid	sliding
speak	speaks	spoke	spoken	speaking
spin	spins	spun	spun	spinning
stand	stands	stood	stood	standing
steal	steals	stole	stolen	stealing
stick	sticks	stuck	stuck	sticking
strike	strikes	struck	struck	striking
swear	swears	swore	sworn	swearing
swim	swims	swam	swum	swimming
swing	swings	swung	swung	swinging
take	takes	took	taken	taking
teach	teaches	taught	taught	teaching
tear	tears	tore	torn	tearing
think	thinks	thought	thought	thinking
throw	throws	threw	thrown	throwing
wake	wakes	waked	waked	waking
wear	wears	wore	worn	wearing
win	wins	won	won	winning
write	writes	wrote	written	writing

All of the verbs in the following sentences are present tense forms of irregular verbs. Underline the verbs. Then write the past tense forms of the verbs on the lines at the right.

EXAMPLE: The convention <u>begins</u> on Thursday.   __began__

1. Jugglers meet once a year at an international convention. _____

2. They come from all age groups and many occupations.   _____

3. Each performer gives a demonstration of a specialty.   _____

4. Everyone makes a unique presentation.   _____

5. These artists throw just about everything from cigar boxes to bean bags up in the air.   _____

6. Some people ride unicycles during their performances.   _____

7. One man even eats parts of an apple and a cucumber in his act.   _____

8. The experts have their names in the *Guinness Book of World Records.*   _____

9. An Italian man holds one of the first such records: ten balls or eight plates in motion at once.   _____

10. Jugglers, amateur or professional, keep things on the move.   _____

Group ACTIVITY

Change the following story to the past tense by writing the past tense form above each underlined verb. Form a group and check your answers with members of the group. Then, as a group, write a paragraph about how you spent a weekend recently. Use the past tense. When you have completed it, underline the verbs. Exchange this paragraph with one written by another group in your class. Change the verbs in that paragraph to the present tense.

Marla and Jack live in an apartment on the third floor. They enjoy the view from their apartment. Marla usually watches TV in the living room while Jack cleans the apartment on weekends. Sometimes they tour the city together when out-of-town visitors come. Jack's stories amuse Marla and the visitors. They often see unusual sights on their tours. One afternoon as they travel, Marla asks Jack if he sees the artist drawing a picture of the scenery. Jack shrugs his shoulders and remarks about the beautiful model who poses for the cameraman nearby. Marla looks angry. She thinks she understands Jack well. But sometimes he disappoints her. She plans to discuss this problem with him soon. Meanwhile she tries to enjoy the rest of the tour of the city.

Lie-Lay and Sit-Set

You may be uncertain at times about how to use these four irregular verbs. Many people confuse lie with lay or sit with set.

Lie-Lay			
Present	**Past**	**Past Participle**	**Present Participle**
lie	lay	lain	lying
lay	laid	laid	laying

To lie down means to recline, to rest in, or to be in a horizontal position.

To lay something down means to put or place it somewhere.

1. After eating, Ryan lay down for a nap. (past tense of lie)
2. He laid his glasses on the table by the couch. (past tense of lay)

Sit-Set			
Present	**Past**	**Past Participle**	**Present Participle**
sit	sat	sat	sitting
set	set	set	setting

To sit means to be seated, to remain in position. To set means to put or to place.

1. Randall unpacked the new computer and set it on the desk. (past tense of set)
2. The empty box and crumpled paper sat in the middle of the floor all week. (past tense of sit)

GRAMMAR TIP

In general, lay and set are followed by a noun or a pronoun, but lie and sit are not. The noun or pronoun, called the **object of the verb,** completes the meaning of the sentence. For a more detailed explanation, see Chapter 3, Lesson 2.

        0
1. Set that heavy package on the counter.   (past tense of set)

       0
2. They laid their plans carefully.   (past tense of lay)

EXERCISE 2C

Write the correct verb choice on the lines at the right.

1. When Derek comes home from work, he (lays, lies) his briefcase on the desk.   _____

2. Sometimes he (sits, sets) it on the floor.   _____

3. Then he goes into the bedroom and (lays, lies) down on the bed.   _____

4. After a short nap, he (sits, sets) up and goes into the kitchen.   _____

5. Yesterday, he (lay, laid) in bed for two hours.   _____

6. When he (sat, set) up, he was surprised that it was dark outside.   _____

7. The daily newspaper was (lying, laying) on the front steps. _____

8. It had (laid, lain) there since the morning.   _____

9. Derek took it inside and (set, sat) down at the kitchen table.   _____

10. He likes to read the newspaper while (sitting, setting) at dinner.   _____

Principal Forms of Verbs

When you change the spelling of a verb, you are changing the form of the verb. All verbs have five principal forms.

1. The **present** or **base form** is the verb without any changes in spelling. It is used with the pronouns I, you, we, and they and with plural nouns.

   EXAMPLES: walk   see

2. The **present + s form** is spelled by adding an **-s** or **-es** to the base form. It is used with singular nouns and with the pronouns he, she, and it.

   EXAMPLES: walks   sees

3. The **past form** is spelled by adding **-d** or **-ed** to a regular verb. Irregular verbs change the base form spelling in different ways. They should be memorized. The past form is used with all pronouns and nouns.

   EXAMPLES: walked   saw

4. The **past participle** is spelled the same as the past form in regular verbs. Irregular verbs that change the spelling should be memorized. The past participle is usually used with a form of the auxiliary verb have.

   EXAMPLES: has walked   has seen

5. The **present participle** is formed by adding **-ing** to the base form of the verb. It is used with a form of the auxiliary verb be.

   EXAMPLES: am walking   am seeing

EXERCISE 3A

Write the principal forms of the following regular verbs on the lines provided. Use your dictionary.

Present	Present + -s	Past	Past Participle	Present Participle
(Base form) Use with I, you, we, they, and plural nouns.	Use with he, she, it, and singular nouns.	Use with all pronouns and nouns.	Use with auxiliary verbs (has, had, have).	Use with auxiliary verbs (is, are, am, was, were).

EXAMPLE:

walk	walks	walked	walked	walking

1. stop _____ _____ _____ _____

2. carry _____ _____ _____ _____

3. watch _____ _____ _____ _____

4. try _____ _____ _____ _____

5. hope _____ _____ _____ _____

SPELLING TIP

All verbs form the **present participle** by adding **-ing** to the present form:

Present	*Present Participle*	*Present*	*Present Participle*
walk	walking	try	trying

Some verbs, however, require a spelling change:

A. Drop a final, unpronounced **e** before adding a suffix beginning with a vowel.

EXAMPLES: like, liking / use, using / come, coming / dine, dining

B. Double a final single consonant before a suffix beginning with a vowel if the consonant ends a stressed syllable or a word of one syllable, *and* if the consonant is preceded by a single vowel.

EXAMPLES: run, running / hop, hopping / begin, beginning / drag, dragging

Spelling Practice

Write the **-ing** forms of these words on the lines provided.

1. let _____

2. jump _____

3. hit _____

4. return _____

5. sleep _____

6. arrive _____

7. live _____

8. manage _____

9. blame _____

10. compete _____

┌───┐
GRAMMAR TIP

Unlike regular verbs, irregular verbs do not form their past and past participles by adding **-d** or **-ed** to the present form. Instead they use some other change in form:

begin/began/begun   go/went/gone   see/saw/seen
└───┘

EXERCISE 3B

Write the principal forms of the following irregular verbs on the lines provided. Use your dictionary or consult the chart of irregular verbs.

EXAMPLE:

see	sees	saw	seen	seeing

1. am, are _____ _____ _____ _____

2. drive _____ _____ _____ _____

3. run _____ _____ _____ _____

4. choose _____ _____ _____ _____

5. do _____ _____ _____ _____

LESSON 4   Auxiliary Verbs

An **auxiliary verb** is a helping verb used with the main verb to form a verb phrase. The present participle and the past participle forms are *not* used alone as the verb in a sentence. They are preceded by an auxiliary verb. This combination of an auxiliary verb and one of the participial forms of the verb is called a **verb phrase.**

Note: When the verb phrase is underlined in this book, one line indicates the auxiliary verb, and two lines indicate the main verb.

EXAMPLE: will be speaking

EXAMPLE: Do not write: Thomas taking his brother to the park.
Do write: Thomas is taking his brother to the park.

The auxiliary verb has two main uses. First, the auxiliary verb indicates shades of meaning that cannot be expressed by a main verb alone.

He <u>might <u><u>go</u></u></u> to college.   He <u>can <u><u>go</u></u></u> to college.
He <u>should <u><u>go</u></u></u> to college.   <u>Would</u> he <u><u>go</u></u> to college?

Second, the auxiliary verb indicates tense—the time the action of the verb takes place.

He <u>is <u><u>going</u></u></u> to college.   He <u>will <u><u>go</u></u></u> to college.
He <u>has <u><u>gone</u></u></u> to college.   He <u>does <u><u>go</u></u></u> to college.

Note that, in a question, the subject separates the auxiliary verb and the main verb.

<u>Will</u> he <u><u>go</u></u> to college?

Auxiliary verbs are commonly divided into two groups.

Group 1: These words are used with main verbs, but they are *not* used as verbs alone except in answer to a question. They usually *signal* the approach of a main verb.

EXAMPLES: Are you going with us? I **<u>may</u>**. I **<u>may</u>** <u><u>go</u></u> with them.

Group 1 Auxiliary Verbs

can	may	shall	will	must
could	might	should	would	ought to

EXERCISE 4A

Underline the auxiliary verb or verbs once and the main verb twice.

EXAMPLE: I <u>would</u> <u><u>like</u></u> to place an order.

1. Can you shop at home?

2. You might have received a mail-order catalog from time to time.

3. Many people would find these catalogs convenient.

4. Years ago farm families could send for clothes and household needs.

5. Today urban shoppers can order a variety of goods from specialty stores.

6. The wide choice of items should appeal to families.

7. They may be surprised to see everything from a twelve-unit condo for birds to a goose-down mask.

8. The order form must be filled out carefully.

9. The merchandise will arrive in good condition.

10. Perhaps you ought to shop by mail.

EXERCISE 4B

Write sentences of your own using the auxiliary verbs listed below. Underline the auxiliary verb once and the main verb twice.

1. will _____

2. can _____

3. should _____

4. may _____

5. would _____

Group 2: These verbs may be used as auxiliary verbs or as main verbs. When they serve as auxiliaries, another form of a verb is used as the main verb of the verb phrase.

Group 2 Auxiliary Verbs			
be	am	have	do
being	is, are	has	does
been	was, were	had	did

Study the way these verbs are used both as auxiliary verbs and as main verbs. As you study, underline the auxiliary verbs with one line and the main verbs with two lines; then label each verb.

GRAMMAR TIP

1. A sentence must always have a main verb, but it may or may not have an auxiliary verb.
2. If the sentence has an auxiliary verb, it is always placed in front of the main verb.
3. In a question, the subject separates the auxiliary verb and the main verb.

EXERCISE 4C

In the following sentences, underline the auxiliary verb or verbs once and the main verb twice. Do not underline the contraction for *not* (*n't*).

EXAMPLE: He didn't understand the procedure.

1. Many injured athletes have been helped by a new instrument called an arthroscope.

2. With the arthroscope, doctors can see inside the knee.

3. The doctor can examine bones and tissues.

4. The surgery may be done within an hour.

5. Without the arthroscope a doctor must cut open the knee.

6. Even then a doctor can't be sure of the diagnosis.

7. Now, many doctors are using the arthroscope for diagnosis and surgery.

8. They don't think of it as miracle surgery.

9. But many injured athletes are playing in games within a week after surgery.

10. Doesn't that seem like a miracle to you?

EXERCISE 4D

Write sentences of your own using the auxiliary verbs listed below. Underline the auxiliary verb once and the main verb twice in each sentence.

EXAMPLE: have read
I have just read a fascinating book.

1. has dreamed _____

_____

2. were wondering _____

_____

3. doesn't think _____

_____

4. are enjoying _____

_____

5. have left _____

_____

Summary of Lessons 3 and 4

1. Present and past participles cannot function alone as the verbs of a sentence.

2. Present and past participles must be accompanied by auxiliary verbs.

3. *Be, have,* and *do* sometimes function as auxiliary verbs.

   I have finished my homework. I didn't speak to him. I was eating.

4. *Be, have,* and *do* often function alone in a sentence as main verbs.

   I have a penny. I do my homework. I was an only child.

EXERCISE 4E

Fill in the correct form of the main verb in parentheses to complete the sentence. Consult the chart of irregular verbs or your dictionary.

1. (run) Since the retirement of his father, Nick has _____ their restaurant.

2. (become) Located downtown in a large city, it had _____ a popular place to eat.

3. (think) For some time Nick had _____ about making a few changes in the business.

4. (begin) As a start he has now _____ faxing his menu to customers on request.

5. (take) Have many people _____ advantage of this service?

6. (hear) New patrons often have _____ of the restaurant's excellent food.

7. (find) Many people who are planning parties have _____ that seeing the menu is very helpful.

8. (make) Businesses have _____ the most frequent requests for these faxed menus.

9. (see) Nick has _____ his take-out orders during the day increase appreciably.

10. (eat) These business customers who have _____ Nick's lunches sometimes bring in their friends to dine in the evening.

Make a habit of consulting your dictionary to find the principal forms of irregular verbs. Do not guess.

Adverbs

An adverb is a modifier that adds further information about verbs, adjectives, and other adverbs. The following adverbs, in addition to others, frequently appear between auxiliary verbs and main verbs. These words are not auxiliary verbs. Do not underline them as verbs.

never	always	often	sometimes
not	still	seldom	completely
just	ever	frequently	also

EXAMPLES: The quarterback <u>will</u> never <u>attempt</u> a pass now.

The football game <u>has</u> just <u>ended</u>.

Contractions

In conversation and informal writing, two words are often joined together with an apostrophe that takes the place of any missing letters. The contraction for *not (n't)* may be added to many auxiliaries, for example:

haven't	doesn't	aren't	can't	isn't	won't

Note: *n't* is not an auxiliary verb; do not underline it as one. It is an adverb.

EXAMPLES: We <u>had</u>(n't) <u><u>driven</u></u> the car for a week.

The mechanic <u>could</u>(n't) <u><u>repair</u></u> the car in one day.

EXERCISE 4F

In the following paragraph, underline the auxiliary verb or verbs once and the main verb twice. Put parentheses around any adverbs or contractions.

EXAMPLE: The past president <u>could</u>(n't) <u><u>serve</u></u> on the new board.

The condo association meeting has just ended. The homeowners have voted for the new officers of the condo board. They have selected some owners who had been complaining about the past president. The owners said that the president had not returned their phone calls when the windstorm had damaged their roofs. The president had been out of town, and when she returned, she didn't want to return all of the irate homeowners' phone messages as she did not have a reply for them. What could she do? The new board members are discussing ways to finance repair of the roofs.

EXERCISE 4G

Underline the auxiliary verbs once and the main verbs twice. Put parentheses around any adverbs or contractions.

EXAMPLE: Mr. Williams <u>has</u> (just) <u><u>seen</u></u> a bear in his backyard.

As Southern California developers have built homes closer and closer to forests and mountains, residents of these communities must often share the territory with its former four-legged inhabitants. Possums are now surveying backyards from utility wires, coyotes are snatching pet cats and small dogs from their owners' patios, and raccoons are accepting nightly handouts from willing human neighbors. Bears in search of food have also appeared. One bear had even found a convenient home in a large tree. He was taking his exercise in nearby swimming pools and his dinner from trash cans. What bear wouldn't enjoy the good life? A crew was finally summoned to convince him that he wasn't welcome. Recently a 300-pound black bear was relocated from a residential area with the aid of a helicopter, three sheriff's deputies, a game warden, and tranquilizing darts. From the bear's point of view, this reception must not have seemed very neighborly.

EXERCISE 4H

Add auxiliary verbs in the blank spaces to complete the following sentences.

1. The students _____ enrolling for the fall semester now.

2. They _____ already received class schedules in the mail.

3. They _____ been given a specific time to telephone the college.

4. Some students _____ not chosen their courses yet.

5. By the time they telephone next week, they _____ _____ chosen their courses for the new semester.

Group
ACTIVITY

Cut out a short article from a newspaper or a magazine. Underline the auxiliary verbs once and the main verbs twice. Put parentheses around any adverbs or contractions. Bring your article to class. Exchange your work with a member of your group to check each other's work.

LESSON 5

Future Tense

The **future tense** is used for sentences about something that will happen in the future. Say "tomorrow" before the subject: "Tomorrow I will walk."

The future tense is formed by using the auxiliary verb will and the base form of the main verb. Here is a chart showing the pattern of all verbs in the future tense.

Model Verb—Walk			
Person	**Singular**	**Person**	**Plural**
First	I will walk	First	we will walk
Second	you will walk	Second	you will walk
Third	he will walk	Third	they will walk
	she will walk		they will walk
	it will walk		they will walk

Although it is correct to express future action by using the present progressive tense (I **am going** to graduate in June.) use only the future tense (I **will graduate** in June.) when you are writing the exercises in this lesson.

EXERCISE 5A

Complete the following sentences by using the future tense of the verb in parentheses.

1. (begin) Tomorrow Linda _____ her new job.

2. (set) Tonight she _____ her alarm clock for 6 A.M.

3. (take) Tomorrow morning she _____ the 7:30 bus to work.

4. (be) She hopes the bus _____ on schedule.

5. (earn) Very soon Linda _____ her first paycheck.

Will and Would

Will points to the future from the present.   **know/will**
Would points to the future from the past.   **knew/would**

   a. You <u>know</u> that you <u>will</u> do well in this class.

In sentence a, "you know" <u>now</u> (in the present) that "you will do well" in the <u>future</u>.

   b. You <u>knew</u> that you <u>would</u> do well in this class.

In sentence b, "you knew" <u>then</u> (in the past) that "you would do well" in the <u>future</u>.

EXERCISE 5B

In the following sentences, fill in <u>will</u> or <u>would</u> to indicate the future.

   1. Herb knows that he _____ win someday.

   2. Herb knew that he _____ win someday.

   3. Wu arrives early so he _____ get the best seats.

   4. Wu arrived early so he _____ get the best seats.

   5. Taylor says that he _____ hire a band.

   6. Taylor said that he _____ hire a band.

EXERCISE 5C

Complete the following sentences with a <u>future</u> form of the verb in parentheses.

   1. (come) Where _____ fish and shrimp _____ from in the future?

   2. (need) The world _____ _____ an additional 16 million tons of fish annually.

   3. (fill) The United Nations hoped that fish farms _____ _____ this need.

4. (supply) Japan and China _____ _____ 1.5 billion pounds of shrimp each year.

5. (raise) The Norwegians had already promised that they _____ _____ salmon in protected fish farms.

LESSON 6   Perfect Tenses

In the lesson on auxiliary verbs, you used the perfect tenses in some of the verbs that you identified or wrote. The phrase **perfect tenses** gives no clue to the uses of these tenses. Study the examples given below to learn how to use the perfect tenses.

A. The **present perfect tense** is formed by using the auxiliary verb **have** in the present tense plus the past participle of the main verb.

Model Verb—Run			
Person	**Singular**	**Person**	**Plural**
First	I have run	First	we have run
Second	you have run	Second	you have run
Third	he has run	Third	they have run
	she has run		they have run

Use the present perfect tense to show that an action began in the past and has continued until now, or that an action has just happened. It is often used to show that an action occurred at an indefinite time in the past. Adverbs such as *just* and *already* are commonly included.

EXERCISE 6A

Fill in the present perfect tense of the verb given in parentheses. Use the chart of irregular verbs or your dictionary.

EXAMPLE: (study) Has Dr. Sandoval studied about Nicaragua?

1. (teach) Dr. Sandoval _____ _____ in the history department for the past five years.

2. (specialize) He _____ _____ in the history of Latin America ever since graduate school.

3. (enjoy) His students _____ always _____ his lectures about Guatemala.

4. (be) For the past semester he _____ _____ on a sabbatical leave.

5. (do) Dr. Sandoval _____ _____ research about his favorite subject in the library.

B. The **past perfect tense** is formed by using the auxiliary verb **had** plus the past participle of the main verb.

Model Verb—Run

Person	Singular	Person	Plural
First	I had run	First	we had run
Second	you had run	Second	you had run
Third	he had run	Third	they had run
	she had run		they had run
	it had run		they had run

Use the past perfect tense to show that one action happened before another action in the past. Use it only when you are writing in the past tense.

EXERCISE 6B

Fill in the past perfect tense of the verb given in parentheses. Use the chart of irregular verbs or your dictionary.

EXAMPLE: After we <u>had</u> <u>seen</u> the play, we went to a restaurant for dessert.

1. (read) The English class _____ already _____ the play last week.

2. (promise) The instructor _____ even _____ to meet the students at the theater.

3. (have) The play _____ _____ a long run in Boston and New York before opening here.

4. (enjoy) The students _____ not _____ reading the play as much as seeing it.

5. (choose) The instructor _____ _____ the play because she had once acted in it.

C. The **future perfect tense** is formed by using the auxiliary verbs **will have** plus the past participle of the main verb.

Model Verb—Run

Person	Singular	Person	Plural
First	I will have run	First	we will have run
Second	you will have run	Second	you will have run
Third	he will have run	Third	they will have run
	she will have run		they will have run
	it will have run		they will have run

Use the future perfect tense to show that something will happen in the future by a specific time.

EXERCISE 6C

Fill in the future perfect tense of the verb given in parentheses. Use the chart of irregular verbs or your dictionary.

EXAMPLE: By the time their trip is over, the Johnsons will have seen most of New England.

1. (buy) By next week the Johnsons _____ _____ _____ a new van for their trip.

2. (read) Before they leave they _____ _____ _____ several travel books about the New England region.

3. (make) Soon they _____ _____ _____ all their plans.

4. (start) By June the family _____ _____ _____ on their way.

5. (return) Toward the end of July, they _____ _____ _____ home with many souvenirs and photos to show their friends.

EXERCISE 6D

In the following sentences, supply the missing verb forms. Use the present perfect, past perfect, or future perfect tenses as needed.

During the past year, our local public schools (spend, present perfect) _____ _____ about $84 billion on supplies. This is an enormous savings over previous years when our schools (spend, past perfect) _____ _____ about 20 percent more than that. The savings occur this year because the schools (buy, present perfect) _____ _____ their supplies on the Internet. They (purchase, past perfect) _____ _____ everything from chalk to microscopes using paper purchase orders in the past. Now, by bidding for supplies on the Internet, schools (save, future perfect) _____ _____ _____ time and money by the end of the school year. Freed of busy work filling out paper forms, the employees (find, present perfect) _____ _____ that ordering online provides faster delivery and lower prices.

Progressive Tenses

Verbs have a progressive form indicating continuing actions. These forms are the same for both regular and irregular verbs. The progressive tenses use a form of the verb "**be**" as an auxiliary verb and the "**-ing**" form or present participle form of the main verb to show that an action is "in progress." For example, the present progressive tense indicates that some action is taking place right now.

Progressive Forms			
Present	is waiting	**Present Perfect**	has been waiting
Past	was waiting	**Past Perfect**	had been waiting
Future	will be waiting	**Future Perfect**	will have been waiting

Group ACTIVITY

Read the following story. Then answer the questions about the story. Answer in complete sentences, using the perfect tenses whenever possible. Compare your answers with those of the group.

Brian had worked as a bagger for several months when the manager asked him to stay late one Saturday night. Brian was worried that the manager had been watching him work and was not satisfied with his performance. Brian had tried to pack the bags carefully, but sometimes he had had difficulty with the fruit. He had never learned the proper way to pack soft fruit, and he had ruined many bags of peaches. Brian said to himself, "By this time tomorrow, I will have lost my job." He was very nervous.

1. What had the manager asked Brian to do? _____

2. Why was Brian worried? _____

3. What had Brian never learned? _____

4. What did Brian predict about the future? _____

LESSON 7   Tense Shift Problems

In the middle of a sentence, a paragraph, or an essay, do not shift tenses unless you have a reason to do so. If you begin writing in the present tense, don't shift to the past. If you begin in the past, don't shift to the present.

Tense Shift: Bike riding is a good way to meet people. They were always willing to join me on a short or a long trip. When I was riding my bike, I enjoyed the company of other bike enthusiasts. (The tense shifts from present to past.)

Revised: Bike riding is a good way to meet people. They are always willing to join me on a short or a long trip. When I am riding my bike, I enjoy the company of other bike enthusiasts. (All the verbs are in the present tense.)

Editing Practice

Some of the following sentences contain shifts in tense. Identify each error by drawing a line under the incorrect verb. Write the correct form above the word.

EXAMPLE: Some villagers from Vietnam worked as fishermen when they
moved
<u>move</u> to Louisiana.

1. In 1975, Nga moved from a fishing village in Vietnam to a large city in southern Louisiana. She finds the climate there similar to that of her native country. She and her husband settled in a suburb of New Orleans along with many other Vietnamese families. He works as a fisherman, and she raises vegetables in a small garden plot. She faced difficulties adjusting to life in a strange land, but before long she feels comfortable in her new home. In 1995, she and her husband proudly attend the college graduation ceremony of their daughter. Today that daughter works as a pharmacist in Atlanta, Georgia.

2. When my neighbor bought a used car, he received a lesson in odometer tampering. He thought he has bought a reliable, low-mileage car, but after he begins driving it, problems develop. His mechanic told him that the car needs a new transmission although the odometer showed only 30,000 miles. The mechanic becomes suspicious. Worn brake and gas pedals suggest that the car had probably been driven over 75,000 miles. Scratches on the odometer further convince the mechanic that the mileage has been changed.

LESSON 8

Sentence Combining

Here is another opportunity to sharpen your skills in the use of verbs as you combine the sentences in this lesson. Notice the way these four sentences have been combined into one sentence.

1. Kevin sorted the papers.
2. He sorted quickly.
3. Kevin put the papers into stacks.
4. Kevin made four stacks.

Combined Sentence: Kevin quickly sorted the papers into four stacks.

A. Combine these four sentences into one sentence.

1. Two hikers climbed the trail to Frog Lake.
2. Their backpacks were heavy.
3. The trail was steep.
4. It was rocky.

B. Combine these four sentences into one sentence.

1. Another strip mall will eliminate our neighborhood park.
2. It will increase traffic.
3. Our streets are narrow.
4. They are already crowded.

C. Combine these four sentences into one sentence.

1. Wynton Marsalis played in an orchestra.
2. It was the New Orleans Civic Orchestra.
3. He played first trumpet.
4. He was in high school.

D. Combine these four sentences into one sentence.

1. Delores has heard the beat of the music.
2. It is rock music.
3. The music and the voices come from the neighboring apartment.
4. She has heard it all night long.

E. Combine these four sentences into one sentence.

1. A reporter interviewed a candidate in the coming election.
2. The candidate was running for mayor.
3. The interview took place last Friday.
4. It was held on a television news program.

Chapter 2 Summary

-d	-ed	third-	forms	past	will	be	do	have	adverbs	never	
always	not										

Choose words from the box above to complete each sentence correctly.

1. Add -s to the verb in the _____ person singular form of the present tense.

2. Regular verbs add _____ or _____ to the present form to make the past tense form.

3. Look in the dictionary to find the principal _____ of irregular verbs.

4. To form the future tense, add the auxiliary verb _____ before the base form of the main verb.

5. To form the perfect tenses, use the auxiliary verb _____ before the _____ participle.

6. Some other examples of auxiliary verbs are _____ and _____.

7. The words that sometimes appear between the auxiliary verb and the main verb are called _____.

8. Some examples of adverbs are _____, _____, and _____.

Writing Assignment

Topic

A neighborhood is more than a collection of people, houses, and stores in the same vicinity. Neighborhoods can differ greatly, each having its own character. In this assignment you are asked to describe an activity in a neighborhood that you knew well in the past.

Step 1. Jot down a list of activities that occurred in your neighborhood.

1. _____

2. _____

3. _____

4. _____

5. _____

Step 2. Focus on a single activity because you cannot describe more than one event in a paragraph. Perhaps the people in your neighborhood were very sociable, and you believe that the Fourth-of-July block party best showed that trait. You might write an opening sentence such as this one: "Every Fourth of July, our neighborhood joined together in a huge dawn-to-dark celebration."

Step 3. Perhaps you prefer to show how a certain person reflected the spirit of your neighborhood. You might write: "Joe Marshall, who lived on our block, was typical of the helpful, friendly spirit in our neighborhood."

Step 4. Remember that you want to make your readers see and hear what you saw and heard in that neighborhood. Don't just write that the man next door was a good guy. Show him helping you change a tire. Let your reader hear his favorite greeting, "Hi, neighbor, come on in. How about a cup of coffee?"

Step 5. Look at your choice of verbs in each sentence of your rough draft. It might help to underline them.

Alternative Writing Assignment

Topic

Describe in detail an activity on your college campus that you have observed firsthand. Follow Steps 2 through 5 in the preceding Writing Assignment as you plan your paragraph. Remember to provide enough specific details to give your readers a clear picture of the activity.

CHAPTER 2
PRACTICE TEST: Verbs

Name _____

Date _____ Class Time _____

Instructor _____

I. **Underline the verb in each sentence. Write the past tense form of each verb on the lines at the right.**

1. Our class plans a reunion for the third weekend in June.   _____

2. Cars spin out of control on the icy streets.   _____

3. Mr. Fuller is a traffic controller at the airport.   _____

4. The shortstop throws the ball to the first baseman.   _____

5. My new job offers a number of advantages.   _____

II. **Underline the auxiliary verbs once and the main verbs twice. Some sentences may have no auxiliary verbs, and others may have more than one auxiliary verb.**

1. Rosa Sanchez has completed her plans already.

2. The senator is campaigning for a second term.

3. All the stores had sales after New Year's Day.

4. Flames were already shooting through the garage roof.

5. Why do so many couples marry in Las Vegas?

6. I have never heard that excuse before.

7. Did the architect finally complete the house plans?

8. Here is one answer to a difficult question.

9. You may need hotel reservations during the holidays.

10. Walter and Tanya had met for the first time at a conference in Dallas.

CHAPTER 2 PRACTICE TEST (Cont.)

III. Write auxiliary verbs in the blanks to make complete sentences.

1. An election _____ _____ held next Tuesday.

2. She _____ never run for political office before.

3. Yesterday we _____ discussing the election issues in class.

4. The candidates _____ speaking at an open meeting now.

5. _____ you vote yet?

IV. Complete the following sentences with the future tense of the verbs in parentheses.

1. (hold) The astronomy club _____ _____ a star watchers' class Friday evenings during January.

2. (serve) Carmen promises that she _____ _____ as chairman of the membership drive.

3. (honor) Many television programs next January _____ _____ Dr. Martin Luther King, Jr.

4. (retire) Our office manager announced that he _____ _____ in July.

5. (receive) Ben hoped that he _____ _____ a promotion soon.

V. In the following sentences, supply an auxiliary and a main verb using the verbs in parentheses. Use one of the perfect tenses.

1. (see) A farmer reported that he _____ _____ an alien spaceship in his pasture.

2. (verify) So far no one else _____ _____ the report.

3. (refuse) His wife _____ already _____ to talk to the press.

4. (make) Several people _____ _____ similar claims last year.

5. (convince) These reports _____ not _____ most people of the existence of alien spaceships.

VI. Write the principal forms of the following verbs.

Present	Present + s	Past	Past Participle	Present Participle
cry	_____	_____	_____	_____
break	_____	_____	_____	_____
am, are	_____	_____	_____	_____
tape	_____	_____	_____	_____
plan	_____	_____	_____	_____

VII. a. In the following sentences, bracket the adverbs and the contractions.
   b. Then underline the main verbs twice and the auxiliary verbs once.

1. Tony has always been a loyal fan of the Broncos.

2. Haven't they ever gone to a rock concert?

3. I can certainly understand the citizens' opposition to the landfill proposal.

4. Troy has recently won a scholarship award.

5. Mr. Loeb will seldom watch situation comedies on television.

Editing
Practice

Some of the following sentences contain shifts in tense. Identify each error by drawing a line under the incorrect verb. Write the correct form above the word.

Working in a legal office is a very demanding job. My job as a legal assistant consisted of processing many felony complaints and other legal documents. These complaints must be filed in court; therefore, they had to be accurate and completed on time. I was working under pressure all the time. I have to be dependable and courteous. Even when I was tired and depressed, I still have to be helpful and polite.

Understanding the Parts of the Sentence

In Chapter 3 you will learn about the main parts of the **sentence.**

Definitions of Terms

Every **sentence** must have at least one subject and one verb and express a complete thought.

The **subject** is the person or thing the verb is asking or telling about. In a sentence with an action verb, the subject is the person or thing doing the action.

The **subject of a command** is the pronoun <u>you</u>.

The **object** is the noun or pronoun that answers the questions "what?" or "whom?" after an action verb.

In the **active voice,** the subject of the sentence names the performer of the action.

In the **passive voice,** the subject of the sentence names the receiver of the action.

A **linking verb** joins the subject and a completer. Common linking verbs are <u>become</u>, <u>feel</u>, <u>seem</u>, <u>appear</u>, and the forms of the verb <u>be</u>.

A **completer** follows a linking verb to describe or rename the subject.

A **compound subject** is two or more subjects joined by a coordinating connective.

A **compound verb** is two or more verbs joined by a coordinating connective.

A **compound object** is two or more objects joined by a coordinating connective.

A **contraction** is a word formed by combining two words with an apostrophe to substitute for the omission of letters.

Prepositions are the words used to show position, direction, or relationship.

A **phrase** is a group of words without a subject and a verb. Examples are noun phrases, verb phrases, and prepositional phrases.

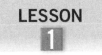

Subjects and Verbs

Fill in the blanks with nouns.

1. _____ land every few minutes at Chicago's O'Hare International Airport.

2. Have _____ claimed their luggage?

You know from Chapter 2 that these word groups have verbs, but they are not complete sentences because the subject of each verb (double underlined) is missing. You have filled in the subjects to make them complete sentences.

The **subject** of a sentence is the person or the thing the **verb** is asking or telling about. The subject may be a **noun** or a **pronoun**.

> **EXAMPLE:**   The tourists have returned home. Subject = tourists. To find the subject of this sentence ask, "Who have returned home?" The answer, The tourists, is the subject of the sentence.

Every **sentence** must have at least one subject and one verb and express a complete thought.

Subject Pronouns

Subject pronouns are used primarily as the subjects of sentences or clauses.

> **EXAMPLE:**   They have claimed their luggage. To find the subject, ask "who" or "what" with the verb: "Who have claimed their luggage?" The answer, They, is the subject of the sentence.

Subject pronouns also are used after all forms of the verb be in formal writing.

> **EXAMPLE:**   It is I. (In conversation most people would say, "It's me.")

Subject Pronouns		
Person	**Singular**	**Plural**
First	I	we
Second	you	you
Third	he, she, it	they

Complete each of the following sentences by supplying a subject pronoun.

1. Tiffany bought bagels and tortillas at the market. _____ served brunch to her friends.

2. The two burritos tasted delicious, but the lox on the bagel was too salty. _____ was left over at the end of the brunch.

3. Anthony traveled to Kansas City by bus. _____ wanted to visit the college campus there.

4. His uncle traveled with him. _____ planned to meet with the football coach.

5. Geneva and I run two miles every morning. _____ are training for the 5k run in September.

Finding Subjects and Verbs

1. First, find the verb. Underline the auxiliary verb once and the main verb twice.

   The children swim. They can play.

2. Then, find the noun or pronoun subject by asking who or what with the verb. Write S above the subject.

S   S
   Who swim? The children swim. Who can play? They can play.

   The answer gives you the noun or pronoun subject identified above.

3. If the sentence asks a question, put the sentence in the form of a statement to help you find the subject and the verb.

S   S
   Can the children play? Change to: The children can play.

   Then ask: Who can play?

                                  S
   The answer gives you the subject. The children can play.

4. Remember that every sentence must have at least one subject and one verb.

EXERCISE 1B

Underline the auxiliary verb once and the main verb twice. Write S above the subject. The last sentence has more than one subject and verb.

S   S

EXAMPLE: I have never traveled to Scotland. Have you ever been there?

1. Americans can experience the Scottish Highland Games without making a trip to Scotland.

2. Similar festivals are held in the United States each year.

3. We have attended the Scottish-American version of the games in our city several times.

4. The numerous events include many tests of strength, such as contests for shot putters, hammer throwers, and caber (pole) tossers.

5. During the caber toss, the contestants are throwing 100-pound, 18-foot poles with remarkable balance and accuracy.

6. The sheep dog trials show another kind of skill on the part of both dog and trainer.

7. In a short time, a small border collie drives the reluctant sheep through a narrow opening.

8. Bagpipers offer yet another diversion at the games.

9. They traditionally have led kilted soldiers into battle and kilted dancers through their steps.

10. Hearing the music of the bagpipers at a festival, you may think that you are in Scotland.

Commands and Requests

Each sentence must have at least one subject and one verb, but the verb can stand alone in a sentence without a stated subject in a **command** or **request**. The subject in such a sentence is the pronoun you.

V   S   V

EXAMPLES: Look! = You look!

$$\text{V} \qquad\qquad \text{S} \quad \text{V}$$
$$\underline{\text{Hurry!}} \ = \ \text{You } \underline{\text{hurry!}}$$
$$\text{V} \qquad\qquad\qquad \text{S} \quad \text{V}$$
$$\underline{\text{Pay}} \text{ the cashier.} \ = \ \text{You } \underline{\text{pay}} \text{ the cashier.}$$

EXERCISE 1C

Fill in the blanks with verbs that command or request.

1. _____ the invitations today.

2. _____ some stamps at the post office.

3. Don't _____ to seal the envelopes.

4. _____ to the party next Saturday.

5. _____ a glass of punch.

The subject of each of these five sentences is the pronoun, _____.

EXERCISE 1D

Write five commands or requests similar to those in Exercise 1C.

1. _____

2. _____

3. _____

4. _____

5. _____

LESSON 2

Objects of Action Verbs

Some action verbs may be followed by an **object** to complete the meaning of the sentence. To find the object of the verb, place <u>what</u> or <u>whom</u> after the subject and the verb.

Finding the Object of the Verb

Here is an example of how to identify a noun used as the object of a verb.

1. Gail's bicycle needs a new tire.
2. Ask: "Gail's bicycle needs what?"
3. The answer is: "Gail's bicycle needs a new tire."
4. Therefore, the noun <u>tire</u> is the object.

Object Pronouns

Here is an example of how to identify a pronoun used as the object of a verb.

EXAMPLE: Gail bought a new tire. She bought it. (<u>It</u> is the object of the verb <u>bought</u>.)

Object Pronouns

Person	Singular	Plural
First	me	us
Second	you	you
Third	him, her, it	them

EXERCISE 2A

Referring to the forms in the Object Pronouns box, write the appropriate object pronouns on the blank lines in the following sentences. Begin by double underlining the main verbs.

EXAMPLE: Matt couldn't go skating. We <u>met</u> ___him___ at the coffee shop later.

1. Last weekend my friends and I skated at the new outdoor ice skating rink. Naida had told _____ about it last week.

2. Her directions to the rink were very clear. We located _____ with no difficulty.

3. None of us had our own skates. However, we rented _____ at the rink.

4. I rode there with Melissa. She asked Cindy, Tracy, and _____ to go with her.

5. Melissa is the best skater in our group. We all admired _____ as she skimmed gracefully over the ice.

a. Write S above the subject, underline the auxiliary verb once, and underline the main verb twice.
b. Write the word that is the object of the verb on the line at the right. If there is no object, leave the space blank.

OBJECT

                                          S
EXAMPLE: All transistors <u>have</u> the same parts: an

                emitter of electrons, a collector of
                electrons, and a base.   _____parts_____

1. In 1947, scientists at Bell Laboratories created the first transistor.   _____

2. The transistor didn't receive much attention in the beginning.   _____

3. Soon it replaced vacuum tubes in radios and televisions.   _____

4. Today tiny transistors power everything from radios to computers, and from jets to satellites.   _____

5. Manufacturers can place millions of transistors on a single computer chip.   _____

Using any tense of the verbs shown, write your own sentences according to the directions in parentheses. Write S above the subjects and underline the verbs. Use your dictionary if you are uncertain about the meaning of any verb.

                                  S
EXAMPLES: 1. (read + object) I <u>read</u> two books about photography this
                   week.
                                         S
                2. (read, no object) I <u>read</u> until midnight last night.

1. (shake + object) _____

2. (paint, no object) _____

3. (vote, no object) _____

4. (do + object) _____

5. (like + object) _____

6. (leave, no object) _____

EXERCISE 2D

Underline the auxiliary verbs once and the main verbs twice. Write the object of the verb on the line at the right. If the verb does not have an object, leave the line blank.

	OBJECT
EXAMPLES: Why <u>don't</u> you <u>have</u> something to eat?	<u>something</u>
We never <u>eat</u> in the school cafeteria.	_____
1. The students read the test instructions carefully.	_____
2. They have been coming to class early this semester.	_____
3. She is writing so fast.	_____
4. Did you pass your test?	_____
5. I will not know the results until tomorrow.	_____
6. Didn't the instructor post the grades by the door?	_____
7. Open the door to the office.	_____
8. Jason has not completed his out-of-class assignment.	_____
9. Where is Jim going for the weekend?	_____
10. Bob and Jim are driving to Philadelphia.	_____

LESSON 3

Prepositional Phrases

Not many sentences have subjects and verbs as easy to recognize as those in the sentences you have been working with. We usually add words to the subject and the verb to give more information about them. Sometimes we use one word. Sometimes we use a group of words. A group of words introduced by a preposition is called a **prepositional phrase**. Prepositional phrases are often used to expand the subject and the verb.

Prepositions are the short words that show position, relationship, or direction. For example, if you were trying to give the location of your pencil, you might say: the pencil is on the desk, or the pencil is under the desk. The prepositions are on and under. The prepositional phrases are on the desk and under the desk.

Every prepositional phrase contains at least two words: a **preposition (P)** and an **object (O)**. The object is always a noun or a pronoun.

               S   P O

EXAMPLE: Paula enjoys a bowl of soup.

Some prepositional phrases contain adjectives that come between the preposition and the object. These words describe the object.

               S   P Adj.   Adj.   O

EXAMPLE: Paula enjoys a bowl of hot minestrone soup.

Notice that the object of the verb enjoys is the noun bowl in both of the examples above.

Finding the Object of the Preposition

Here is an example of how to identify a noun used as the object of a preposition.

1. She is competing in the race.
2. Ask, "In what?"
3. The answer is race.
4. Therefore, race is the object of the preposition in.

Pronouns can also be used as objects of prepositions.

EXAMPLE: She is competing in the race. She is competing in it. (It is the object of the preposition in.)

Commonly Used Prepositions

Position	Direction	Relationship
about	at	as
above	beyond	because of
across	down	but
after	from	by
against	in	except
along	into	for
before	on	like
during	to	of
near	toward	since
until	up	with

In the following exercises, bracket all prepositional phrases in the sentences to help locate the subjects and verbs of the sentences. The main reason for learning to recognize prepositional phrases is to help find the subject and the verb of a sentence. One common mistake in identifying the subject of a sentence is confusing it with a noun used as the object of the preposition. The subject of the sentence cannot be the object in the prepositional phrase.

EXERCISE 3A

Bracket all prepositional phrases in the following sentences. Use the Commonly Used Prepositions chart to help you identify the prepositions.

1. The Erie Canal, which opened the way to the Midwest, was the first important national highway built in the United States.

2. The laborers who installed the locks were working in the wilderness with no roads to haul the equipment needed to build the canal.

3. Their champion was De Witt Clinton, who by the time of the canal's opening had been mayor of New York City and governor of the state.

4. The canal cut travel time between Albany and Buffalo to six days from two weeks by wagon.

5. The Erie Canal opened in 1825 with the booming of a line of cannons stationed along the way and down the Hudson.

Prepositions of Two or More Words

These prepositions are made up of two or more words as in the sentence: I made the cake according to those directions.

according to	in addition to	in spite of
along with	in case of	on account of
because of	in front of	on top of
by means of	in the middle of	out of
contrary to	in place of	together with
for the sake of	instead of	with reference to

EXERCISE 3B

Bracket all the prepositional phrases in the following sentences. Use the preposition charts to help you identify the prepositions.

EXAMPLE: The rain began [in the middle of the game].

1. Last week I went to a baseball game along with two friends.

2. We didn't believe it would rain, contrary to the weather forecast.

3. On account of the large crowd, we waited at the box office.

4. A man in front of us complained loudly about the long wait in line.

5. After six innings the baseball game was called because of rain.

GRAMMAR TIP

1. Learn to recognize the prepositional phrase as a unit. The preposition comes first, and the object of the preposition comes last.

2. When you are doing exercises in this workbook or correcting your written assignments, remember to bracket all the prepositional phrases before trying to identify the subject and verb.

3. Next, find the verb.

4. Then, find the subject. Ask "who" or "what" to find the subject.

EXERCISE 3C

In the following sentences, first bracket all the prepositional phrases. Then underline the auxiliary verb once and the main verb twice, and write S above the subject.

EXAMPLE:

Grizzly bears [at Glacier National Park] are thriving [on cow parsnip].

1. The rangers in Glacier National Park must inform campers about cow parsnip.

2. The cow parsnip, a member of the parsley family, is the favorite food of the grizzly bears.

3. Grizzlies graze like cattle on moist slopes of cow parsnips.

4. At the time of year when backpackers are entering the park in large numbers, the grizzlies are looking for cow parsnips.

5. According to the park rangers, the grizzly bears are never far from the campers.

EXERCISE 3D

a. Place brackets around all the prepositional phrases in the paragraph below.
b. Underline the auxiliary verbs once and the main verbs twice. Write S above the subjects.

EXAMPLE: The guitars are hanging [on the wall] [behind that display].

Central Guitar is located along with a number of other guitar stores and studios on one long block in the middle of a large city. Last month Jerry Montgomery, a college sophomore, started a part-time job at Central. Rock 'n' roll music has always been one of Jerry's enthusiasms, and his record collection includes artists from Les Paul and Roy Orbison to Eddie Van Halen and the Wallflowers. The store's customers vary widely. A beginning player with only six weeks of instruction may be standing in front of the counter beside a star performer. One is shopping for a $95 guitar, and the other admires the finish on a $20,000 instrument. Autographed pictures of the top rock stars decorate the walls while the sound of guitar music surges into the shop from the studios just down the street. Jerry posts a notice of a rock concert above a rack of music and turns toward his next customer. Jerry, at this particular time, has found the perfect job.

LESSON 4
Active and Passive Forms of the Verb

Action verbs that can be followed by objects have active and passive voice forms.

Reggie caught the fly ball. (The object <u>ball</u> tells us what Reggie caught.)

Kiesha has bought another guitar. (The object <u>guitar</u> tells us what Kiesha bought.)

In the **active** form, the subject names the performer of the action.

Reggie <u>caught</u> the fly ball. (Reggie performs the action.)

Kiesha <u>has</u> <u>bought</u> another guitar. (Kiesha performs the action.)

In the **passive** form, the subject names the receiver of the action. Change the active to the passive by adding a form of **be** as a helping verb and the past participle form of the main verb.

The fly ball <u>was caught</u> by Reggie. (The subject <u>ball</u> is the receiver of the action.)

Another guitar <u>has been bought</u> by Kiesha. (The subject <u>guitar</u> is the receiver of the action.)

Using the passive is appropriate in the following instances:

1. Use the passive when the receiver or the result of an action is more important than the person performing the action:
   Her diamond necklace <u>was stolen</u>.   The thief <u>was captured</u> two months later.
2. Use the passive in scientific writing to stress the importance of an experiment:
   Tiny electrodes <u>were attached</u> to fruit flies to discover whether insects actually <u>sleep</u>.

3. Use the passive when the person performing the action is unknown or difficult to identify:
Charges regarding irregularities in the campaign funds <u>were</u> <u>leaked</u> to the press.

For the most part, use the **active** form of the verb in your writing. You will write more directly and clearly than if you use the passive. Compare the two sentences below:

Passive: Several reasons <u>were</u> <u>given</u> by the candidate for his failure to win re-election.

Active: The candidate <u>gave</u> several reasons for his failure to win re-election.

You can choose to use either the active or the passive form for stylistic reasons by considering which form is appropriate to your purpose.

EXERCISE 4A

Rewrite the following sentences changing the verbs from the passive to the active form.

1. Flying status was earned in the French Air Service by Eugene J. Ballard, the first African American airman, in 1917.

2. The group called Tuskegee Airmen was founded by General Benjamin Davis at Tuskegee, Alabama, in 1941.

3. These first African American combat pilots were commanded by General Davis during World War II.

4. Fifteen hundred missions over Europe were flown by these airmen beginning in 1943.

5. Bombers were escorted to their missions by the flyers of this new unit.

6. Not one bomber was lost to enemy action by these escorts.

7. The first enemy plane credited to the 99th Pursuit Squadron was shot down by Lieutenant Charles Hall in June of 1943.

8. Enemy power stations and trains also were bombed by the group.

9. The successful movement to end racial segregation in the military in 1948 during the Truman administration was strengthened by the outstanding performance of these airmen.

10. Today, minority students interested in flying careers are assisted by Tuskegee Airmen, Inc., established in 1972 by the veterans of the 99ᵗʰ Pursuit Squadron.

Group ACTIVITY

A. Before you come to class, underline the verbs and analyze each sentence to see whether the active or the passive form of the verb has been used.
B. During class, in groups of three or four, compare your answers and then explain why the writer of each sentence used the passive or the active form.
C. Which of the sentences can you improve by changing the form?
D. Which of the sentences contain both active and passive verbs?

1. Although the planet Saturn was identified in 1656, Pluto was not discovered until 1930.

2. Mario whacked the piñata hard and knocked the candies to the floor.

3. In 1955, Rosa Parks defied a bus driver's order and was taken promptly to a Montgomery jail.

4. An error was made in calculating the expenses for the advertising campaign.

5. After the parade, litter was scattered all over the streets.

6. Arnie was honored at a banquet after he won the tournament.

7. It is rumored that the treasurer is being investigated.

8. During the Bosnian conflict, thousands of families were uprooted from their towns.

LESSON 5 Linking Verbs

Action verbs tell what the subject does, did, or will do.

Linking verbs do *not* tell what the subject does. Linking verbs are verbs of being. They include all forms of the verb be—am, is, are, was, were, been, and being—and other verbs such as seem, feel, become, and appear, which can be substituted for forms of be.

Linking verbs link the subject with another word in the sentence that is called the **completer.**

1. The verb links the subject (S) to a noun or pronoun completer (C) that *renames* the subject.

    EXAMPLES: Judy is a dancer. Mr. Bradley is our football coach.

2. The verb links the subject to an adjective completer that describes the subject.

    EXAMPLES: Judy is graceful. Mr. Bradley is enthusiastic.

The Verb Be

The verb be is the most commonly used linking verb.

Present (Base Form)	Present + -s	Past	Past Participle	Present Participle
am, are	is	was, were	been	being

| Tense | Singular | | Plural | |
	Person	Form	Person	Form
Present	First	I am	First	we are
	Second	you are	Second	you are
	Third	he is	Third	they are
		she is		they are
		it is		they are
Past	First	I was	First	we were
	Second	you were	Second	you were
	Third	he was	Third	they were
		she was		they were
		it was		they were
Future	First	I will be	First	we will be
	Second	you will be	Second	you will be
	Third	he will be	Third	they will be
		she will be		they will be
		it will be		they will be

(continued)

Tense	Singular		Plural	
	Person	**Form**	**Person**	**Form**
Present Perfect	First	I have been	First	we have been
	Second	you have been	Second	you have been
	Third	he has been	Third	they have been
		she has been		they have been
		it has been		they have been
Past Perfect	First	I had been	First	we had been
	Second	you had been	Second	you had been
	Third	he had been	Third	they had been
		she had been		they had been
		it had been		they had been
Future Perfect	First	I will have been	First	we will have been
	Second	you will have been	Second	you will have been
	Third	he will have been	Third	they will have been
		she will have been		they will have been
		it will have been		they will have been

Linking Verbs

appear	become	grow	remain	taste
be	feel	look	seem	turn

In the following examples, S = subject, C = completer, and LV = linking verb.

            S   LV   C

1. The velvet feels soft.

             S   LV   C

2. Has this milk turned sour?

                    S   LV   C

3. Nevertheless, she will remain our president.

        S   LV   C

4. Darrell had become a pole vaulter in college.

                                S   LV   C

5. On the surface the coach's decision seemed reasonable.

Some of these linking verbs can also be used as action verbs with or without objects. Study the following examples:

Linking Verbs

        S   LV   C
a. The corn grows tall.

        S   LV   C
b. The cake tasted delicious.

        S   LV   C
c. The patient appeared better.

Action Verbs

        S   V   O
d. The farmer grows corn.

        S   V   O
e. Marla tasted the cheesecake.

        S   V
f. Richard appeared in a play on Broadway. (no object or completer)

In sentences d and e, the action verbs are followed by objects. In sentence f, the action verb is not followed by an object. Remember that these verbs are linking verbs only when they are followed by a word that renames or describes the subject of the sentence, as in sentences a, b, and c.

EXERCISE 5A

Write S above the subject, underline the auxiliary verbs and the main verbs, and label the completers (C) in each of the following sentences.

                S   C
EXAMPLES: The mango is a tropical fruit.

                S   C
           This mango looks ripe.

1. My daughter is a freshman at Jackson Community College.

2. She is a physical education major.

3. The traffic light is finally turning green.

4. The pedestrians seemed impatient.

5. Can you be the moderator of our next discussion?

6. The discussion should be interesting.

7. Is Mrs. Chavez your friend?

8. During high school Mrs. Chavez was both a friend and an adviser to me.

EXERCISE 5B

Write five sentences and label them according to the following example. You may use any tense of the verb and change it according to the sense of your sentence.

S   LV   C

EXAMPLE: (is + completer) Your report is excellent.

1. (become + completer) _____

   _____

2. (taste + completer) _____

   _____

3. (appear + completer) _____

   _____

4. (feel + completer) _____

   _____

5. (remain + completer) _____

   _____

EXERCISE 5C

Underline the auxiliary verb in each sentence once and the main verb twice. Write S above the subjects as shown in the examples. Write the word that is the object of the action verb or the completer of the linking verb on the lines at the right. If there is no object or completer, leave the line blank.

OBJECT or COMPLETER

               S

EXAMPLES: Isn't dinner ready yet?   _____ready_____

               S

Would you like some help in the

kitchen tonight?   _____help_____

1. Marla has just arrived home from work.   _____

2. Her last appointment at the office was late.   _____

3. Jack has been waiting for her for an hour.   _____

4. They both feel tired and hungry.   _____

5. The refrigerator looks almost empty.   _____

6. Marla finds some leftover chicken in the meat saver.   _____

7. Jack makes a tossed salad and slices some French bread.   _____

8. The bread tastes a bit stale.   _____

9. Marla prepares some fresh fruit for dessert.   _____

10. Jack does not seem very enthusiastic about the dessert.   _____

11. Marla comes to the rescue.   _____

12. She discovers a pint of chocolate ice cream in the freezer.   _____

Group ACTIVITY

Read the following paragraph. First, bracket the prepositional phrases. Then, underline the verbs and identify the subjects. Meet with two other students from your class to check each other's work. As a group make a list of the subjects and verbs and completers or objects in each sentence. Compare your list with the list prepared by another group in your class.

Although the achievements of W.E.B. Du Bois were many, his life ended sadly. Du Bois was born in Massachusetts in 1868. Before the turn of the century, he received a doctorate from Harvard University. He pioneered experimental sociology with *The Philadelphia Negro,* a book about his interviews with thousands of Philadelphia natives. With that book, he may have started American sociology. Later he became the editor of *The Crisis,* the NAACP magazine. Along the way he wrote *The Souls of the Black Folk* and *Black Reconstruction in America.* He clashed with

Booker T. Washington, champion of manual training for black youths; with Marcus Garvey, the black nationalist; and with the National Association for the Advancement of Colored People. In the last years of his life, Du Bois applied for membership in the Communist Party and then fled from America. He died in Ghana in 1963, a day before the Rev. Martin Luther King, Jr.'s March on Washington. In the past, W.E.B. Du Bois was admired as teacher, model, and inspiration by many black scholars. However, some scholars do not admire him today.

LESSON 6 — Compound Subjects, Verbs, and Objects

Until now most of the sentences in this book have had simple subjects and simple verbs. Many sentences, however, have **compound subjects** and **compound verbs**. A compound subject is made up of two or more subjects joined by coordinating connectives, such as and or or. A compound verb is made up of two or more verbs joined by coordinating connectives, such as and or or.

Simple Subject

S   LV   C
The melons are ripe.

Compound Subject

S   S   LV C
The melons and bananas are ripe.

Simple Verb

S   V
The car skidded.

Compound Verb

S   V   V
The car skidded and stopped.

GRAMMAR TIP

Objects and completers can also be compound.

Compound Object

S V   O   O   O
She brought fresh beans, squash, and tomatoes from her garden.

Compound Completer

S LV C   C
He is an actor and a musician.

EXERCISE 6A

Write five sentences with compound subjects. Underline and label the subjects (S) and the verbs (V).

1. _____

2. _____

3. _____

4. _____

5. _____

Write five sentences with compound verbs. Underline and label the subjects (S) and the verbs (V).

1. _____

2. _____

3. _____

4. _____

5. _____

EXERCISE 6B

Write S above the compound subjects, and underline the compound verbs in the following paragraph.

When I was in the second grade, my brother and I attended a Japanese class every day after our regular school. I resented Japanese school and complained frequently to my parents. The Japanese language and customs meant nothing to me. I wanted to play after school and envied the other children who did not have to go. Mother and Dad were sympathetic but firm. However, as I continued going to Japanese school, my interest and enjoyment grew. After a while I was able to communicate with my relatives in Japan and also act as a translator at school when a new student arrived from Japan. In time I realized that knowing two languages well and communicating with people were very important skills to me. Today I have decided to major in the Japanese language, and I hope to become a translator. Therefore, I am attending a community college and preparing myself for the university. I also speak Japanese daily while working part-time at a Japanese import company. Mother and Dad, meanwhile, recall my complaints about Japanese school and smile.

Pronouns in Compound Subjects and Objects

Compound subjects and objects can be a problem when they include pronouns. For example, what pronouns would you place in these blanks?

1. Bob and _____ (me, I) went to the game Friday.

2. We waited for Tom and _____ (he, him) after class.

I is correct in sentence 1 because I is the subject of the verb. Him is correct in sentence 2 because him is the object of the preposition for.

When you are in doubt about the form of a pronoun in sentences like these, leave out the noun subject or the noun object and the connective and read the sentence with the pronoun by itself.

1. Bob and I went to the game Friday. (You read, "I went to the game Friday." You wouldn't say, "Me went to the game Friday.")

2. We waited for Tom and him after class. (You read, "We waited for him after class." You wouldn't say, "We waited for he after class.")

Sometimes you might have to change the sentence slightly:

Bob and _____ (me, I) have been friends for years.
Change to: I have been Bob's friend for years.

When you read the following sentences aloud, leave out **one** of the subjects (or the objects) and connectives; then write the correct form of the pronoun on the line.

EXAMPLE: The supervisor asked Carol and me (I, me) to work an extra hour on Saturday. (Read aloud, "The supervisor asked me to work an extra hour on Saturday.")

1. Jean has been working as a volunteer in the hospital. Carol first met Donna and _____ (she, her) at the hospital last year.

2. I asked Jean to meet Donna and _____ (I, me) at the hospital cafeteria for lunch.

3. Andy and Donna drive to work together. Carol met Andy and _____ (she, her) when they were walking to the hospital parking lot.

4. Carol thanked Donna and _____ (he, him) for the ride home.

5. _____ (We, Us) parents should be concerned about our children's low test scores.

6. The principal and several teachers came to the PTA meeting. The parents asked the teachers and _____ (she, her) to explain the drop in test scores.

7. Victor and Wes tried out for the team last week. Both Victor and _____ (he, him) made the varsity squad.

8. Brian asked Wes and _____ (he, him) to meet him after football practice.

9. Carmen and _____ (I, me) misunderstood the directions.

10. The instructor gave Carmen and _____ (I, me) another day to complete our assignments.

LESSON 7

Contractions

In writing contractions, be sure to use an apostrophe. Note in the following examples that the apostrophe replaces the letter or the letters that have been omitted.

Omitting Letters in a Verb

EXAMPLES: She is my sister. She's my sister.

She will have to explain. She'll have to explain.

In each of the examples above, a pronoun (she) and a verb (is, will) have been combined. The apostrophe takes the place of the letter *i* in is and the letters *wi* in will. She is = she's; she will = she'll.

Omitting the *i* in Here Is and There Is

Contractions may also be formed by combining there with is and here with is.

EXAMPLES: There is John now. There's John now.

Here is your book. Here's your book.

In both cases the apostrophe takes the place of the letter *i* in is.

Note: There are and here are are not written as contractions. Furthermore, when a sentence begins with the words here is or there is, the noun that follows the verb is the subject.

EXERCISE 7A

Supply the contractions for these words.

1. she will   _____she'll_____   6. I am   _____

2. they have   _____   7. we have   _____

3. he had   _____   8. here is   _____

4. he is   _____   9. it is   _____

5. I will   _____   10. we are   _____

EXERCISE 7B

A. Supply the missing apostrophes.

1. Hell meet us in an hour.

2. Well shoot some baskets.

3. Heres your basketball.

4. After dinner theyre going to a play.

5. Theres the entrance to the theater.

6. Shell be late for the first act.

7. Theyll have some dessert after the play.

8. Youre wanted on the telephone.

9. Whos calling please?

10. Were not interested in subscribing to that magazine.

B. Now write the subjects and the complete verbs of the sentences. Omit the apostrophes and supply the missing letters of the verb if necessary. The first one has been completed for you.

	S	AV	MV		S	AV	MV
1.	he	will	meet	6.			
2.				7.			
3.				8.			
4.				9.			
5.				10.			

It is a good idea to limit the use of contractions to informal writing. Do <u>not</u> use contractions in formal letters, essays, or term papers.

LESSON 8

Sentence Combining

Practice using compound subjects and compound verbs in this exercise. Study the way the writer combined the following sentences into one sentence before you begin writing.

1. It was Sunday evening.
2. Ashley settled down.
3. Eric settled down.
4. They were on the couch.
5. They were in front of the television.
6. They watched their favorite program.

Combined Sentence: On Sunday evening Ashley and Eric settled down on the couch in front of the television and watched their favorite program.

Notice that the writer has used a compound subject in addition to prepositional phrases to combine six sentences into one.

On Sunday evening = prepositional phrase
Ashley and Eric = compound subject
in front of the television = prepositional phrase

A. Combine these four sentences into one sentence with a compound subject.

1. The members of the cast took their bows.
2. The members of the orchestra took their bows.
3. They took their bows to the applause of the audience.
4. It was the final performance of the play.

B. Combine these four sentences into one sentence with a compound verb.

1. The gardener finished his work.
2. He loaded his tools on his truck.
3. He loaded them quickly.
4. He drove off to his next job.

C. Combine these five sentences into one sentence with a compound subject.

1. I am going on a trip.
2. My friend is going too.
3. We are going on a barge.
4. We are going in November.
5. We are going through the French countryside.

D. Combine these six sentences into one sentence with a compound verb.

1. The sports car skidded on the road.
2. The sports car spun around.
3. The road was a mountain road.
4. The road was icy.
5. The sports car nearly rear-ended a truck.
6. The truck was huge.

E. Combine these five sentences into one sentence with a compound verb.

1. The driver of the sports car was frightened.
2. He turned the wheel sharply.
3. He brought the car to a stop.
4. It was a skidding stop.
5. He brought the car to a stop just in time.

Chapter 3 Summary

prepositional	subject	links	verb
object	compound	"You"	

Complete these sentences by choosing the appropriate words from the box.

1. In order to write complete sentences, remember to write a complete

   _____ and a noun or pronoun _____.

2. To help you find the verbs and their subjects, get in the habit of brack-

   eting _____ phrases.

3. Some action verbs may be followed by a noun or pronoun that is called

   the _____ of the verb.

4. A special group of verbs _____ the subject to a completer.

5. Two or more subjects or verbs joined by a coordinating connective are called _____ subjects or verbs.

6. The subject of a verb that commands or requests is the pronoun _____.

Writing Assignment

Topic

Read the paragraph in Exercise 6B in this chapter by the student whose parents sent her to Japanese school despite her protests. Write a paragraph about a past activity of yours that gave you little sense of purpose or no good reason for participating in it at the time. Today, however, the experience has proved valuable to you, and you are glad that you made the effort.

If you do not wish to write about yourself, perhaps you know someone you can interview who has had such an experience and is willing to serve as your subject.

Step 1. When you are planning your paragraph, jot down questions that lead to an evaluation of the experience rather than just telling a story about it. To begin, make a list by answering these questions:

1. What specifically was the activity? Where and when did it take place? Is this an unusual activity? Will your reader require any special definitions?
2. Did someone else persuade you to participate in it, or was it your own idea?
3. What pressures, your own or someone else's, did you face?
4. Why did you continue despite your negative feelings and objections?
5. Why do you now regard this as a valuable experience?

Step 2. Decide how many items on your list you will include in your paragraph. For each item jot down specific details and examples that you will need to include to give your reader a clear picture of your experience.

Step 3. Write a topic sentence summing up the change in your thinking that took place.

For example, "As I continued going to Japanese school, my interest and enjoyment grew."

The topic sentence should give your opinion about the subject. Read the discussion of the topic sentence in Chapter 10 to help you write the topic sentence.

Step 4. Write S above the subjects, underline the auxiliary verbs once, and underline the main verbs twice in your rough draft. Attach the rough draft to your completed paragraph.

Alternative Writing Assignment

Topic

Look back at the Group Activity in Lesson 5. After reading over the paragraph about W.E.B. Du Bois, you might be reminded of a friend or acquaintance who is outstanding in some ways but has difficulty getting along with colleagues and friends.

Step 1. Begin by writing the name of the person you are going to write about in the middle of a piece of paper. Draw a circle around the name. Then make a cluster of circles listing the achievements or good qualities on one side of the central circle and a cluster of circles listing the problems or difficulties on the other side of the central circle. (For further discussion of "clustering," see Chapter 10.)

Step 2. Decide how many achievements and how many character problems you will include from your cluster diagram.

Step 3. Then write a topic sentence containing an evaluation of your subject's strengths and weaknesses. For example, although the achievements of W.E.B. Du Bois were many, his life ended sadly.

The topic sentence should give your opinion about the subject. Read the discussion of the topic sentence in Chapter 10 to help you write your sentence.

Step 4. Write S above the subjects, underline the auxiliary verbs once, and underline the main verbs twice in your rough draft. Attach the rough draft to your completed paragraph.

CHAPTER 3

PRACTICE TEST: Understanding the Parts of the Sentence

Name _____

Date _____ Class Time _____

Instructor _____

I. Write the subjects, the auxiliary verbs, and the main verbs on the lines at the right. Some sentences may have more than one auxiliary verb, and some may not have any auxiliary verb, but all the sentences have main verbs and subjects.

	S	AV	MV
1. Jesse's license plates have expired.	_____	_____	_____
2. Why didn't he renew them last month?	_____	_____	_____
3. Pull over to the curb!	_____	_____	_____
4. The officer listens politely to Jesse's excuse.	_____	_____	_____
5. He is smiling and writing a citation.	_____	_____	_____
6. Nola has recently been to traffic school.	_____	_____	_____
7. She had been driving over the speed limit.	_____	_____	_____
8. Across the street from the police station is the library.	_____	_____	_____

CHAPTER 3 PRACTICE TEST (Cont.)

9. Traffic school is
    usually held in the
    library.   _____   _____   _____

10. Nola's class met
    for six hours.   _____   _____   _____

II. **a. First, bracket the prepositional phrases and underline the verbs.**

    b. Then, write the word that is the object of the verb on the line at the right.

    c. If there is no object of the verb, leave the space blank.

OBJECT

1. May I ride with you to school on Wednesday?   _____

2. Write the objects on the lines at the right.   _____

3. Eddie will be working for a tax consultant during
    March.   _____

4. The students in the political science class recently
    heard some startling facts.   _____

5. Tina studies French daily from 10 A.M. until noon.   _____

III. **Write a word of your choice in each blank. The words that are called for are linking verbs (LV) and completers (C). Do not use any form of a verb more than once, including the verb <u>to be</u> (<u>am</u>, <u>is</u>, <u>are</u>, <u>was</u>, <u>were</u>).**

1. (C) Did Joanna feel _____ about the interview?

2. (LV) The rent for the apartment _____ too high.

3. (C) Bert will probably be (a/an) _____ next year.

4. (LV) The children _____ hungry again soon after lunch.

5. (LV) The circus bear _____ harmless.

IV. 1. Write a sentence with a compound verb.

_____

_____

2. Write a sentence with a compound subject.

_____

_____

3. Write a sentence with a compound object or a compound completer.

_____

_____

V. In the following sentences, underline the correct form of the pronoun in the parentheses.

1. Brenda, her brother, and (me, I) have decided to buy tickets for a concert.

2. (Her, She) and her brother have been saving money for the tickets.

3. Her brother will drive Brenda and (I, me) downtown to the box office.

4. I like to go to concerts with Brenda and (he, him).

5. (He, Him) and Brenda enjoy going to concerts together with me.

VI. In the following sentences, bracket the prepositional phrases.

1. Aretha has been practicing tennis with her coach for many months.

2. Despite the pain in her arm, Aretha comes to the court every morning.

3. After a half hour, she puts an ice pack on her shoulder.

4. Aretha, together with her coach, runs around the track in the afternoon.

5. She cannot play in the tournament because of the injured shoulder.

CHAPTER 3 PRACTICE TEST (Cont.)

VII. a. Supply the missing apostrophe.

1. Well help you with those heavy suitcases.

2. Theyre too heavy for you to carry alone.

3. Youre going to drive us to the airport.

4. Ive been looking forward to this vacation for a long time.

5. Youll get a postcard from us soon.

b. Now list the subjects and the complete verbs of the sentences in VII. a. Omit the apostrophes and supply the missing letters of the verb if necessary.

	Subject	Auxiliary Verb(s)	Main Verb
1.	_____	_____	_____
2.	_____	_____	_____
3.	_____	_____	_____
4.	_____	_____	_____
5.	_____	_____	_____

Editing Practice

Some of the pronouns in the following sentences are incorrect. Underline the pronouns you think are incorrect and write the correct ones above them.

I
EXAMPLE: My brother and <u>me</u> want to buy a condominium together.

We want to find one that has a bedroom for him and one for me. Him and I have been sharing one bedroom for a long time. There has never been any trouble between he and I. The real estate agent asked whether my brother and I need two bathrooms. My brother said that him and I need two bedrooms and two bathrooms. Between you and I, I think that is a good idea. The agent told my brother and me to consider sharing a bathroom to save money. We're going to inspect some condominiums that her and her partner have listed. Now me and my brother may have to compromise in order to find a place we can afford. I hope that my brother and me can find one we like.

Adjectives and Adverbs

In Chapter 4 you will learn about several ways to expand the sentence using modifiers, such as adjectives and adverbs.

Definitions of Terms

An **adjective** modifies a noun or pronoun by limiting or describing it.

A **verb phrase** is the combination of an auxiliary verb and one of the principal forms of the verb. It is used as the verb of the sentence.

A **participle** is a verb form that may function as part of a verb phrase (was winning) or as an adjective (the winning team).

The **comparative** form of the adjective or adverb is used to compare two people, places, ideas, things, or actions.

The **superlative** form of the adjective or adverb is used to compare three or more people, places, ideas, things, or actions.

An **adverb** can modify verbs, adjectives, or other adverbs. It answers one of the following questions: When? How? Where? Why?

Verbals are formed from verbs but cannot function as main verbs. They are used as nouns, adjectives, and adverbs. A **verbal phrase** includes a **verbal** plus a noun and/or a prepositional phrase.

A **modifier** describes, limits, or makes specific another word in the sentence.

A **misplaced modifier** is an adjective or adverb that has been placed next to a word it does not modify.

A **dangling modifier** is an adjective or adverb that does not modify any word in the sentence.

LESSON
1

Adding Details with Adjectives

The sentences you have written for the exercises in Chapters 1 through 3 are just a beginning. Readers usually ask more of the writer: more color, more variety, more information, more specific details. **Modifiers** (adjectives and adverbs) give the reader additional information by further describing and qualifying nouns and verbs.

Functions of Adjectives

1. An adjective (A) makes a noun (N) or pronoun (P) specific or concrete by limiting and describing it:

   N   N   N
   Ginseng grows in the forests of the United States.

   A   N   A   A   N   A
   Wild ginseng grows in the dense mountain forests of the southeastern

      N
   United States.

2. To give the reader a mental picture of a subject, the writer chooses adjectives that describe the qualities or characteristics of it:

        N   N   N
   a. This plant is valued for the properties of its roots.

            A   N   A   N
   b. The unusual roots are valued as a medical remedy.

          P   A   A   A
   c. They are yellow, gnarled, and knotted.

Position of Adjectives

1. The adjective usually appears before the noun:

   A   N   A   N   A   N
   long assignment   busy weekend   difficult exam

2. But the adjective can follow the noun it modifies:

      N   A   A   N   A   A
   his refusal, firm but courteous,   her manner, confident and friendly,

3. Adjectives can also follow linking verbs:

          N   LV   A
   The challenger seemed eager for the match to begin.

Special Forms of Adjectives

1. Sometimes present and past participles are used as adjectives:

   <u>excited</u> fans   <u>winning</u> pass   <u>opening</u> game   <u>defeated</u> team

   (A N) (A N) (A N) (A N)

2. When a noun directly precedes another noun, the first noun serves as an adjective to describe or limit the second noun:

   <u>canvas</u> tent   <u>circus</u> performance   <u>lion</u> trainer   <u>cotton</u> candy

   (A N) (A N) (A N) (A N)

3. Prepositional phrases are also used as adjectives. (Review Chapter 3, Lesson 3.)

   Toshiro sent five letters <u>of application</u>.

   (N A N A)

   <u>Of application</u> specifies the kind of letters that Toshiro sent; therefore, the phrase is an adjective.

4. The noun markers that you studied earlier can also be classified as adjectives. These include **articles, demonstrative pronouns, indefinite pronouns, numerals, possessive nouns,** and **possessive pronouns.** (Examples may be found in **noun markers**, Chapter 1, Lesson 4.)

GRAMMAR TIP

Remember to consult your dictionary when you have difficulty identifying a part of speech. Assigning a part of speech to a word depends on its use in the sentence. For example, in the special forms of adjectives described in the examples above, the word <u>circus</u>, which generally functions as a noun, serves as an adjective in the phrase "circus performance." Look up the word <u>circus</u> in your dictionary and then look up the word <u>fast</u>. How many parts of speech do you find listed in each entry?

EXERCISE 1A

In the following sentences, bracket all the participles and nouns used as adjectives.

EXAMPLE: Alex spent an [exciting] time at the [football] game.

1. In his reserved seat, Alex watched a closely fought game on a chilly night.

2. During intermission he bought a hot dog with mustard and relish and a paper cup of hot coffee.

3. Victory came for the home team during the closing minutes of the game.

4. The fans cheered the rookie quarterback as he carried the ball into scoring territory.

5. As he left the sports stadium, Alex hoped that this game marked the beginning of a winning streak.

6. The wind was cold, so he zipped up his nylon parka, pulled on his leather gloves, and wished he had worn a wool sweater under his parka.

7. But Alex's evening ended on a low note, for he could not find his car in the crowded lot.

8. A stadium guard had called a truck to tow Alex's car from the no-parking zone.

Ways to Identify Adjectives

When writers choose adjectives to create a picture for the reader, they are asking themselves questions about their subjects. Questions like these can help writers to add details to a sentence.

1. What kind?

   EXAMPLE: dancing lessons   "Dancing" tells what kind of lessons.

2. How many?

   EXAMPLE: ten lessons   "Ten" tells how many lessons.

3. Which one?

   EXAMPLE: the last lesson   "The" and "last" tell which lesson.

4. Whose?

   EXAMPLE: Mitra's lesson, her lesson   "Mitra's" and "her" tell whose lesson.

Fill in each blank with an adjective.

1. Frida Kahlo was a _____ artist.

2. _____ paintings are in the collections of many large museums.

3. She had a _____ accident when she was a young girl.

4. To show her _____ feelings, she painted herself weeping.

5. Many of her paintings depict her _____ pain.

6. A few of her paintings show her with a monkey on _____ shoulder.

7. She was married to _____ painter, Diego Rivera.

8. A number of her paintings reveal her _____ relationship with Rivera.

9. _____ books have been written about Kahlo's _____ life.

10. As a woman painter, she received _____ recognition during her lifetime.

Punctuating Adjectives Before a Noun

Use commas to separate two or more adjectives that modify the same noun if a coordinating connective such as <u>and</u> or <u>but</u> can be inserted between the adjectives. For a more detailed explanation, see Chapter 8, Lesson 5.

EXAMPLES: a. The enthusiastic candidate spoke in a loud <u>and</u> excited voice.
            b. The enthusiastic candidate spoke in a loud, excited voice.
            (A comma separates the adjectives.)

Insert commas as needed in the following sentences.

1. The scenic rugged lands of northeastern Arizona attract tourists from everywhere.

2. Glowing sunsets illuminate the purple red and blue-gray sediments in the curving mounds of the Painted Desert's surreal landscape.

3. Steep red sandstone cliffs surrounding Lake Powell provide a stark contrast to its clear intense emerald-green water.

4. The mineralized rainbow-colored giant stone trees now lie exposed upon the floor of the Petrified Forest through the action of wind and water.

5. Some of the most remarkable breathtaking and memorable views of secluded sandstone canyons, rivaling those of the Grand Canyon, perhaps not in immensity, but surely in beauty, await the visitor to Canyon de Chelly (de shay).

Group ACTIVITY

Part A: First, bracket all the adjectives in the following paragraph as shown in the first sentence. Then, together with members of your group in class, check each other's work.

It is [a] [beautiful], [sunny] day in [a] [popular] [theme] park in [the] United States. Mr. and Mrs. Tomita, on their first trip to this country, listen attentively to a tour guide's claim that 35,000 adults and children visit the park every day. Most visitors to this magical place are attracted by an amazing variety of shows, rides, exhibits, and restaurants. Both Mr. and Mrs. Tomita, however, are impressed by the clean surroundings. They are staying at the vacationland's hotel where the rooms have immaculately clean, blue plastic furniture, green and beige walls, and beds covered with purple-green spreads. The hotel's parking lot, with its carefully planted vegetation, is also sparkling and clean. The smallest scrap of litter is sucked underground and rushed via pipes to an efficient trash compactor. Even the friendly birds do their part by picking some bread crumbs off the restaurant's patio at the hotel. Mr. and Mrs. Tomita know that they will enjoy themselves in this spotless American tourist attraction.

Part B: Working together with your group, write five sentences about a theme park that you have visited. In these five sentences, use at least one possessive pronoun, one possessive noun, one noun marker, one color, and one number, as adjectives. You, of course, may use more of these words if you wish. Exchange your sentences with those of another group in the class. Check each other's work by bracketing the adjectives in each sentence.

1. _____

_____

_____

2. _____

_____

_____

3. _____

_____

_____

4. _____

_____

_____

5. _____

_____

_____

LESSON 2

Adding Details with Adverbs

Another kind of modifier is an **adverb**. Adverbs offer additional information about verbs, adjectives, and other adverbs. The adverb tells the time the action happened, the place it happened, the manner in which it happened, and the purpose of the action.

GRAMMAR TIP

Recognizing Adverbs

1. Although you may identify many adverbs by the -*ly* ending (examples: quickly, slowly, softly), not all words ending in -*ly* are adverbs. (Lonely and lovely are adjectives.)

2. In fact, many adverbs do not end in -*ly* (examples: otherwise, soon, almost, very, rather, not).

3. Some adjectives and adverbs have the same form (examples: fast, hard, only, right, straight).

4. Learn to identify adverbs by determining their use in sentences and by consulting your dictionary.

Ways to Identify Adverbs

Study the following questions for adverbs.

1. Ask the question, When?

   EXAMPLE: I ran five miles yesterday.

   The word yesterday tells *when* I ran five miles.

2. Ask the question, How?

   EXAMPLE: I ran five miles slowly.

   The word slowly tells *how* I ran five miles.

3. Ask the question, Where?

> **EXAMPLE:**   I ran five miles <u>around the track</u>.

The words <u>around the track</u> tell *where* I ran five miles.

4. Ask the question, Why?

> **EXAMPLE:**   I ran five miles <u>for my health</u>.

The words <u>for my health</u> tell *why* I ran five miles.

From the examples given above, you can see that an adverb can be a single word (yesterday) or a phrase (around the track). To determine if a word or group of words is an adverb, ask *when, where, how,* or *why.* Adverbs answer these questions.

Function of Adverbs

Adverbs are usually added to a basic sentence to give the reader more information.

> **EXAMPLE:**   She arrived.   basic sentence
>
> She arrived <u>early</u>.   tells <u>when</u> she arrived
> She arrived <u>suddenly</u>.   tells <u>how</u> she arrived
> She arrived <u>at my door</u>.   tells <u>where</u> she arrived
> She arrived <u>to stay with me</u>.   tells <u>why</u> she arrived

Some sentences need additional information to make them more interesting to your reader. Adverbs add interest and information.

Note: A few words that are usually nouns sometimes function as adverbs.

They tell where he walked: He walked <u>home</u>.
They tell how far: He walked <u>a mile</u>.
They tell when: He walked <u>yesterday</u>.

Position of Adverbs

The position of an adverb in a sentence is flexible; that is, it can be moved around in a sentence. The position of the adverb <u>occasionally</u> is correct in all the sentences in the following example:

EXAMPLE: Occasionally she eats in the cafeteria.
She occasionally eats in the cafeteria.
She eats occasionally in the cafeteria.
She eats in the cafeteria occasionally.

A limited number of adverbs and the contraction for not (n't) may appear between the auxiliary verb and the main verb.

EXAMPLE: He has often eaten in the cafeteria, but he wouldn't eat there today. For a partial list of these adverbs, review Chapter 2, Lesson 4.

EXERCISE 2A

In the following sentences, fill in the blanks with one-word adverbs or adverbial prepositional phrases of your choice. The sentences form a paragraph.

EXAMPLE: Kimiko had been planning her vacation for six months.
                                                          (when)

1. Kimiko arrived _____ after a long flight _____.
                        (when)   (where)

2. The pilot landed the plane _____ and _____.
                                        (how)   (how)

3. All the passengers _____ applauded _____.
                                (where)   (how)

4. Kimiko walked _____ toward the exit door _____.
                        (how)   (where)

5. She was thrilled to be _____ after so many years.
                                    (where)

Misuse of Modifiers

Adjectives and adverbs are both modifiers, but they modify different parts of speech. Speaking informally, we do not always observe the distinction between the two. When we say, "Come here quick!" we use the adjective "quick" instead of the adverb "quickly," which should modify the verb "Come." Such expressions have become common and are generally accepted by most people.

For school and business writing, however, follow these guidelines:

1. Adjectives modify only nouns and pronouns.
2. Adjectives follow linking verbs.
3. Adverbs modify verbs, adjectives, and adverbs.

So you would write: The children come <u>quickly</u> when their mother calls them.

Commonly Misused Modifiers

Adjectives	Adverbs
well (healthy)	well (satisfactorily)
bad	badly
real	really
good	

EXERCISE 2B

In the sentences below, underline the correct form of the modifier in parentheses.

EXAMPLE: Jason drove very (careful, <u>carefully</u>) through the school zone.

1. While shopping, Shana tried on several dresses before she found one that fit her (perfect, perfectly).

2. Jill sings off key, but she plays the piano (good, well).

3. Sergio won the golf tournament (easy, easily) with a score of 15 under par.

4. After talking to his counselor, Martin felt (well, good) about his prospects for a scholarship.

5. The engine ran (smooth, smoothly) after the mechanic tuned it.

6. Antwaan studied (real, really) hard for his chemistry final.

7. Yolanda was feeling (good, well) after recovering from the flu.

8. The weather looked so (bad, badly) that we decided to stay home.

9. Jennifer was running so (quick, quickly), she got to the bus stop before the light turned red.

10. Garrett told Tonya that she should take her work more (serious, seriously).

Completing this exercise will give you a further review of adjectives and adverbs. Combine the sentences in each part according to the directions. Sections A, B, and C focus on adjectives, and sections D and E focus on adverbs.

A. Combine these five sentences into one sentence. Use a prepositional phrase to describe the sale. Use a participle to describe the books and the customers.

1. The bookstore was having a sale.
2. They were selling reduced books.
3. The books were slightly soiled.
4. But the customers didn't mind the smudge marks.
5. The customers were delighted.

_____

_____

_____

B. Combine these six sentences into one sentence in which the subject is compound. Use salesman's to modify the noun briefcase.

1. Books filled the briefcase.
2. Magazines filled the briefcase.
3. The briefcase belonged to a salesman.
4. The briefcase was large.
5. It was brown.
6. It was leather.

_____

_____

_____

C. Combine these seven sentences into one sentence that shows a contrast. Use modifiers to describe the nouns bicycle and roads.

1. Ervin has a bicycle.
2. The bicycle is lightweight.
3. But it is strong enough.
4. He can ride it on city streets.
5. The streets are paved.
6. He can ride it on country roads.
7. The roads are unpaved.

_____

_____

_____

D. Combine these six sentences into one sentence.

1. It was Monday.
2. The foreign minister arrived.
3. He was a new one.
4. He arrived early.
5. It was in the morning.
6. He arrived in Helsinki.

_____

_____

_____

E. Combine these six sentences into one sentence.

1. Mrs. Konitz joined her friends.
2. She usually met them every Sunday afternoon.
3. They sat on the same bench.
4. The bench was just inside the gate.
5. It was the gate to the park.
6. The gate was at the south end of the park.

_____

_____

_____

The Comparative and Superlative Forms of Adjectives and Adverbs

LESSON 3

We use the **comparative** form when comparing _two_ people, places, things, or actions. We use the **superlative** form when comparing _three_ or more people, places, things, or actions. You can form the comparative and superlative forms of adjectives and adverbs in a number of different ways as the following explanation shows.

Forming Comparatives and Superlatives

Adjectives

One Syllable: Most one-syllable words add -er and -est (rich, richer, richest).

Two Syllables: Many two-syllable words add -er and -est (happy, happier, happiest).

SPELLING TIP

Note that in the comparitive forms of words ending in -y, the y changes to i before you add the endings.

Three (or More) Syllables: All three-syllable words add more and most (plentiful, more plentiful, most plentiful).

Adverbs

One Syllable: Most one-syllable words add -er and -est (fast, faster, fastest).

Two (or More) Syllables: Most two-syllable words add more and most (carefully, more carefully, most carefully).

Note: The following adjectives and adverbs have irregular comparative and superlative forms.

Positive	Comparative	Superlative
Adjectives		
bad	worse	worst
good	better	best
well (healthy)	better	best
Adverbs		
badly	worse	worst
well (satisfactorily)	better	best

EXERCISE 3A

Change the adjective in parentheses into the comparative or superlative form as indicated. The first sentence is completed as an example.

1. Buying a computer for home or business may be the __most important__ purchase you will make in the next ten years. (important, superlative)

2. The computer you choose for the home is almost _____ to use than the telephone. (easy, comparative)

3. It enables you to have a _____ method of controlling the family budget. (good, comparative)

4. You should be sure to buy a computer that can be upgraded to a _____, _____ model sometime in the future. (big, comparative) (powerful, comparative)

5. The data-processing computer has become the _____ addition to the business world. (recent, superlative)

6. Some computerized information systems offer businesses _____ productivity. (great, comparative)

7. They even promise _____ use of energy. (efficient, comparative)

8. The use of computers encourages _____ business procedures. (simple, comparative)

9. The _____ computer systems are powerful enough to process company payrolls. (large, superlative)

10. The computer you buy for home or business should be the _____ quality at the _____ price. (good, superlative) (low, superlative)

EXERCISE 3B

Change each adverb in parentheses into the comparative or superlative form. The first sentence is completed as an example.

1. Shalita Grant, a night school student and the mother of three children under the age of ten, had decided __most reluctantly__ to give up her full-time job. (reluctantly, superlative)

2. She wanted to perform all three roles _____. (efficiently, comparative)

3. The inability to organize her activities was not the problem; she planned each day _____ than the last. (systematically, comparative)

4. Her supervisor arranged a flexible schedule that allowed her to _____ fulfill her obligations at home, at school, and at work. (easily, comparative)

5. Mrs. Grant is one of an increasing number of white-collar workers with staggered working hours who now fare _____ at home and at work. (well, comparative)

6. The companies adopting flexible scheduling for employees _____ benefit as well. (often, superlative)

7. Absenteeism drops _____ as employees request less time off for medical and dental appointments. (significantly, superlative) In addition, many companies find that flexible scheduling improves production and raises worker morale.

Less and Least Less and least may be substituted for more and most to show a lesser degree in a comparison.

Comparative (followed by than)	**Superlative** (followed by of or other prepositions)
less dangerous less comfortable	least dangerous least comfortable

EXERCISE 3C

Fill in the blanks with words that show a lesser degree of comparison.

> **EXAMPLE:** The driver's account of the accident was __less__ factual than the traffic officer's.

1. The speaker was _____ interesting than I had expected.

2. Highway 10 is the _____ dangerous way of all through the mountains.

3. That house is _____ expensive than the one we looked at this morning.

4. I am the _____ creative member of our family.

5. The baby seems _____ sleepy than she was an hour ago.

Look at the chart below comparing the costs of a day at the stadium. Answer the following questions in complete sentences. Use the comparative or superlative form of adjectives to compare the costs.

Comparison of the Costs of a Day at a Stadium

Team	Hot Dog	Soda	Ticket	Parking
MILWAUKEE LIONS (Milwaukee Stadium)	$3.00	$1.50	$30.00	$4.00
TENNESSEE EAGLES (Memphis Stadium)	$2.75	$1.25	$27.50	$5.00
MANCHESTER MOLES (New Hampshire Forum)	$2.50	$1.75	$25.00	$3.00
TEXAS TIGERS (Austin Astrodome)	$3.25	$1.95	$20.00	$10.00

1. How does the total cost compare between the Austin Astrodome and the

   Milwaukee Stadium? _____

   _____

2. How does the cost of a hot dog compare between the New Hampshire

   Forum and the Memphis Stadium? _____

   _____

3. How does the cost of a soda compare between the Memphis Stadium and

   the Austin Astrodome? _____

   _____

4. How does the cost of a ticket compare between the teams in Milwaukee and

   Memphis? _____

   _____

5. Compare the cost of parking in all four stadiums. Where would you prefer

to park your car? Explain why. _____

_____

EXERCISE 3E

In the following paragraph, change the adjectives in parentheses into the comparative or superlative form as indicated.

EXAMPLE: Many people think that the _____best_____ ritual of all is the
                                                (good, superlative)
    lighting of the seven candles.

1. Kwanzaa is the holiday that has received the _____ response from
                                                        (enthusiastic, superlative)
    African Americans.

2. Since its origin around 1965, many people are joining in a _____
                                                                (active, comparative)
    celebration of Kwanzaa every year.

3. The _____ children receive gifts that are supposed to be home
           (young, superlative)
    made.

4. Each night of the week, another candle is lit to represent one of the seven

    _____ principles by which people should live.
    (high, superlative)

5. One of the _____ symbols is the Unity cup.
                (unusual, comparative)

6. The Unity cup is used to pour libations for all the people at the celebration

    to share in the _____ ideal of the unity of the people.
                        (important, superlative)

Group ACTIVITY

A. Read the following paragraph. First, bracket all words used as adverbs in the paragraph as shown in the first sentence. Then, together with members of your group, check each other's work.

A baseball can carry [farther] in some stadiums than in others. Most hitters already know that fact. There is also evidence that, on some days and in some stadiums, a ball will go even farther. The ideal day would be very hot and very humid. The stadium in Denver, located at an altitude of 5,280 feet, is the ideal place. Many players hit best of all in Denver's stadium, and they hit worst of all in the stadium in San Diego. The stadium in that city is at sea level, and there is almost no humidity. A baseball travels fastest and farthest on hot, humid days and at high altitudes. So if you are seriously interested in becoming a "home-run king," you should travel to Denver on an exceptionally hot day in August, and you should be able to hit the ball harder and faster.

B. Working as a group, write five sentences about a campus activity that you have attended. Use at least one comparative and one superlative adverb or adjective.

LESSON 4

Adding Details with Verbal Phrases

Verbal phrases can be indispensable additions to a basic sentence. These phrases can add interest and paint a clearer picture for the reader.

EXAMPLE: Ardella waited.
Exhausted, Ardella waited to hear the choreographer's opinion.

Ardella waited, forgetting her exhaustion.

Verbals are formed from verbs but cannot function as main verbs. They introduce verbal phrases and usually include a noun and/or a prepositional phrase. They are used as nouns, adjectives, and adverbs in sentences.

Verbal Phrase

to choose a pet	The verbal is to choose, formed from to plus the present form of the verb.
chosen for its intelligence	The verbal is chosen, the past participle.
choosing a guard dog	The verbal is choosing, the present participle.

Pay special attention to the first type of verbal phrase (to choose a pet) because it looks like a prepositional phrase. Read the following Grammar Tip carefully.

GRAMMAR TIP

The word to is used to introduce both verbal phrases and prepositional phrases.

to + a Verb = a Verbal Phrase (Infinitive Phrase)

> **EXAMPLE:**   to send

to + a Noun and Its Modifiers = a Prepositional Phrase

> **EXAMPLE:**   to the moon

EXERCISE 4A

Complete the following sentences by writing verbal phrases on the lines. Form the verbal from the verb in parentheses.

EXAMPLE: (hike) Laurel likes to hike in the mountains every summer.

1. (begin) Curtis has decided _____.

2. (reduce) Mr. Gleason has increased the company's profits by

   _____.

3. (drive) _____, Robin listened to her CD player.

4. (encourage) The author, _____, began work on a second book.

5. (understand) Mrs. Rodman tried _____.

In the following paragraphs, bracket the verbal phrases and prepositional phrases. Then, answer the questions following the paragraph, using complete sentences that include verbal phrases wherever possible.

The water in the Amazon is muddy. It is hard to see just a few feet down, and twenty feet down, it is impossible to see anything. But electric fish are able to navigate at that depth without vision. They use electric organs to generate electric fields around their bodies to sense other living things. Catfish, using feelers, probe the muddy waters. They also have taste buds all over their bodies, allowing other senses to dominate over sight. Researchers have found many eyeless fish swimming at the bottom of the Amazon. They survive by eating the tails of other fish. The fish can then grow new tails.

Another unusual group of fish found in the Amazon survive by eating dead wood found along the banks of the river. Hoping to discover more rare species, researchers are dragging nets along the bottom of the muddy river to bring them to the surface for study. The nets have brought in a tiny transparent catfish that is only one-third of an inch long. It is also blind, but it has thickened bones and armored plates on its sides to protect it from larger fish. So far the waters of the Amazon are estimated to harbor at least 200 million fish species. That number is nearly twice the number of fish species in all of North America.

1. What special adaptation do electric fish have to navigate the muddy waters of the Amazon River?

_____

_____

2. How do the catfish "see" in the dark? Describe two different methods.

_____

_____

3. How do these eyeless fish survive? Describe at least two different survival tactics.

_____

_____

4. Why does the tiny transparent catfish have protective armor?

_____

_____

Punctuating a Verbal Phrase

At the beginning of a sentence, use a comma after an introductory verbal phrase.

EXAMPLES: Standing at the end of the line, I had little hope of getting a ticket.
Discouraged by the long line, I gave up and went home.

EXERCISE 4C

Insert commas after the introductory verbal phrases.

1. Hoping to make a profit Carolyn invested in the stock market.

2. Trying to get to the airport on time Josephine got a ticket for speeding.

3. Snowed in for a week in the mountains we couldn't get back in time to take our final exams.

4. Having spent the day shopping unsuccessfully for shoes Tina decided to wear her old ones to the party.

5. Finding a wallet on his way to school Jerry had visions of a generous reward.

For a more detailed discussion of this use of the comma, see Chapter 8.

Misplaced Modifiers and Dangling Modifiers

When you use modifiers in your sentences, be sure that the word order of each sentence is clear and logical. Placing a modifier in an incorrect position can change or confuse the meaning of the sentence. Modifiers should be placed close to the words that they describe or qualify. Learn to identify and correct **misplaced modifiers** and **dangling modifiers**.

Misplaced Modifiers

Misplaced modifiers are exactly what the term suggests. These modifiers are called misplaced because they have been incorrectly placed next to words that they are not intended to modify.

EXAMPLES:

a. I <u>nearly</u> ate all the brownies. (misplaced modifier)

This sentence suggests that you didn't eat anything at all. You should place <u>nearly</u> in front of <u>all the brownies</u>.

I ate <u>nearly</u> all the brownies. (revised)

b. I heard that our nation needs additional preschool teachers <u>on the television news</u>. (misplaced modifier)

The preschool teachers are not needed on the television news, are they? You should place <u>on the television news</u> after the verb <u>heard</u>.

I heard <u>on the television news</u> that our nation needs additional preschool teachers. (revised)

c. Coretta bought a German shepherd dog <u>alarmed by the robberies in the neighborhood</u>. (misplaced modifier)

   If the dog is alarmed by the robberies, it is not going to make a good watchdog. You should place the verbal phrase modifier in front of <u>Coretta</u>.

   <u>Alarmed by the robberies in the neighborhood</u>, Coretta bought a German shepherd dog. (revised)

EXERCISE 5A

Revise the following sentences by placing the words or phrases in parentheses next to the words that they modify.

EXAMPLE: Eileen ran after the bus. (carrying a heavy briefcase)
                 <u>Carrying a heavy briefcase, Eileen ran after the bus.</u>

1. Nick saved $100 by making his own repairs on his car. (almost)

   _____

2. The candidate promised that he would reduce unemployment. (at the political rally)

   _____

3. Alfredo ordered a pizza to go. (with mushrooms and pepperoni)

   _____

4. The painters told us that they would begin painting the house. (on Wednesday)

   _____

5. Rex saw a woman in the front row jump up and run out the side exit. (suddenly)

   _____

EXERCISE 5B

Rewrite the following sentences, placing each misplaced modifier as close as possible to the word it modifies. The first sentence is completed as an example.

1. Riding around in a black and white patrol car marked K-9 Patrol, everyone noticed the new police unit in town, Barney and Fred.

   Everyone noticed the new police unit in town, Barney and Fred, riding

   around in a black and white patrol car marked K-9 Patrol.

2. Unfortunately, Barney drove the car, and Fred, sitting in the back seat, was a bit too eager for action.

   _____

   _____

3. Barney would hear Fred's growls, stopping the car at a traffic light or an intersection.

   _____

   _____

4. Putting his head out of the window, Fred snarled and barked at pedestrians frequently who passed close to the car.

   _____

   _____

5. Disgruntled citizens said that Fred was supposed to protect them, not attack them in their complaints to the police department.

   _____

   _____

6. The police chief sent Barney and Fred back to training classes, hoping to restore peace and order.

   _____

   _____

7. Fred is no longer an embarrassment to Barney, trained to control his enthusiasm.

   _____

   _____

8. Now when Barney stops the patrol car, Fred sits facing the front of the car in the back seat calmly.

_____

_____

9. His eyes move—from left to right and from right to left only.

_____

_____

10. He doesn't bark at the cats even that he sees on the prowl.

_____

_____

Dangling Modifiers

A word or a phrase is called a dangling modifier when there is no word in the sentence for it to modify.

EXAMPLE: Showing an interest in computers, personnel offices are flooded with applications.

Were the personnel offices showing an interest in computers? Of course not. The verbal phrase modifier, Showing an interest in computers, is left dangling. There is no word in the sentence for it to modify. To correct this problem, write the sentence as follows:

Showing an interest in computers, students are flooding personnel offices with applications.

Add a noun and a complete verb, not just the word "students" to eliminate the dangling modifier. Another method of eliminating dangling modifiers changes the dangling word or phrase into a subordinate clause. So you could correct the example given above as follows:

Since students are showing an interest in computers, personnel offices are flooded with applications.

┌───┐
│ **GRAMMAR** TIP
│
│ You cannot correct a dangling modifier by moving it around in a sentence. Since there is
│ no word in the sentence for it to modify, you must rewrite the sentence and add the word
│ that the phrase modifies.
└───┘

EXERCISE 5C

Complete these sentences by adding a subject and a verb. Do not leave any modifiers dangling. Notice that these sentences form a paragraph.

EXAMPLE: <u>Walking to the front of the courtroom</u>, the defense attorney objected to the judge's ruling.

1. Summoning another witness, _____

2. Turning to face his client, _____

3. Frowning and looking annoyed, _____

4. To make his point clear, _____

5. Calling for a conference, _____

Editing Practice

Rewrite this paragraph on the lines below, correcting the dangling modifiers in each sentence.

   Expecting a robot like R2D2, the robot that was demonstrated to Willy was disappointing. Propelling itself on large wheels, Willy had hoped for useful arms and legs. Having limited mobility, stairs could not be climbed. Responding to voice command, a distance of less than seventy feet was necessary between the robot and its owner. Frustrated by the poor quality, his decision to buy a robot would have to be delayed.

_____

_____

_____

_____

_____

_____

_____

LESSON 6 **Sentence Combining**

Now that you have completed the exercises in this chapter, you understand how useful modifiers can be for adding details to your sentences. As you combine the following sentences, see if you can include adjectives or adverbs to add details to each sentence.

EXAMPLE:

1. There was a council meeting.

2. It was held on Wednesday.

3. Mr. Washington pointed out the failure of the city government.

4. The government had not found one solution.

5. There are many inner-city problems.

Combined Sentence: At the council meeting on Wednesday, Mr. Washington pointed out the failure of the city government to find one solution to the many inner-city problems.

You might add the adjectives, *an angry,* to describe Mr. Washington. Or perhaps you would rather insert the adverb, *angrily,* before the verb *pointed out* to show the manner in which Mr. Washington spoke.

Your sentence would read: At the council meeting on Wednesday, Mr. Washington angrily pointed out the failure of the city government to find one solution to the many inner-city problems.

A. Combine these five sentences into one sentence.

   1. It was late summer.
   2. Thunderstorms flooded the region.
   3. More than seventeen inches of rain fell in places.
   4. The thunderstorms sent people to higher ground.
   5. There were hundreds of people.

B. Combine these five sentences into one sentence.

   1. The opponents were determined.
   2. They circulated a petition.
   3. The opponents stirred up public opinion.
   4. The public was against the location of the plant.
   5. The plant makes chemicals.

C. Combine these six sentences into one sentence, using a verbal phrase for sentence 4.

   1. Julia told us about her trip.
   2. It was a recent one.
   3. She had gone to China.
   4. Julia emphasized her boat ride.
   5. It was exciting.
   6. It was up the Yangtze River.

D. Combine these six sentences into two sentences. Change sentence 2 into a prepositional phrase. Change sentences 4 and 6 into verbal phrases.

   1. Sage Ranch was a popular movie location.
   2. Its big red boulders served two purposes.
   3. They sheltered the good guys.
   4. They were camping out.
   5. They concealed the bad guys.
   6. They were hiding out.

E. Combine these six sentences into one sentence, using a verbal phrase for sentence 2.

1. The city was destroyed.
2. It was located on the Bay of Naples.
3. The city was an ancient one.
4. It was named Pompeii.
5. An earthquake destroyed it.
6. The earthquake occurred in A.D. 79.

Chapter 4 Summary

how?	what kind?	verbs	superlative
when?	how many?	adjectives	
where?	which one?	adverbs	
why?	misplaced modifiers	comparative	

Choose words from the box above to complete the following sentences.

1. To test a word to see if it is an adjective, ask ＿＿＿＿＿＿,

    ＿＿＿＿＿＿, or ＿＿＿＿＿＿.

2. The form of some adjectives and adverbs can be changed to show the

    ＿＿＿＿＿＿ form and the ＿＿＿＿＿＿ form.

3. Adverbs add further information about ＿＿＿＿＿＿, ＿＿＿＿＿＿,

    and other ＿＿＿＿＿＿.

4. To see if a word is an adverb, ask, ＿＿＿＿＿＿, ＿＿＿＿＿＿,

    ＿＿＿＿＿＿, or ＿＿＿＿＿＿.

5. Modifiers that are placed near words they are not intended to modify are

    called ＿＿＿＿＿＿ ＿＿＿＿＿＿.

Writing Assignment

Read the following paragraph:

Gambling provides big profits for Indians. It has become the biggest source of income for Native Americans all over the country. They believe that it is the only way they can overcome the poor quality of their lands and their out-of-the-way locations. Tribal members have used the profits to better their lives. They have built homes and water treatment plants, and they operate day-care centers and medical centers. Their grandparents used to walk miles to a creek to bring back a bucket of water. But today they have decent plumbing and enough money to pay for their groceries. In Florida the Seminole Indians living on a reservation near Tampa have defied the law of their state. They have been selling cigarettes without charging sales tax for many years. And now they are operating large bingo parlors built on the Tampa reservation. The bingo parlors have flourished and attracted many tourists by offering super jackpots. When the members of Congress passed the Indian Gaming Act in 1988, they gave the Indians the right to operate casinos on their reservations. Indian slot machines are actually illegal in many states, but the states cannot do anything about them. Only the federal government can do something, and the federal law enforcement agencies are reluctant to act.

Topic

What is your opinion about Indian-sponsored gambling casinos? Try to persuade your reader to agree with your views.

Step 1. Start by jotting down all the ideas that come to mind about the benefits and the problems associated with gambling. Do not try to write in sentences. Make lists of your thoughts as they occur to you. You will edit them later.

Step 2. Once you have a long list, look it over to decide what items you want to write about.

Step 3. Select two or three major reasons to support your opinion. Then, write out your opinion to serve as your topic sentence.

Step 4. Provide sufficient support for each reason you give. Refer to Chapter 10 for a discussion of how to develop specific support for the main idea of the topic sentence. You might refer to the many years of genocide of the Native Americans and the policy of neglect followed by the American government, or you might refer to the influence of mobsters in gaming casinos in the past.

Step 5. Whichever side of the issue you decide to write about, you should stay with one side for the duration of your paragraph. It is too difficult to write about both sides in one paragraph. You would have to write a longer essay to consider both sides.

As You Write: Try to include verbal phrases in your sentences. Pay special attention to your choice of adjectives and adverbs as discussed in this chapter.

Alternative Writing Assignment

Topic

As we know, people from all over the world have immigrated to the United States. Although they now are Americans, many do not wish to lose their cultural heritage and seek to keep old customs and beliefs alive in various ways. Write a paragraph about one group's efforts in this regard.

Step 1. Read about the Scottish Highland Games in Chapter 3, Exercise 1B, and consider what makes these games uniquely Scottish. In Exercise 3E of this chapter, read again about the Kwanzaa ceremony—a recent attempt to bring a people together in the pursuit of moral excellence. If you have participated in a Kwanzaa rite, you may want to expand upon the brief paragraph in this chapter and give a detailed personal account.

Step 2. Assume that your reader is not a member of the group you have chosen as your subject. Start by jotting down all the ideas that come to mind about your topic. Describe the ceremony, celebration, or whatever form the activity assumes. When did this observance begin, years ago or recently? What are its distinguishing characteristics? Are any costumes, foods, props, or symbols used that reflect aspects of the culture? Is the group seeking to preserve specific values and beliefs? Would the ceremony be meaningful to someone outside the group? In what ways is it memorable?

Step 3. Once you have a long list, look it over to decide which items you want to write about. Select two or three major reasons to support your opinion. Then write out your opinion to serve as a topic sentence.

Step 4. Provide sufficient support for each reason you give. Refer to Chapter 10 for a discussion of how to develop specific support for the main idea of the topic sentence.

As You Write: Try to include verbal phrases in your sentences. Pay special attention to your choice of adjectives and adverbs as discussed in this chapter.

Suggested Subjects

Cinco de Mayo	Japanese Oban Festival	St. Patrick's Day Parade
Korean or Chinese celebrations of the New Year		Kwanzaa

> ► **CHAPTER 4**
> **PRACTICE TEST:** Adjectives and Adverbs

Name _____

Date _____ Class Time _____

Instructor _____

I. Bracket all adjectives, including noun markers, in the following sentences.

EXAMPLE: Lori borrowed [her] [roommate's] [new] earrings.

1. The judges presented three winners with gold medals.

2. Scrambled eggs won't stick to that Teflon skillet.

3. Jayne distrusts her ex-husband's good intentions.

4. The warranty covers replacement of any damaged parts.

5. His signature was smudged and illegible.

II. In the following sentences, bracket the adverbs. Each sentence has one adverb.

1. The hotel elevator suddenly lost power.

2. Laurel frequently skips her lunch.

3. We mustn't forget to make our reservations.

4. Ed politely refused her unreasonable request.

5. The music class has just started.

III. Change the adjective in parentheses into the comparative or superlative form.

1. Brenda is the _____ of all her sisters during the evening

    hours. (energetic, superlative)

CHAPTER 4 PRACTICE TEST (Cont.)

2. My brother is a _____ cook than I am. (good, comparative)

3. Mr. Greer is the _____ supervisor anyone ever had. (bad, superlative)

4. Who is the _____ salesperson in the office? (competitive, superlative)

5. Casey soon had become _____ at repairing a fender than his instructor. (expert, comparative)

IV. Change the adverb in parentheses into the comparative or superlative form.

1. Of all the members on the panel, the district judge spoke the _____ about the issues. (intelligently, superlative)

2. Fred worked the _____ of anyone on the project. (hard, superlative)

3. Arthur studies _____ alone than he does with his friends. (well, comparative)

4. Farley has invested his inheritance _____ than his brother has. (prudently, comparative)

5. The more the other children laughed at my son's misbehavior, the _____ he acted. (badly, comparative)

V. Correct the misplaced modifier in each sentence by placing it next to the word it should modify.

1. Some of the parents shouted at the members of the school board, angered by the new busing plan. ───────────────

   ───────────────────────────────

2. Leaking air slowly, I knew that the bicycle tire would soon be flat.

   ───────────────────────────────

   ───────────────────────────────

3. The defendant watched the jury return with its verdict without much hope. ───────────────────────

   ───────────────────────────────

VI. Correct the dangling modifier by rewriting the sentence and adding the word or words that it should modify.

1. Looking at the opposite shore, the telescope brought the waterfront buildings into focus. ──────────────

   ───────────────────────────────

2. Only two years old, my uncle took me to my first major-league baseball game. ──────────────────────

   ───────────────────────────────

3. The orange squirted juice all over Tricia's new silk blouse while eating lunch. ────────────────────

   ───────────────────────────────

Editing
Practice

Underline any errors in adjectives and adverbs that you find in the following paragraph. Write the correct form in the space above the underlined words.

New Yorkers, who are usually surrounded by tall buildings, cannot even glimpse the sky between the towers. But now, with the completion of the New York Rose Center at the American Museum of Natural History, they can get a real good view of the heavens. The $210-million center is the world's most advanced planetarium. It contains the largest and powerfulest virtual-reality site in the world. Of all the new attractions, visitors seem more impressed by the planetarium's 429-seat theater, where they are taken on a trip to the edge of the universe. Visitors sit in seats like those in spaceships and feel the seats vibrate, as they lift off on the most grandest tour, passing planets and the Milky Way, and going on a journey of a billion light-years. The solid sidewalks of the neighborhood look more better to the visitors when they come out of the planetarium. Don't feel badly if you cannot make a trip to New York soon. The spectacularest building in New York will be attracting visitors for years to come.

Main Clauses

In Chapter 5 you will learn about the **main clause**.

Definitions of Terms

A **main clause** (also called an **independent clause**) is a group of words with a subject and a verb that can stand alone as a sentence if the first word is capitalized and the clause ends with a mark of punctuation such as a period or a question mark.

A **simple sentence** contains one main clause.

A **compound sentence** contains two or more main clauses joined by a coordinating connective and appropriate punctuation.

Coordinating connectives (and, or, but, for, nor, so, yet) are words used with a comma to join words, phrases, and main clauses. They are also called **coordinating conjunctions**.

A **semicolon** (;) is a mark of punctuation that can be used to connect main clauses.

Adverbial connectives (however, nevertheless, then) are words used with a semicolon and a comma to join main clauses. They are also called **adverbial conjunctions** or **conjunctive adverbs**.

Parallel structure is the placing of similar items in similar grammatical form.

A **comma splice** is a grammatical error made when main clauses are joined with only a comma and no coordinating connectives.

A **run-on sentence** is a grammatical error made when main clauses are joined with no punctuation or coordinating connectives between them.

Identifying Main Clauses

When you studied prepositional phrases and verbal phrases, you learned that a phrase is a group of related words without a subject and a verb. A group of related words with a subject and a verb is called a **clause**. There are two kinds of clauses, **main** and **subordinate**, but this chapter will deal only with the **main clause** (also called an independent clause).

To identify a main clause, look first for the verb and then for the subject. The main clause can stand alone as a sentence if the first word is capitalized and the clause ends with a punctuation mark such as a period or a question mark. The main clause may also contain words or phrases in addition to the verb and the subject.

EXERCISE 1A

In the following sentences, identify the underlined group of words as a phrase (P) or a main clause (MC). Write your answer on the lines at the right.

1. Conservationists are trying <u>to reintroduce wild wolves into the woods.</u>   _____

2. <u>They have already returned some wolves</u> to the Rockies.   _____

3. Wild gray wolves are moving <u>from Quebec into the United States.</u>   _____

4. <u>They are returning</u> to parts of Maine.   _____

5. A wolf sometimes travels as far as 500 miles <u>in search of a mate.</u>   _____

EXERCISE 1B

In the following sentences, write a main clause in the blanks.

EXAMPLE: _____ in the campus theater.
<u>The spring play opens this weekend</u> in the campus theater.

1. After finishing his midterm examination, _____ to relax.

2. _____ at Fiona's party Saturday night?

3. Friday night _____ during the basketball game.

4. _____ at the last student council meeting.

5. Tomorrow afternoon _____ .

6. Standing in line for half an hour _____ to pass the time.

LESSON 2

Connecting Main Clauses

The Simple Sentence

In Chapters 1 through 4, you have been working primarily with the **simple sentence**. The simple sentence has one main clause. Which of the following two sentences is a simple sentence?

1. Lamar Hughes has dreamed of graduating.
2. For a long time since building his first race car nineteen years ago, Lamar Hughes has dreamed of graduating to the NASCAR Grand National Circuit.

Both sentences are **simple** sentences. Although the second sentence contains several phrases, it has only one main clause: one subject and one verb. Both sentences have the same subject and verb:

```
        S        AV     V
Lamar Hughes has dreamed
```

The Compound Sentence

Which of the following two sentences has *more than one* main clause and, therefore, is not a simple sentence?

1. Thousands of drivers like Lamar Hughes test themselves on America's hundreds of small dirt tracks, hoping to win $1,000, $100, or even just a trophy.

2. The race-car drivers hope to make it to the big-league tracks, and they love the thrill of driving at very high speeds.

The first sentence has only one subject and one verb.

S   V

Thousands <u>test</u>

It is a **simple** sentence with one main clause. The second sentence, containing two main clauses, is a **compound sentence.** It has two subjects and two verbs:

S   V   S   V

drivers <u>hope</u> . . ., and they <u>love</u>

> A simple sentence has *one* main clause.
>
> A compound sentence has *two* or more main clauses.

EXERCISE 2A

Label the subjects and underline the verbs in the following sentences. Identify them as simple or compound. If the sentence has only one main clause, write S (simple) on the line at the right. If the sentence has two or more main clauses, write C (compound) on the line at the right.

                     S   S

EXAMPLE: David <u>wanted</u> a new bicycle, but he <u>didn't</u>

have enough money for one.   C

1. Some people think of Iowa as flat, but some bicyclists know better.   _____

2. Every year about seven thousand bicyclists ride slowly and painfully across the state of Iowa.   _____

3. The ride begins at the Missouri River along the state's western border, and it ends at its eastern edge along the Mississippi River.   _____

4. Many riders complain about injured knees as well as sunburns.   _____

5. The bicyclists are surprised by the hills of Iowa, for
    the land had looked flat to them.   _____

Joining Main Clauses

There are three ways to join the main clauses of compound sentences:

  1. a coordinating connective
  2. a semicolon
  3. an adverbial connective

Coordinating connectives (sometimes called coordinating conjunctions) are
words used to join words, phrases, or clauses together.

EXAMPLES: Words: typhoons **and** hurricanes
               Phrases: in the Pacific Ocean **and** along the Atlantic
                         coastline
               Clauses: In the Atlantic Ocean, a tropical cyclone is called
                         a hurricane, **but** in the western Pacific Ocean, it
                         is known as a typhoon.

Coordinating Connectives			
and	for	or	yet
but	nor	so	

All seven words contain two or three letters.

Place a comma before the coordinating connective when it joins two main
clauses into a compound sentence.

EXAMPLE: Formerly, hurricanes were named exclusively for women**, but**
              today men's names are also used.

EXERCISE 2B

Change the following simple sentences into compound sentences by joining the
main clauses with a comma and the coordinating connectives in parentheses.

EXAMPLE: (for) Formed in the sea, hundreds of miles from land, hurricanes become most destructive along the Atlantic seaboard. They increase their speed on their northward journey.
Formed in the sea, hundreds of miles from land, hurricanes become most destructive along the Atlantic seaboard, **for** they increase their speed on their northward journey.

1. (yet) No more than ten hurricanes of great strength develop in a year. Of these, only about six become a threat to our eastern coastline.

2. (so) Hurricanes require a high sea-surface temperature of at least 82 degrees to spawn. They usually occur in the late summer or early fall.

3. (but) Many storms follow a fairly straight path. Others make sharp turns, loops, and reversals before pursuing a more predictable course.

4. (and) By Columbus' fourth voyage to this part of the world, he was familiar with the native population's hurricane lore. Thus he drew upon this knowledge to save his ships from a coming storm.

5. (for) Many Seminole Indians in Florida still accurately predict storms by noting the height of saw grass, the flight pattern of birds, and the alligators' move to deep water. These Seminoles have more faith in their own observations than in those of the official weather forecasters.

A **semicolon (;)** may be used to connect main clauses.

EXAMPLE: Many tourists are afraid to travel around the city of New York by themselve**s;** a volunteer Big Apple Greeter makes such travel a little less frightening.

EXERCISE 2C

On the lines at the right, identify each sentence as simple (S) or compound (C). Join the main clauses of the compound sentences with semicolons.

1. The young couple on their honeymoon in New York expected to find muggers and thieves on the streets, instead they found a woman by the name of Lucy Littlefield. _____

2. Ms. Littlefield welcomed the couple to New York with free subway tickets and city maps. _____

3. She also gave them several hours of her time guiding them around New York she is a member of a group called the Big Apple Greeters.   _____

4. The Big Apple Greeters help visitors discover the joys of this large metropolis no other American city offers such a service.   _____

5. To the honeymooners, it seemed as though they had Mom along on their trip.   _____

The **adverbial connectives** (sometimes called adverbial conjunctions) also may be used to join main clauses. Use a semicolon before the connectives and a comma after them.

Adverbial Connectives

Addition:	also	further	in addition	moreover
Contrast:	however	instead	nevertheless	otherwise
Time:	meanwhile	then		
Result:	as a result	consequently	thus	therefore
In Reality:	in fact	indeed		

EXAMPLE: In the 1926 hurricane, the Seminoles avoided harm by moving out of the path of the storm**; however,** loss of life and property was high among the rest of the state's population.

You may need to consult your dictionary to be sure you are using these words correctly.

EXERCISE 2D

Write five compound sentences using the words in the box below as adverbial connectives. Study the previous example to help you punctuate the connectives.

however	meanwhile	furthermore	instead	nevertheless

1. _____

2. _____

3. _____

4. _____

5. _____

Choose an appropriate adverbial connective from the words in the box to connect the main clauses in the following sentences. Use each connective only once. Punctuate the sentences correctly.

consequently	in addition	in fact	instead	then

1. Samuel Clemens' formal education ended at the age of twelve. This noted author represents the model of a self-made man to many people.

2. At seventeen, leaving the small town of Hannibal, Missouri, he worked for a time as a river pilot. He traveled West to try his hand at gold mining.

3. Clemens did not make a fortune as a miner. He found his vocation as a journalist and, more importantly, the identity of Mark Twain.

4. Leaving the West, he became a popular writer, a lecturer, and an Eastern gentleman. He won an audience among Europeans as well.

5. As an internationally known writer, Twain did not entirely leave his Midwest origins behind. Hannibal and the Mississippi River provided the material for his most widely read books.

┌───┐
│ **GRAMMAR** TIP   │

Three Ways to Connect Main Clauses

1. Use a coordinating connective and a comma (, but).

2. Use a semicolon (;).

3. Use an adverbial connective and punctuation marks (; however,).
└───┘

Punctuating Main Clauses

In simple sentences some connective words serve as adverbs and are enclosed by commas. These adverbs do not join main clauses in a sentence as adverbial connectives do.

EXAMPLE: Eric sometimes guesses correctly the meanings of words.
He should, nevertheless, consult a dictionary.

EXERCISE 2F

Punctuate the sentences in the following paragraph correctly. The first sentence is punctuated as an example.

A dictionary, indeed, can tell you the meaning of a word. Besides that a dictionary shows you how to spell a word. A dictionary in addition shows you how to divide a word into syllables. It can tell you furthermore the origin and development of a word. A dictionary in fact is a good source of biographical information. Moreover if you want to know about the location of any college in the United States, just look in your dictionary. You should in fact keep a dictionary in several rooms of your house. Thus you will have a handy reference tool always at hand. You must however develop the habit of consulting it frequently.

Connect the two main clauses in each of the following groups of sentences by using the method suggested in parentheses. Correct the punctuation and change the capital letters to lowercase letters.

1. Alan wanted to play in the Rose Bowl. His team's record was 0–10 for the season. (coordinating connective)

2. Alan's team will try harder next year. Perhaps they will have a better record. (coordinating connective)

3. Playing in the Rose Bowl is every football player's dream. Few achieve that goal. (adverbial connective)

4. On New Year's Day Alan will watch the game on TV. His teammates will be there too. (semicolon)

Group
ACTIVITY

Read the following paragraph and respond to the questions that follow using complete sentences. Together with two or three classmates, check your sentences. Then, select the best sentences from your group and exchange your work with that of another group to pick the best answers.

1. In 1989, European scientists sent up a satellite to measure the position of 120,000 stars. 2. The satellite failed to reach its correct orbit after its launching, but it was reprogrammed from the ground. 3. It has been operating perfectly since 1993, and the scientists have been surprised by its findings. 4. In fact, they have had to change their thinking about the size of the universe. 5. The universe may be much bigger than the previous estimates.

Answer the following questions using the sentence numbers 1–5 to identify the sentences:

1. Which sentences are simple sentences? _____

2. Which sentences are compound sentences? _____

3. What coordinating connectives are used? _____

4. How many verbal and prepositional phrases can you find? _____

5. How did the European scientists plan to measure the size of the universe?

   _____

6. What was the original problem with the satellite, and how was it corrected?

   _____

7. How long has the satellite been operating successfully?

   _____

8. What have been the results of the satellite's findings?

   _____

LESSON 3 — Parallel Structure

Coordinating connectives join words, phrases, or clauses that are of equal importance. The word to notice in this definition is "equal." Parallel structure, the placing of similar items in similar grammatical form, gives the writer another strategy for expanding a sentence in a balanced way.

EXAMPLE A: Ann Nguyen is now a student in a small community college.
Ann Nguyen, former gardener, secretary, and short-order cook, is now a student in a small community college.
The three parallel nouns (gardener, secretary, and short-order cook) give the reader more information about Ms. Nguyen.

EXAMPLE B: She participates in student activities.
She enjoys working in the college library, serving on student council, and writing for the school newspaper.
Parallel verbal phrases (working . . ., serving . . ., writing . . .) supply additional information about the nature of Ms. Nguyen's participation in student activities.

Faulty Parallelism

When you use parallel structure, always put the parts of the sentence that you are joining in the same grammatical form. For example, placing a noun before or, and, or but requires that another noun follow the connective (a swimmer, a golfer, or a jogger). Failure to do so results in **faulty parallelism** (a swimmer, a golfer, or jogging).

Faulty Parallelism: Ann liked swimming, dancing, and <u>to play basketball</u>.

Revised: Ann liked <u>swimming, dancing, and playing basketball</u>.

(or)   Ann liked <u>to swim, to dance, and to play basketball</u>.

Editing Practice

Underline the part of each sentence that is not parallel. Then, in the space provided, rewrite this part to match the other items listed, as in the preceding examples.

1. On a crowded highway, driving too slow is almost as bad as to drive too fast.

   _____

2. My doctor told me to stop smoking and that I should go on a diet.

   _____

3. After a week of studying, preparing for finals, and the worry about finances, I look forward to the weekend.

   _____

4. Amy and her husband decided to take guitar lessons, to learn how to play tennis, and to take golf lessons.

   _____

5. Veronica left home, drove to work, and was parking her car in the parking lot.

   _____

Write five sentences using the group of parallel words or phrases given for each sentence.

EXAMPLE: Jim was on a flight to New York.
(dozing, working a puzzle, reading a book, listening to music)

Your Sentence: During the flight to New York City, Jim passed the time by dozing, listening to music, reading a book, and working a puzzle.

1. He was met by a volunteer from the Big Apple Greeters.
   (friendly, energetic, attractive)

   Your Sentence: _____

   _____

   _____

2. His plans included riding on the subway.
   (climb to the top of the Statue of Liberty, eat at the Hard Rock Café, see Rockefeller Center)

   Your Sentence: _____

   _____

   _____

3. Jim was amazed by the sights of New York.
   (crowds in Times Square, weirdos around SoHo, traffic on every avenue)

   Your Sentence: _____

   _____

   _____

4. He walked around with his new camera.
   (equipped with a zoom lens, finished in black and chrome, fitted with a small automatic flash)

Your Sentence: _____

_____

_____

Punctuating Items in a Series

Use commas to separate three or more items in a series. The items may be single words, phrases, or clauses.

EXAMPLE: Winslow Homer, an American artist of New England origins, was a master of three mediums: wood engraving, oil, and watercolor.

EXERCISE 3B

Insert commas where necessary.

Winslow Homer's love of the natural world is apparent in his choice of subjects: the sea the woods and the mountains. His regard for the people who lived close to this natural world also may be seen in his depiction of the simple pleasures of American life: young couples at a picnic an ice skating party on a pond and a berry-picking expedition in the woods. Children figure in many of his rural and seaside paintings. They sit on rail fences share watermelons raid sand-swallow nests and build a fire for a clambake on the beach. Making their living from the sea, their parents unload boats mend gear and haul in nets of fish. He is, perhaps, best known for his sea paintings which frequently portray a storm at sea—the power the danger the violence

and the beauty of the spectacle.

See Chapter 8 for a more detailed explanation of the use of the comma in a
series.

LESSON 4 — Correcting Comma Splices and Run-on Sentences

Main clauses may be joined with connecting words and appropriate punctuation
marks, as summarized in the Grammar Tip in Lesson 2 of this chapter. But sometimes writers join main clauses with commas or without using any connecting
words or punctuation marks.

            S   V   S   V

1. The team won the tournament, they received a trophy.

            S   V   S   V

2. The team won the tournament_ they received a trophy.

The error in sentence 1 is called a **comma splice** (**CS**). Sentence 2 is called a **run-on sentence** (**RO**).

A **comma splice** is a grammatical error made when main clauses are joined with
only a comma and no coordinating connective. A **run-on sentence** is a grammatical error made when main clauses are joined with no punctuation or coordinating connectives. Correct comma splices and run-on sentences in any one
of the following ways:

1. Use a comma and a coordinating connective.
   The team won the tournament, and they received a trophy.

2. Use a semicolon.
   The team won the tournament; they received a trophy.

3. Use an adverbial connective with a semicolon and comma.
   The team won the tournament; therefore, they received a trophy.

4. Use a period and a capital letter.
   The team won the tournament. They received a trophy.

```
                                                     EXERCISE 4A
```

Identify the subjects and underline the verbs. On the lines at the right, write CS for comma splice or RO for run-on sentence. Then punctuate the sentences correctly.

1. The long line of weather watchers, turning for assistance from birds, may have begun with Noah, he sent out a raven and a dove from the ark, hoping for an end to the long rain.   _____

2. According to some, the distinctive calls of woodpeckers and robins signal rain the unusual silence of other birds supposedly makes the same prediction.   _____

3. Hawks, perched high on power poles, are another indicator of coming rain they wait to catch small creatures heading from low creek beds to the safety of higher ground.   _____

4. On some days, sea gulls remain on the shore, seeming to avoid the ocean, fishermen once took the gulls' behavior as a sign of a coming storm and also stayed in port.   _____

5. Birds themselves are weather watchers during the time for migration needing good weather to navigate, they postpone their departure during uncertain weather conditions.   _____

```
                                                     EXERCISE 4B
```

Correct the comma splices and run-on sentences by using coordinating connectives, semicolons, or adverbial connectives with correct punctuation.

1. More corporations are beginning to open day-care centers for their employees' children, the centers are open from nine to five.

2. With their children in these centers, working parents worry less about them these parents take fewer days off.

3. Two-paycheck families appreciate the cost benefits, the price of a full-time baby-sitter would use up an entire salary.

4. Single-parent families especially appreciate the convenience of quality child-care programs child-care programs help to recruit high-quality employees.

5. Government support helps the corporations build special facilities, preschool playgrounds and indoor classrooms are often too expensive for smaller corporations to construct.

Editing Practice

Rewrite the following paragraph correcting the comma splices and run-on sentences. The paragraph contains two comma splices and three run-on sentences.

Americans of all ages are chocolate addicts each year the per capita consumption of this sweet is about nine pounds. Of course American chocolate lovers still have to catch up with the Swiss, number-one consumers of chocolate in the world, however, Americans are well on their way. Chocolate fanciers who want to be current on the latest news about their weakness subscribe to a bimonthly publication it is appropriately printed on brown, chocolate-scented paper. Shops specializing in expensive chocolate are thriving, some "chocoholics" will pay up to $30.00 a pound to satisfy their craving. No one should ever offer a carob bar or a dish of jelly beans to a chocolate-loving friend nothing but deep brown, rich chocolate appeals to a true "chocophile."

_____

_____

_____

_____

_____

_____

_____

LESSON 5 Sentence Combining

These sentences will give you practice in using compound sentences and parallel structure in addition to prepositional phrases and single-word modifiers.

Combine these six sentences into one compound sentence. Use a verbal phrase and a prepositional phrase in parallel structure for sentence 2.

1. College students are showing an interest in computers.
2. They are showing an interest in other math-related fields.
3. Personnel offices are flooded.
4. They are flooded with applications.
5. The applications are for work.
6. There are only a few jobs available.

Combined Sentence: Showing an interest in computers and other math-related fields, college students are flooding personnel offices with applications for work, but only a few jobs are available.

A. Combine these six sentences into one compound sentence. Sentences 4, 5, and 6 should be in parallel structure.

1. Shana was looking for a job.
2. She was looking for a job in the computer field.
3. The computer field is rapidly growing.
4. She sent her résumé to software developers.
5. She sent it to manufacturing companies.
6. And she sent it to health maintenance organizations.

B. Combine these five sentences into one compound sentence. Use a coordinating connective that shows a contrast between the main clauses.

1. Astronomers have known about five planets.
2. These planets are in our solar system.
3. Astronomers have known about these planets for centuries.
4. An astronomer did not discover Pluto until 1930.
5. The astronomer was at Lowell Observatory in Arizona.

C. Combine these six sentences into one compound sentence. The first sentence should be used as a verbal phrase. Sentences 4, 5, and 6 can be put in parallel structure.

1. Keiko walks onto one of Tokyo's new commuter trains.
2. She notices a television screen above the door.
3. The screen is in English as well as Japanese.
4. The screen shows the current stop.

5. It shows the next stop.
6. It also gives some news and some commercials.

D. Combine these six sentences into one sentence. Use verbal phrases in parallel structure for sentences 4, 5, and 6. Use a verbal phrase for sentences 1 and 2.

1. The governor called a press conference.
2. He called it on Friday.
3. He announced his education plan.
4. He wants to provide more computers.
5. He wants to reduce class size.
6. He wants to expand the intern program for teachers.

Chapter **5** Summary

compound	semicolon	parallel
main	subject	

Select words from the box to complete the following sentences correctly.

1. A clause is a group of related words with a _____ and a verb.

2. A _____ clause can stand alone as a simple sentence.

3. Two or more main clauses may be joined to form a _____ sentence.

4. A _____ may be used to connect two main clauses.

5. _____ structure is the placing of similar items in similar grammatical form.

Writing Assignment

Topic

Turn to the Editing Practice at the end of the Chapter 5 Practice Test. Read the paragraph about the problems that shoppers sometimes experience with poor service. Think about recent encounters you have had that resemble the experience described in that paragraph. If you prefer, write about a pleasant shopping experience and describe in detail the good service you received.

Step 1. Before you begin to write about your experiences, jot down the name of the store you were in, the description of the item you wanted to buy, and what happened in your encounter with the salespeople.

Step 2. Include in your notes your analysis of the reasons why there has been a breakdown in the service offered by most retailers. Is there something that can be done to improve the service? Can you do anything about it?

Step 3. Describe in specific terms the improvements you recommend to solve the problem by giving some concrete suggestions.

Step 4. As you write, look back at Lesson 2 in this chapter. Try to use adverbial connectives in your sentences.

Step 5. See Chapter 10 to learn how to use transitional words and phrases to connect ideas in your paragraph. The use of transitional expressions will help you incorporate your shopping experiences into the paragraph.

Alternative Writing Assignment

Topic

What should be done to improve your school environment? What experiences have you had that made you wish you could make some changes? Do you have any suggestions regarding participation in student government, peer counseling opportunities, availability of tutors, the library, instructional facilities, food services, the bookstore, financial aid, or student contributions to curricula planning? When you have completed your assignment, you might consider sending it to the student newspaper.

Step 1. Jot down the difficulties you have encountered or observed.

Step 2. Now list the improvements you would suggest.

Step 3. Next list the ways you think each improvement could be made. If you can, decide who should be responsible for making the changes.

Step 4. If you find that you have too many items to develop in a paragraph or two, focus on several major improvements.

Step 5. First state the problem and give the reader a clear picture of the situation. Then describe in specific terms the improvements you recommend by making some concrete suggestions. Look back at Lesson 2 in this chapter. Try to use adverbial connectives in your sentences.

Step 6. See Chapter 10 to learn how to use transitional words and phrases to connect ideas in your paragraph. The use of transitional words will help you incorporate your own experiences and observations into the paragraph as well as make your recommendations for improvement.

► CHAPTER 5

PRACTICE TEST: Main Clauses

Name _____

Date _____ Class Time _____

Instructor _____

I. On the lines at the right, write MC for main clause or P for phrase.

1. Solving the puzzle was not so easy _____

2. Trained in the art of self-defense _____

3. From the scientist's point of view _____

4. Remember this _____

5. The commuters waited impatiently for their
   train to arrive _____

II. Identify each sentence as simple (S) or compound (C).

1. Martin wanted to eat at Bruno's restaurant, but
   Valerie was tired of eating pasta. _____

2. Did they go to Bruno's or to her favorite Japanese
   restaurant? _____

3. Outraged parents planned to attend the Board
   of Education meeting and to protest against the
   schedule for the school year. _____

4. The Board of Education may vote to operate
   schools on a year-round schedule despite strong
   opposition to the plan. _____

5. Federal surpluses of food have been reduced; as
   a result, severe cuts will be made in many
   school-lunch programs. _____

CHAPTER 5 PRACTICE TEST (Cont.)

III. **The following sentences contain words that can be used as adverbs or adverbial connectives.**

   a. **Begin by labeling the subjects and verbs.**

   b. **Next write (S) for simple sentence or (C) for compound sentence on the lines at the right.**

   c. **Punctuate the sentences correctly.**

   1. Lewis subscribes to several magazines however he rarely reads them.   _____

   2. His wife meanwhile finds time to read them all.   _____

   3. Molly must take the placement test in addition she must submit an essay.   _____

   4. The deadline for admission applications had already passed consequently the university refused to accept Molly's essay.   _____

   5. She must reapply therefore in a few months.   _____

IV. **Underline the part of each sentence that is not in a parallel form. Then, rewrite this part by making it parallel to the other items.**

   1. The Eastern Importing Company sells Oriental carpets, lamps made of brass, and many unusual gift items.

   2. Shoppers appreciate the courteous salespeople, the reasonable prices, and an atmosphere that is pleasant.

   3. Rashid believes that learning a second language is as important to his career plans as to know the techniques of marketing.

   4. Marilisa is not only a successful businesswoman but also coaches her daughter's soccer team.

   5. LeBron's job requires him to travel to several countries in South America and opening new company offices there.

V. The following sentences contain errors.

    a. Identify the errors by writing CS (comma splice) or RO (run-on) on the lines at the right.

    b. Then correct the sentences using the method suggested in parentheses.

1. We could attend the anthropology lecture tonight, we could study in the library. (coordinating connective) _____

2. Charlene prefers classical music Howard likes rock, jazz, and reggae. (semicolon) _____

3. They buy many classical CDs, they also go to rock concerts. (adverbial connective) _____

4. That book has been on the best-seller list for six weeks I haven't read it yet. (coordinating connective) _____

5. The rent for the apartment was high, Calvin was looking for a roommate to share expenses. (adverbial connective) _____

Editing
Practice

Read the following paragraph and underline all examples of parallel structure.

How many times has this happened to you? You walk into a store knowing exactly what you want to buy. You have studied the store's advertisements, and you have decided exactly what color and size you need. You even have your credit card ready to facilitate the purchase. But you cannot find anyone to help you. You wander around the store for a while in search of a salesperson. Finally, disappointed, you give up, return your credit card to your wallet, and head for the exit. Or else, you may find a salesperson who has no idea what item you want to buy nor where to find it in the store. Retailers deny that they have reduced their sales staff, but they do admit that they have reduced their sales costs. That translates to fewer salespeople on the floor and fewer well-trained people to serve you. Of course, there are exceptions, but customers these days cannot count on careful attention in the lingerie department, knowledgeable service in the fine china department, or cheerful service at the lunch counter.

Subordinate Clauses

In Chapter 6 you will learn about **subordinate clauses.**

Definitions of Terms

A **subordinate clause** (dependent clause) is a group of words with a subject and a verb that is introduced by a subordinator. It makes an incomplete statement, so it must be attached to a main clause to be a complete sentence.

A **subordinator** is a word that is used to introduce a subordinate clause. Examples are because, that, and although.

A **complex sentence** has a main clause and one or more subordinate clauses.

A **comma splice** joins main clauses with only a comma and no coordinating connective between them.

A **run-on sentence** joins main clauses with no punctuation or coordinating connective between them.

A **sentence fragment** is a group of words that begins with a capital letter and ends with a period, but the words do not express a complete thought or contain a main clause.

Identifying Subordinate Clauses

A main clause is a group of words with a subject and a verb. It is called a simple sentence when the first word is capitalized and it ends with a period, a question mark, or an exclamation point.

                                    S
EXAMPLE: We enjoy eating ice cream. (main clause or simple sentence)

A **subordinate clause** contains both a subject and a verb yet cannot stand on its own as a complete sentence because it begins with a subordinating word. For this reason, a subordinate clause is sometimes called a dependent clause; that is, it depends on the main clause to which it is attached.

                (subordinator) S
EXAMPLE: because we enjoy eating ice cream

EXERCISE 1A

If the group of words is a subordinate clause, put an "X" on the line at the right. If it is a simple sentence, leave the line blank.

1. We listened to the debate.   _____

2. Before we listened to the debate.   _____

3. Because the candidates answered questions from
   the audience.   _____

4. The candidates answered questions from the audience. _____

Although the subordinate clauses you have just marked make incomplete statements, the subjects and verbs are not missing. What is missing is a main clause. To complete the statement in the subordinate clause, you must join it to a main clause. Then you will have a complete statement or, in other words, a sentence.

The following subordinate clause is incomplete by itself. It should not be followed by a period.

                                S
EXAMPLE: While the band took a break

It leaves a question unanswered. You want to ask: What happened while the band took a break?

It needs another clause, the main clause, to answer this question. You might complete the sentence as follows: While the band took a break, I soaked my feet.

The difference between a main clause and a subordinate clause is often only the addition of one word at the beginning of the clause. If you add a subordinator to a main clause, you make a subordinate clause.

EXAMPLE: the band <u>took</u> a break (main clause)
s

<u>while</u> the band <u>took</u> a break (subordinate clause)
s

EXERCISE 1B

Study the words listed in the Subordinators box. Underline the subordinator in each of the following clauses. Complete the sentence by adding a comma and a main clause.

1. After the band had been rehearsing for two hours _____

2. When the director told us to keep marching _____

3. Although everyone complained _____

4. Because we were going to march in the parade _____

5. Before we went home that day _____

Subordinators

Place: where, wherever

Time: after, before, when, whenever, as, since, until, as soon as, while, as long as

Cause or Purpose: so that, in order that, as, because, since, that, why

Condition: if, as if, unless, when, whether

Contrast: although, even though, though, while, whereas

Comparison: than

Identification: that, who, what, whom, whose, which

Some of the words listed in the preceding box function as **subordinators** in some sentences and as **prepositions** in other sentences. The subordinator is followed by a subject and a verb.

                              S

EXAMPLE: before Tyrone goes to his work = subordinate clause

The preposition is followed by a noun and its modifiers.

                 Prep   N

EXAMPLE: before his work = prepositional phrase

EXERCISE 1C

Referring to the subordinators listed in the previous box, change the following main clauses to subordinate clauses by adding a subordinator to the beginning of the clause. Do not use the same subordinator twice.

1. _____ the rain became heavy

2. _____ the players left the field

3. _____ the groundskeepers covered the infield

4. _____ the crowd ran for protection under the covering

5. _____ some people had brought umbrellas

EXERCISE 1D

Write a complete sentence by adding a main clause to each of the subordinate clauses in Exercise 1C. The first sentence is completed for you as an example.

1. They delayed the game after the rain became heavy.

2. _____

3. _____

4. _____

5. _____

The sentences you have written in Exercise 1D are complex sentences. A **complex sentence** has a main clause and one or more subordinate clauses.

In the following paragraph, write the appropriate subordinators in the blanks, choosing each from the list of subordinators in the box following the paragraph.

EXAMPLE: <u>Although</u> many older Japanese have had an aversion to buying used merchandise, many young people now make weekly trips to their favorite "recycle shops" <u>where</u> they buy secondhand bargains.

Japanese women _____ were enthusiastic buyers of expensive imported goods _____ times were good have turned to "recycle shops," _____ offer used luxury items at reduced prices. _____ a young Japanese woman may have less money to spend during these years of recession, she hasn't lost her desire for a Gucci handbag _____ original price may have been $800. Their grandmothers, concerned with cleanliness and the possibility _____ the spirit of the former owners remained with their possessions, avoided secondhand objects, but these young women seem undisturbed by such concerns. The stores _____ they shop were formerly pawn shops _____ were located in back alleys. _____ they hope to attract an entirely different clientele, owners of these stores have redecorated them and restocked them with used luxury brand names. _____ many young Japanese women live at home, they can spend up to 90 percent of their income on luxuries. Consequently, they shop _____ they can find a $200 dress or accessory at the discount price of $30.

Subordinators

because	when	although	whose	that
where	which	wherever	who	since

NOTE: "That" is used more than once in the paragraph.

Sentences with More Than One Subordinate Clause

The following sentence has one subordinate clause. It begins with the word "When."

When the Aztecs designed their cities, each street was half roadway and half canal.

The next sentence has two subordinate clauses. They begin with the words "which" and "that."

The Aztecs used canoes to transport their crops, which were grown along the banks of the lake in small terraced plots that climbed the mountain slopes.

GRAMMAR TIP

The subordinator is sometimes used as the subject of the subordinate clause. You can see examples of which and that used as subjects of the subordinate clauses they introduce in the last sentence of the paragraph above (which were grown, that climbed). In Exercise 2D, sentences 1 through 6, have additional examples of who, which, and that used as subjects of subordinate clauses.

EXERCISE 1F

In the following complex sentences, underline the subordinate clauses and put parentheses around the subordinators. Begin by writing S above the subjects and underlining the verbs.

1. When the Aztecs arrived in the Valley of Mexico in 1325, they became farmers who were forced to create their farmland artificially.

2. They settled on an island that was in the middle of Lake Texcoco, and after they dredged mud from the bottom of the lake, they piled it along the shores to create "floating" gardens.

3. Since water continuously seeped up through the mud, the soil was kept moist, allowing plants to grow and protecting the crops from drought before the rainy season began.

4. As the Aztec population expanded, the "floating" gardens were used for urban development, while food production was moved to the southern end of the valley.

5. The Aztecs' settlement developed into a city of thousands of small islands, which were divided by canals that formed the basis of their transportation system.

Group ACTIVITY

Place parentheses around the subordinators and underline the subordinate clauses in the following paragraph. Then get together with two of your classmates and, as a group, write a paragraph about a fruit that you might find in your local grocery store. Try to follow the pattern of sentences in this paragraph. Use complex sentences. Place parentheses around the subordinators and underline the subordinate clauses. Exchange your work with that of another group to check your sentences.

Do you know (what) a kiwi is? It is a plum-sized fruit that has become popular all over America. When you look at the outside, you see a dull brown, fuzzy exterior. When you cut it open, the fruit is bright green and fragrant. While some people who have tasted it think that it tastes like a banana, others find the flavor hard to describe. It is considered nutritious because it contains more vitamin C than an orange does. Kiwi growers also say that the juice can be sprinkled on tough meat as a tenderizer. Although it was first cultivated in China about 300 years ago, it was not known in the western hemisphere until the twentieth century. Now, most kiwis come from New Zealand where they grow all year round. If you have not tasted a kiwi yet, you may be in for a surprise. They are, however, quite expensive, so they may strain your budget while they tingle your tastebuds.

Using Subordinate Clauses

Subordination, the use of subordinate clauses, gives writers another option for adding ideas to their sentences and variety to their writing. In addition, the subordinator shows the precise relationship between the subordinate clause and the main clause of the sentence.

EXAMPLES:

S (main clause)   S (main clause)

1. Mario was in Rome. A thief stole his wallet.

(subordinate clause)   (main clause)
S   S

2. (When) Mario was in Rome, a thief stole his wallet.

By using subordination in sentence 2, the writer makes the time and place of the theft exact and emphasizes one idea—the theft of the wallet. Combining these two main clauses into one complex sentence also improves the style.

3. The people on the bus had offered to help him, and
    S

    Mario thanked them. (two main clauses)

    S

4. Mario thanked the people on the bus (who) had offered

    to help him. (one main clause and one subordinate

    clause)

Sentence 4 improves an awkward compound sentence by subordinating the first clause in sentence 3 to the second clause. The subordinate clause clarifies the situation by restricting the word people to those who helped Mario.

WRITING TIP

We often combine ideas by coordinating them—that is, by linking them with one of the following words: or, but, and. Coordination works well when the parts are of equal importance, but when the ideas are not of equal importance, it is better to subordinate one idea to another.

In the following paragraph, the writer uses many subordinate clauses, but he has omitted the subordinator. As you read the paragraph, choose the subordinator that best fits the sentence from the box at the end of the paragraph. Then answer the questions at the end of the paragraph.

_____ Blanche attended a lab technician's convention in Vancouver, British Columbia, she was delighted. _____ she came from a small town in Missouri, she had never seen such a big city with so many tall buildings. The city was surrounded on all sides by water, _____ caused the sunlight to sparkle as it bounced off the surface of the waves in the harbor. The glass and steel skyscrapers shimmered _____ they reflected the dazzling sunlight. She enjoyed a visit to the Anthropology Museum at the University of British Columbia, _____ enormous totem poles overwhelmed the large gallery rooms and stood in an outdoor courtyard, memorials of the ancient Indians _____ had carved them. She then ate a picnic lunch on the grass outside the museum with her friends _____ enjoyed the view of Vancouver framed by the mountains. _____ she drove to Queen Elizabeth Park, she went to the Bloedel Conservatory to see the many different plants and colorful little birds that flew around inside the domed garden. In the evening she went to Stanley Park _____ she wanted to eat at the Teahouse Restaurant, _____ she sat outdoors and admired the sunset over the harbor. The next day she took a sea-bus across the water _____ she could look back at the city's skyline from the shore of North Vancouver. _____ she left Vancouver, she drove to Granville Island to shop at the outdoor markets for souvenirs, _____ she brought back to her family in Missouri.

Subordinators

after	so that	before	which
when	who	where	because

NOTE: Some subordinators are used twice in the paragraph.

Answer the following questions in complete sentences. Practice using subordinate clauses in the sentences you write.

> **EXAMPLE:**   Where did Blanche come from? <u>Blanche came from a small town in Missouri where she had never seen a city as big as Vancouver.</u>

1. Why did Blanche go to Vancouver? _____
   _____

2. What did she especially like about the city? _____
   _____

3. Why did she go to Stanley Park? _____
   _____

4. What did she do when she took the sea-bus? _____
   _____

5. Why did she go shopping on Granville Island? _____
   _____

Using Subordination to Correct Comma Splices and Run-on Sentences

In Chapter 5, Lesson 4, you learned to correct comma splices and run-on sentences by using one of the following methods:

1. Use a comma and a coordinating connective.
2. Use a semicolon.
3. Use an adverbial connective with a semicolon and a comma.
4. Use a period and a capital letter.

Subordination gives you another way to correct comma splices and run-on sentences by placing one idea in a subordinate clause and the other in a main clause.

EXAMPLE: (because) According to legend, Navajos are fine weavers, the Spider Woman taught a young Navajo girl the art of weaving. (comma splice)

REVISION: According to legend, Navajos are fine weavers because the Spider Woman taught a young Navajo girl the art of weaving.

EXERCISE 2B

Correct the following comma splices and run-on sentences. On the lines provided, join the ideas in the main clauses into complex sentences by changing one main clause to a subordinate clause. Use the subordinators in parentheses. On the lines at the left, identify the errors as CS (comma splice) or RO (run-on). Punctuate the sentences correctly.

_____   1. (although) Spiders are of great benefit to our environment many people, unfortunately, dislike and fear them.

_____

_____   2. (while) Several species are quite poisonous these represent a very small fraction of the 30,000 species of spiders in the

world. _____

_____   3. (since) Spiders are invaluable to us, they devour more

insects than all other insectivores together. _____

_____

_____   4. (because) According to many scientists, spiders keep the balance of nature, without spiders, these insect pests would

eliminate man by destroying his food supply. _____

_____

_____   5. (when) Spiders, in general, appear in a favorable light they appear in folk tales, myths, and legends throughout the

world. _____

Punctuation of Subordinate Clauses

Use Commas After Introductory Subordinate Clauses

> **EXAMPLE:** When schools add computer-aided instruction, teachers are able to send their students to the lab for individualized tutoring.

See Chapter 8 for a more detailed discussion of this use of the comma.

EXERCISE 2C

Insert commas where they are needed. Some sentences do not need commas added.

1. Although many people might laugh at the idea of computers belonging in every classroom others will accept the reality.

2. While some critics prefer an excellent teacher many people would vote for an excellent multimedia computer system.

3. Generations of pupils who have learned from textbooks are protesting against the expense of electronic installations.

4. If you wanted to improve the quality of education in America you would keep computers out of the classroom.

5. That slogan has been adopted by those parents whose children need more textbooks, teachers, and traditional values.

Use Commas to Set Off Nonessential Clauses

Use commas to enclose a clause containing nonessential material. The information may add some details, but the reader can understand the main idea of the sentence without the clause.

> **EXAMPLE:** Stan, who arrived late, had to sit in the last row.

Omit the words enclosed by commas, and the sentence reads: Stan had to sit in the last row.

The main idea of the sentence is unchanged.

Do not use commas to enclose clauses that are essential to the meaning of the sentence.

EXAMPLE: The people <u>who arrived early</u> had the best seats.

If the subordinate clause is omitted, the main idea of the sentence is lost: The people had the best seats. The subordinate clause is needed to identify the people—those who arrived early.

When "that" or "which" introduces a subordinate clause, follow the same rule for enclosing nonessential material.

EXAMPLES: The seat that Stan preferred was in the first row.

Stan's seat, which was most unsatisfactory, was in the last row.

Blanche wanted to see the little birds that flew around inside the domed garden.

Blanche wanted to shop at the outdoor markets for souvenirs, which she brought back to her family in Missouri.

EXERCISE 2D

Insert commas where necessary. Some sentences do not need commas added.

1. The sled dog race that is run between Whitehorse and Fairbanks should not be confused with the more widely publicized Iditarod.

2. The Iditarod Trail Sled Dog Race which is a 1,150-mile race in Alaska from Anchorage to Nome began in 1973.

3. The race that is known as the Yukon Quest International Sled Dog Race made its first appearance in 1983 and covers about 1,060 miles.

4. The fifteen mushers who complete the race share a purse of $125,000.

5. Promoters of the Yukon Quest which shares many similarities with the Iditarod maintain that their race is more challenging and less commercial than its competitor.

6. Both races in the subarctic wilderness are endurance contests which test both human and canine ability to face the extreme hardships and isolation imposed by the courses.

LESSON 3

Sentence Fragments

A **sentence fragment** is part of a sentence treated as a complete sentence, with a capital letter and a period at the end. A sentence fragment may lack a subject or a verb, thus confusing the reader by leaving out an essential element. Some professional writers use fragments in magazines and books. We hear sentence fragments used in conversation, as in the following example:

> "Did you leave school early yesterday?"
> "Yes, after my music class."

Although the last bit of dialogue begins with a capital letter and ends with a period, it is not a complete sentence. It is a sentence fragment. If you do use a fragment in your writing, be sure to make your meaning clear, or you may confuse your reader.

Four Types of Sentence Fragments

It will be easier for you to correct fragments in your own writing if you learn to recognize these four types of fragments:

1. Subordinate clauses punctuated as sentences
2. Missing subjects or missing verbs
3. Using verbals instead of verbs, or using participles without auxiliary verbs
4. Lists and examples not connected to a subject and verb

Subordinate Clauses Punctuated as Sentences

Identifying the Fragment: When Jean came home.

This is the most common form of fragment. This subordinate clause is punctuated like a sentence.

Revising the Fragment: When Jean came home, she turned on the stereo.

1. You can, of course, simply remove the subordinator, and you will have a complete sentence.
2. More than likely, however, the fragment will appear among the sentences of a paragraph you are writing. In that case, you should connect the fragment to a sentence that is before or after the subordinate clause and change the punctuation.

(Fragment) When Jean came home. We had just finished dinner.
(Revised) We had just finished dinner when Jean came home.
(Fragment) When Jean came home. She turned on the stereo.
(Revised) When Jean came home, she turned on the stereo.

EXERCISE 3A

If the following sentence fragments were complete sentences, they could be connected to form a paragraph about Tina Turner. You can turn these fragments into sentences by adding a main clause to each one. Place a comma after subordinate clauses if necessary. Correct the punctuation and change the capital letters to lowercase letters as needed.

1. _____ Because Tina Turner has made a great comeback.

2. While she is loved by rock 'n' roll fans _____.

3. If she can also sing rhythm and blues _____.

4. Although Tina worked to escape her past _____.

5. _____ After they were married.

6. _____ Since she has great talent.

7. _____ Who is very popular.

8. Before she became a star _____.

9. _____ As much as she could.

10. _____ That Tina Turner's story was true.

Missing Subjects or Missing Verbs

Identifying the Fragment: Swims for an hour in the pool. Swims is a verb, but both nouns (hour and pool) are objects of the prepositions for and in. So this is a fragment because there is no subject.

Add a subject to make a sentence.

S
Revising the Fragment: Janelle swims for an hour in the pool.

EXERCISE 3B

Change the following fragments into sentences. Write your sentences on the lines. Do not leave out any words in the phrases. Change the punctuation and capitalization as necessary.

1. Transferred to the university this fall. _____

_____

2. A dorm on campus or a room in town. _____

_____

3. Enrolling in classes. _____

_____

4. To make an appointment with a counselor. _____

_____

5. Michelle has almost completed all the courses required for her major. Except for English 101, Psychology 2, and History 17. _____

_____

6. The instructor reviewed the material to be covered in the chapter test. Especially calling our attention to the last three pages. _____

_____

Using Verbals Instead of Verbs

Identifying the Fragment: Riding our bicycles on the bike path.

In this case, the writer mistakes the verbal for a main verb and also leaves out the subject.

1. Supply an auxiliary verb and, if necessary, a subject.

   S

   Revised: We <u>were</u> <u>riding</u> our bicycles on the bike path.

2. Attach the fragment to the sentence preceding it or to the one following it.

   S   (verbal phrase)

   Revised: We <u>enjoyed</u> ourselves, riding our bicycles on the bike path.

   (verbal phrase)   S

   Revised: Riding our bicycles on the bike path, we <u>stopped</u> to talk to several friends.

3. Supply a verb and a completer or an object. The verbal phrase <u>riding our bicycles</u> serves as the subject of the sentence.

   (verbal phrase)

   Revised: Riding our bicycles on the bike path <u>is</u> good exercise.

Lists and Examples Not Connected to a Subject and Verb

Identifying the Fragment: 1. Such as, Harry Truman, Richard Nixon, Lyndon Johnson, Gerald Ford, and George Bush.

Identifying the Fragment: 2. For example, my College Algebra final last semester.

A sentence fragment is frequently a list or an example explaining some thought that the writer has just expressed. This kind of fragment often begins with one of the following words:

also	especially	except
first	for example	including
such as		

You could turn the fragment into a sentence by supplying a subject and a verb. In most cases, however, you should connect the fragment to the sentence preceding it.

Revising the Fragment: 1. A number of US vice presidents have become presidents, such as Harry Truman, Richard Nixon, Lyndon Johnson, Gerald Ford, and George Bush.

Revising the Fragment: 2. Some examinations are not fair, for example, my College Algebra final last semester.

Mark F for sentence fragment or S for sentence on the lines at the right. Then revise the fragments on the answer lines following the exercise.

1. Kim's sister wants to move to Chicago. _____

2. Concerned with the view from her apartment. _____

3. She needs to be near the central business district. _____

4. Whenever she does the shopping. _____

5. And will come home every weekend. _____

6. First by cutting down on unnecessary purchases. _____

7. She is studying the newspaper advertisements. _____

8. The location that she wanted. _____

9. Wondering what she would do until moving day. _____

10. Because she would not be able to find a parking space. _____

_____

_____

_____

_____

_____

_____

_____

_____

_____

LESSON 4

Sentence Combining

As you combine the sentences in this lesson, you will learn how to add variety to your writing by using subordinate clauses, verbal phrases, and prepositional phrases. You also will be writing more concisely by subordinating one idea to another, as the following example shows.

EXAMPLE: Use a verbal phrase, a prepositional phrase, and a subordinate clause.

1. I have attached two pictures to my paper.
2. The pictures bring back memories.
3. Some of the memories are good.
4. Some of the memories are bad.
5. The memories are of Fort Benning, Georgia.
6. At Fort Benning, Georgia, I trained to be a parachutist.

Combined Sentence: The attached two pictures bring back some good and some bad memories of Fort Benning, Georgia, where I trained to be a parachutist.

We have combined the six sentences into one by subordinating one of the main clauses and reducing the number of verbs. This technique allows the writer to express the six ideas more concisely.

In the following exercise, combine the short sentences into longer ones by following the suggestions given.

A. Use compound subjects and verbal phrases.
   1. I still remember the fear I felt.
   2. I remember the fear of looking down at the earth.
   3. I remember the fear of leaping into space.
   4. I remember the joy of landing safely.
   5. I remember the joy of seeing my buddies.

B. Use a subordinate clause and a prepositional phrase.
   1. I float gently downward.
   2. I'm afraid that I'll land in the river.
   3. I have 80 pounds of equipment on my back.

C. Use a subordinate clause, a compound verb, and a prepositional phrase.
   1. I fall to the ground.
   2. I land on the river bank.
   3. I gather my chute.

    4. I bury it.

    5. I bury it in the jungle.

    6. I run to the waiting truck.

D. Use a subordinate clause, a verbal phrase, and a prepositional phrase.

    1. We are in enemy territory.

    2. We are alone now.

    3. We have only our skills to keep us alive.

    4. We also have walkie-talkies.

    5. The walkie-talkies keep us in touch with our commanders.

Chapter **6** Summary

complex	subordinator	subject
sentence	attach	auxiliary
subordinate		

Choose words from the box above to complete these sentences.

1. A subordinate clause is a group of words with a subject and a verb that cannot stand alone as a _____ because it makes an incomplete statement.

2. A sentence that has a main clause and at least one subordinate clause is called a _____ sentence.

3. You can correct comma splices and run-on sentences by making one of the clauses a _____ clause.

4. You learned four ways to correct sentence fragments in your writing. First, you can remove the _____ to change a subordinate clause to a main clause.

5. A second way to correct sentence fragments is to _____ the fragment to a sentence that is before or after the subordinate clause and change the punctuation.

6. A third way to correct a sentence fragment is to supply the missing _____ or verb.

7. A fourth way to correct a sentence fragment is to supply an _____ verb and, if necessary, a subject.

Writing Assignment

Topic

Many people believe that every student should have access to the information that is available through the use of computers and modems. Do you agree that every classroom should be connected to the World Wide Web if we are to improve our schools? Or would it be better to spend the money on basic textbooks and excellent teachers? How important is the use of computers in the classroom?

Step 1. Begin by listing, freewriting, or making a cluster to generate your ideas. After you have finished, talk about the subject with several of your classmates.

Step 2. State your position in a topic sentence. You may want to revise the sentence later, but knowing the direction you want to take will help you plan your paragraph.

Step 3. When you talked to your classmates, you may have found that you didn't have enough support to defend your point of view. Go back over your notes. Write down two or three main reasons and develop examples and details to support each one.

Step 4. Making a simple outline before you write your rough draft will help you decide the order in which to present each supporting point. (See the discussion of outlining in Chapter 10.)

Step 5. When you have completed the rough draft, check it carefully and correct any sentence fragments, comma splices, and run-on sentences you find before writing the final copy.

Alternative Writing Assignment

Topic

What is music to your ears? Write about the music you listen to regularly. Explain in specific detail why this particular music appeals to you or what associations it may have for you.

Step 1. Begin by listing, freewriting, or making a cluster to generate your ideas. Answering the following questions should help you get started, but don't feel limited by them.

> When and where do you listen?
> Is this music a part of your daily life? In other words, how important is it to you?
> Do you listen to the radio at home, in the car, or on headphones while you exercise?
> Do your friends also enjoy this music?
> Do you have a collection of videos, tapes, or CDs?
> Do you have a favorite instrumental group or a singer that you especially like to hear perform this music?
> Do you associate a musical selection with a person, a place, or an event?

Step 2. State your opinion in a topic sentence. You may want to revise the sentence later, but knowing the direction you want to take will help you plan your paragraph. For example, you may want to write about a specific singer. Be sure that you have expressed an opinion about your subject.

1. I have quite a few of _____'s CDs. This sentence leads nowhere.

2. As a singer, _____'s greatest appeal to me is the wide variety of her selections. Using this sentence, you can explain what you mean by "wide variety." (See also Chapter 10.)

Step 3. Review your notes and select three or four main points of support for your thesis. For each of these points, include details and examples to expand your ideas. (See Chapter 10.)

Step 4. To help you decide the most effective order in which to present these main points, make a simple outline before you write your rough draft. (See Chapter 10.)

Step 5. When you have completed the rough draft, check it carefully and correct any sentence fragments, comma splices, and run-on sentences you find before writing the final copy.

CHAPTER 6

PRACTICE TEST: Subordinate Clauses

Name _____

Date _____ Class Time _____

Instructor _____

I. Put parentheses around the subordinators. Then underline the subordinate clauses.

    1. Although Mr. Barr tried to stop in time, his brakes were not working properly.

    2. The driver who changed lanes abruptly in front of Mr. Barr caused the accident.

    3. Fortunately Mr. Barr was wearing a seat belt because he always remembered to "buckle up."

    4. When he saw the damage to his car, he knew he would have to call a tow truck.

    5. Both drivers, who had only minor bruises, were not seriously hurt.

II. a. Change the following main clauses into subordinate clauses by adding a subordinator to the beginning of the clause. Do not use the same subordinator twice.

    1. _____ we went to the community center to hear the candidates

    2. _____ Mr. Wayne was the moderator of the meeting

    3. _____ my friend asked a question

    4. _____ the candidate refused to recognize him

    5. _____ some reporters for the local newspaper covered the meeting

CHAPTER 6   PRACTICE TEST (Cont.)

II. b. Make complete sentences by adding main clauses to each subordinate clause you made in question II. a. Your sentences must include both clauses.

1. _____

2. _____

3. _____

4. _____

5. _____

III. Write three sentences that have one main clause and at least one subordinate clause. Place parentheses around the subordinate. Punctuate the sentence correctly.

1. _____

2. _____

3. _____

IV. In the following sentences, identify comma splices (CS) and run-on sentences (RO) on the lines at the left. Then, join the ideas in the main clauses into a complex sentence by changing one main clause to a subordinate clause, using the subordinators in parentheses.

_____ 1. (if) Morgan's TV reception is poor he may have to install a

satellite dish. _____

_____

_____ 2. (that, omit "it") The Picasso painting is valued at $10 million,

it was bought by a Japanese investor. _____

_____

_____ 3. (so that) Megan bought a new car, she can have reliable

transportation. _____

_____

_____ 4. (as long as) We may as well buy a new dishwasher we are

remodeling the kitchen. _____

_____

_____ 5. (who, omit "they") Many listeners enjoy listening to National

Public Radio they show their appreciation by giving financial

support to their local stations. _____

_____

V. a. There are five incomplete sentences in the following paragraph. Indicate on the lines following the paragraph whether a sentence is complete (S) or a sentence fragment (F).

   1. Muzak is difficult to escape unless city dwellers stay out of many public places. 2. Such as shopping malls, supermarkets, offices, restaurants, and elevators. 3. Even if people do stay out of public places, Muzak invades their homes via the telephone. 4. When they are put "on hold" while waiting for the completion of a call. 5. Although most people hear canned music almost daily. 6. Few of them actually listen to it. 7. The sound of Muzak has changed little in 60 years. 8. The musical selections have always been carefully chosen to blend into the background of any activity. 9. By playing well-known tunes that would appeal to a mass audience. 10. This music is intended to make people feel good. 11. In the belief that they will then be productive workers and willing buyers. 12. Many people, however, regard Muzak as another form of noise pollution.

1. _____	7. _____
2. _____	8. _____
3. _____	9. _____
4. _____	10. _____
5. _____	11. _____
6. _____	12. _____

CHAPTER 6 PRACTICE TEST (Cont.)

V. b. On the lines below, rewrite the incomplete sentences that you identified as sentence fragments (F) above. Write complete sentences by combining the fragments with other sentences next to them.

1. _____

2. _____

3. _____

4. _____

5. _____

Editing Practice

Underline and correct the seven sentence fragments in the following paragraph.

Pirates are often portrayed as inhuman. Quick to kill someone in pursuit of treasure. In movies and novels, they often sank helpless ships. Forcing prisoners to walk the plank. But scholars in recent years have said that most of the mythology is wrong or misleading. They were less cruel and more democratic than previously thought. They carefully divided up the distribution among crew members. Including rare jewelry from the African gold trade. From recent finds on pirate ships located on the ocean bottom, scientists have learned that real pirates had no time for such ceremonies. As sending victims walking down the plank. They imprisoned some sailors and even treated them well. Also, pirates were not exclusively European. Perhaps as many as 30 percent of them were black slaves who had escaped from captivity. Or been freed by pirate gangs to join in the attacks on organized trade. These crews had established democratic principles aboard ship. Even the most feared captain, the famous Captain Blackbeard, shared equally with the members of the crew. As he could not receive a larger portion of the booty. Blackbeard's ship has now been located off the coast of Beaufort, North Carolina. Where it had lain since 1718. When the divers searched that ship, they hoped to find further proof of the lack of accuracy in the typical portrayal of pirates.

_____

_____

_____

_____

Agreement

In Chapter 7 you will learn about the **agreement** of subjects and verbs and of pronouns and antecedents.

Definitions of Terms

Agreement is the matching in number, gender, and person between subjects and verbs or between pronouns and antecedents.

An **antecedent** is the noun or pronoun to which a pronoun refers.

Compound antecedents are two or more antecedents joined by a coordinating connective.

Collective nouns name groups of people, places, things, ideas, or activities (for example, family).

Indefinite pronouns refer to people, things, or ideas in general rather than to specific antecedents (for example, anyone or someone).

LESSON 1 Subjects and Verbs

By now you probably can identify the subject and verb of a sentence accurately and confidently. Identifying the subject and the verb is the first step in correcting subject-verb agreement errors.

The Subject and the Verb Must Agree in Person and Number

A third-person <u>singular</u> subject (one person or thing) takes a <u>singular</u> verb.

The pear tastes sweet.	It tastes sweet.
The woman waits patiently.	She waits patiently.
The boy learns quickly.	He learns quickly.

A third-person <u>plural</u> subject (more than one person or thing) takes a <u>plural</u> verb.

The pears taste sweet.	They taste sweet.
The women wait patiently.	They wait patiently.
The boys learn quickly.	They learn quickly.

In the sentences in the box above, you can see that the singular verb in the present tense ends in **-s** when the subject is a singular noun that can be replaced by <u>he</u>, <u>she</u>, or <u>it</u>. The plural verb in the present tense drops the **-s**.

EXERCISE 1A

Write five sentences using the present tense of the verbs in parentheses and a singular common noun as the subject.

EXAMPLE: (fly) The airplane <u>flies</u> nonstop to Chicago.

1. (make) _____

2. (turn) _____

3. (use) _____

4. (lend) _____

5. (play) _____

EXERCISE 1B

Now rewrite the sentences that you just completed. Change the subjects from singular to plural. Make sure the verbs agree with the subjects.

EXAMPLE: (fly) The airplanes <u>fly</u> nonstop to Chicago.

1. (make) _____

2. (turn) _____

3. (use) _____

4. (lend) _____

5. (play) _____

LESSON 2	# Subjects and Verbs—Four Difficult Patterns

Words That Come Between the Subject and the Verb

Words that come between the subject and the verb do *not* affect subject-verb agreement.

EXAMPLES: 1. Today the purpose of many zoos in large cities is not the same as in the past.

The subject "purpose" is third-person singular, so the verb "is" is singular. The words "of many zoos in large cities" that come between the subject and the verb do not affect the agreement.

2. Until this century the people visiting the zoo were the first consideration, not the animals.

The subject _____ is plural, so the verb _____ is plural. The words "visiting the zoo" that come between the subject and the verb do not affect the agreement. (The subject is "people" and the verb is "were.")

┌─ **GRAMMAR** TIP ───

When you are identifying subjects and verbs, bracket any verbal phrases or prepositional phrases. Phrases that come between the subject and the verb can present a special problem. A verbal can be mistaken for a verb, and an object of a preposition can be mistaken for a subject.

EXAMPLE: The new programs started last spring provide information on endangered species to schoolchildren.

Bracket "started last spring." "Started" is a verbal and not a verb although it is nearer to the subject of the sentence than the verb "provide."

Bracket "on endangered species to schoolchildren." "Species" and "schoolchildren" are objects of prepositions. The subject is "programs."

(continued)

> **EXAMPLE:**   The high quality of these innovative zoo programs accounts for their success.
>
> Bracket "of these innovative zoo programs." "Programs" is the object of the preposition and not the subject of the sentence although it is nearer to the verb "accounts" than the subject "quality."

EXERCISE 2A

In the following sentences, write S above the subject and bracket any words that come between the subject and the verb. Then underline the correct form of the verb. The first sentence serves as an example.

1. Open-range quarters, [like those in San Diego's Wild Animal Park], (gives, give) animals the room to live naturally.

2. The zookeeper, whenever possible, (works, work) to preserve and protect exotic species.

3. Endangered species, such as the condor, (is, are) bred in the zoo and later set free.

4. These fully grown animals, released into their natural habitats, (seems, seem) to have a good chance of survival.

5. Obviously not every zoo in the country (plays, play) this important role.

6. Only zoos that have the money, space, and time (conducts, conduct) these programs.

EXERCISE 2B

In the following sentences, write S above the subject. Underline the verb that best completes each sentence.

1. The effects of the recent cold weather (lingers, linger) on.

2. The fruit trees, which were just beginning to flower, (has, have) withered.

3. The flowers that had appeared (is, are) turning brown.

4. The farmers, who could lose millions of dollars, (is, are) using several methods to protect the crops.

5. The hope of everyone concerned (is, are) for the early arrival of spring weather.

Reversed Word Order

A verb agrees with the subject even if the subject comes after the verb.

EXAMPLE: Here are some reasons for testing the air in your home.

The plural subject reasons comes after the verb.

In general when sentences begin with there, here, and where, the subject follows the verb. Rearrange the sentence to find the subject:

Here are some reasons for testing the air in your home.

Some reasons for testing the air in your home are here.

EXERCISE 2C

In the following sentences, write S above the subject. Underline the correct form of the verb. In two of the sentences, the verb is in a subordinate clause. Some of the sentences have the subject before the verb, and some have the subject after the verb.

1. There (is, are) disagreement on the seriousness of indoor air pollution.

2. Some researchers say that there (is, are) much to be learned about controlling indoor air quality.

3. Experts agree that there (is, are) greater chances of problems developing in older homes.

4. The first clue that a home may have a problem (is, are) often increased humidity.

5. Increased humidity in an insulated home (signals, signal) that the rate of air change is low and other air pollutants may be building up.

6. There (is, are) devices that can eliminate the problem.

7. One widely used device in new homes (is, are) the air-to-air heat exchanger.

8. A problem that can occur with heat exchangers (is, are) condensation.

9. Here (is, are) the best way to lower indoor pollution.

10. Electric appliances (is, are) best to prevent pollution from developing inside a home.

EXERCISE 2D

Write six sentences, two beginning with <u>Here is/are</u>, two with <u>There is/are</u>, and two with <u>Where is/are</u>. Write S above the subject and underline the verb in each sentence. When you have completed this exercise, get together with two or three classmates to check each other's work.

1. (Here is) _____

2. (Here are) _____

3. (There is) _____

4. (There are) _____

5. (Where is) _____

6. (Where are) _____

Compound Subjects Joined by <u>and</u>

Compound subjects joined by <u>and</u> usually take a <u>plural</u> verb.

EXAMPLE: Both the clock radio and the toaster need to be repaired.

The subjects in the clause are "clock radio" and "toaster." They are joined by "and," so the verb "need" is plural.

EXCEPTION: When two nouns joined by "and" describe a single person or thing, use a singular verb.

EXAMPLES: Tuna and noodles seems to be a popular casserole at potluck suppers.

My best friend and neighbor is also my business partner.

EXERCISE 2E

Write six complete sentences, using the words at the left as the subjects of your sentences. Use the present tense of the verbs.

EXAMPLE: (video store and book shop) The video store and the book shop attract many customers to the mall.

1. my desk and my bookcase _____

   _____

2. spaghetti and meatballs _____

   _____

3. standing in line and waiting _____

   _____

4. the summer heat and the street noise _____

   _____

5. Toby's ambition and hard work _____

   _____

6. the Washington Monument and the Lincoln Memorial _____

   _____

Compound Subjects Joined by <u>or</u>, <u>neither. . .nor</u>, or <u>either. . .or</u>

When subjects are joined by these connectives, the verb agrees with the subject *closer* to the verb.

EXAMPLE: Neither the tenants nor the landlord <u>expects</u> the door bell to be fixed today.

"Landlord," is singular, so the verb "expects" agrees with it.

EXERCISE 2F

Insert the form of the verb <u>have</u> that best completes each sentence below. Choose either <u>has</u> or <u>have</u>.

1. The telephone and the front door bell in an apartment _____ not been working.

2. The tenants and the landlord _____ tried unsuccessfully to solve the problem.

3. The electrician and the telephone repairman _____ been trying to make an appointment to fix the door bell and the telephone.

4. Neither the landlord nor the tenants _____ been able to hear the knock on the door.

5. Because the workers cannot get into the apartment, neither the telephone nor the front door bell _____ been fixed.

6. Either the tenants or the landlord _____ to stay outside to wait for the repairmen.

EXERCISE 2G

Write complete sentences using the words at the left as the subjects of the sentences. Use a verb in the present tense in each sentence.

1. Neither the library nor the book store _____

2. Either the customers or the sales person _____

3. Magazines or newspapers _____

4. Neither the radio nor the television _____

5. Tutors or instructors _____

LESSON 3

Subjects and Verbs— Special Problems

Subjects That Are Singular

When used as subjects, the words below take singular verbs. These **indefinite pronouns** refer to no particular person, thing, or idea.

anybody	either	neither	one
anyone	everybody	nobody	somebody
anything	everyone	no one	someone
each	everything	nothing	something

In the following paragraph, write S above the subjects. Underline the correct forms of the verbs in parentheses.

S
EXAMPLES: Everyone (<u>is</u>, are) <u>going</u> to work during summer vacation.

S
Each of us (<u>has</u>, have) a job.

No one who is a college student today (need, needs) to read a survey to know that the cost of a college education has risen. Almost everyone I know at school (work, works) during the school year, and nobody (take, takes) the summer off. Neither of my two closest friends (receive, receives) any financial support from home. In addition to working, each (depend, depends) on student loans to help cover the increased costs of tuition, lodging, and books. If either (plan, plans) to attend graduate school, she must expect to make monthly student loan payments for some years following graduation.

Subjects That Can Be Singular or Plural

When used as subjects, the following six words can be singular or plural, depending upon the noun or the pronoun they refer to.

all	any	more	most	none	some

S
EXAMPLES: (plural) Where are your photographs? <u>Have</u> any of them <u>been damaged</u> yet?

(singular) The work of moving the photos must be com-
S
pleted soon. <u>Has</u> any of it <u>been started</u>?

Read the following paragraph about saving your family photos. Answer the questions at the end of the paragraph, using complete sentences. Follow the suggestions given for subjects of your sentences.

Your old family photographs are probably resting in a box right now. Or they are secure in an album you bought to preserve them for decades. Well, according to experts, your peace of mind is an illusion. Here are some recommendations for protecting your photos for future generations. First, all photographs benefit from the lack of extreme temperatures and humidity in an acid-free environment. Acid is present in wood, cardboard, photo-finishing envelopes, album pages, and unpainted or stained wooden shelves. Most photograph albums are especially hazardous to your photos because the typical heavy black paper is just cheap paper with a lot of wood in it. If you want to mount your photos on paper, you should get good museum-quality paper. Second, if you have snapshots glued to black paper, remove them carefully. It's not just the paper you have to worry about; the glue is even worse than the paper. Also, paper clips, transparent tape, and rubber bands will harm your photos. The best method for saving pictures is to use plastic sleeves and acid-free paper that fit into three-ring binders. The shelving is also important. You should never store photographs on unpainted wood shelving. Acid can migrate from the wood. But if you are throwing pictures in a cardboard box, it won't matter much about the shelf. The box itself is not good. Another warning is that you should never use ink on the back of a picture. Ink will eventually bleed through the paper. To identify a picture, write on the back with a pencil no harder than a No. 2. To save some

of your damaged photos, you may have to make a new copy from the neg-

ative, so be sure to keep your negatives in acid-free envelopes.

1. Where are most of your pictures stored right now?

   Use "most" as the subject of a sentence.

   Most _____

2. What do experts say about using photo albums?

   Use "some" as the subject of a sentence.

   Some _____

3. What do all photographs need as to temperature and humidity?

   Use "all" as the subject of a sentence.

   All _____

4. What do the experts say about using glue, tape, or rubber bands?

   Use "none" as the subject of a sentence.

   None _____

5. How important is the shelf where you store your photos?

   Use "any" as the subject of a sentence.

   Any _____

6. What is the best method of identifying your photos?

   Use "all" as the subject of a sentence.

   All _____

7. Do you have any damaged photos?

   Choose either "none" or "some" as the subject of a sentence.

   None _____

   or

   Some _____

8. What can you do to restore damaged photographs?

Use "any" as the subject of a sentence.

Any _____

Collective Nouns

Collective nouns represent a collection of people, places, things, ideas, or activities.

audience	college	crowd	band
committee	family	class	company
government	group	jury	management
number	school	society	team

It is often difficult to decide whether a collective noun is singular or plural. Most of the time, use a singular verb or rewrite the sentence to make the subject clearer. Instead of saying, "The band are tuning their instruments," you could say, "The band members are tuning their instruments."

EXAMPLES: 1. The number of courses offered this semester is small.

2. My favorite musical group is playing at the club all week.

Nouns Ending in -s That Are Not Plural

Some nouns, such as physics, economics, mathematics, measles, mumps, and news are considered singular even though they end in -s, and they take singular verbs.

EXAMPLE: Measles is caused by a virus and usually occurs during childhood.

Underline the correct verbs in the sentences below.

1. Mathematics (is, are) required for all engineering students.

2. Politics (was, were) viewed as the motive for the senator's vote against the tax bill.

3. Gymnastics (has, have) become a popular event in the Olympics.

4. The news of a recent archaeological discovery (was, were) announced by the university today.

5. Physics (include, includes) the study of optics.

> Consult your dictionary whenever you are in doubt about whether a particular word is singular or plural.

Time, Money, and Weight

Words that specify *time, money,* or *weight* require singular verbs when they are considered as a unit even if they are plural in form.

EXAMPLES:
   1. Two semesters is really a short time.

   2. Five dollars is a modest fee for an entrance exam.

Titles

Titles of songs, plays, movies, novels, or magazine articles require singular verbs even if the titles are plural.

EXAMPLE: *The Hours* is both a novel and a movie.

Names of Organizations and Businesses

The names of organizations and businesses that are plural in form but singular in meaning require singular verbs. Substitute a pronoun for the proper noun to determine which verb to use.

EXAMPLES: Century Cleaners has been in the same location for 45 years.
(It has been . . .)

The House of Representatives is in session today. (It is in session today.)

GRAMMAR TIP

If you are having difficulty finding the subject or determining whether the subject is singular or plural, the following four suggestions may help you.

1. Consult a dictionary.

2. To find the subject, rearrange the sentence when appropriate.

   EXAMPLE: Here are several ways of preventing indoor pollution.
   Rearrange: Several ways of preventing indoor pollution are here.

3. To decide whether a subject is singular or plural, substitute a pronoun for the subject.

   EXAMPLE: *The Hours* is both a novel and a movie.
   Substitute the pronoun "it." It is both a novel and a movie.

4. Identify any noun completers. The verb must agree with the subject in number and not with the noun completer.

   EXAMPLE: A major expense is the salaries for a large staff.
   The subject "expense" is singular although the noun completer "salaries" is plural.

   EXAMPLE: The salaries for a large staff are a major expense.
   The subject "salaries" is plural although the noun completer "expense" is singular.

EXERCISE 3D

Write five sentences on the lines below, using the words at the left as the subjects. Use the present tense of the verbs.

1. *The Stone Diaries* _____

2. The League of Women Voters _____

3. Five pounds of bananas _____

4. Twenty dollars a month _____

5. *Underground Voices,* a short film about African-American poets, _____

_____

Special Problems of Agreement

Who, That, **and** *Which* **as Subjects:** Who, that, and which used as subjects take singular verbs if the words (antecedents) they refer to are singular. They take plural verbs if the words they refer to are plural.

EXAMPLES: 1. Mark taped the tennis matches that <u>were</u> on CBS while he watched the baseball game on NBC Saturday afternoon. In the subordinate clause, the verb "were" is plural because it agrees with its subject "that." "That" is plural because it refers to the plural noun "matches."

2. Mark's friend who <u>works</u> every Saturday came over to watch the tape that night. In the subordinate clause, the verb "works" is singular because it agrees with its subject "who." "Who" is singular because it refers to the singular noun "friend."

EXERCISE 3E

Write the noun that <u>who</u>, <u>which</u>, or <u>that</u> refers to on the lines at the right. Then underline the correct form of the verb in parentheses.

EXAMPLE: Businesses that (<u>sell</u>, sells) products for leisure activities compete with television.   ___businesses___

1. The television set has become a home-entertainment center for Americans who (seeks, seek) recreation during their leisure time.   _____

2. The family of four that usually (goes, go) to a movie theater once or twice a week can now save money, watching cable television at home.   _____

3. People with DVDs, which (plugs, plug) into the television set, schedule their favorite programs to watch at hours most convenient for the family.   _____

4. Instead of going to a video-game arcade, many consumers play video games that (hooks, hook) up to their own televisions.   _____

5. And, of course, commercial television, which (has, have) been keeping Americans at home for years, continues to consume one billion hours of their time each day.   _____

Group
ACTIVITY

A. In the following paragraphs, the words "who," "that," and "which" used as subjects of the subordinate clauses have been placed in parentheses. Read the sentences carefully and put brackets around the words (antecedents) these subordinators refer to. Then underline the verbs in the subordinate clauses. The first sentence has been completed for you.

The blossoming of the cherry [trees] (that) surround the Jefferson Memorial on the Tidal Basin is one of the loveliest signs of spring in the nation's capital. The 3,700 trees of several varieties, (which) were a gift of Japan in 1912, grow in two parks in Washington, D.C. Most of the trees, (which) are the Yoshino variety, produce a white, cloud-like blossom, while the Akebonos, fewer in number, contribute a delicate pink to the sea of color, appearing briefly for two weeks each year. A weeklong Cherry Blossom Festival, (which) opens with the lighting of a 300-year-old, 8½-foot Japanese stone lantern, includes a parade and many other activities. The blossoms, as might be expected, do not appear on schedule every year on a specific day; the time ranges somewhere between March 15, the earliest date, and April 18, the latest one recorded. The hundreds of thousands of tourists, (who) arrive in expectation of the event, will be disappointed if the trees do not flower during their visit. Moreover, the festival plans, (which) await completion, depend upon the estimated blossoming time.

The question (that) arises for most of us concerns how the date can be predicted with a high degree of accuracy. Fortunately, the National Park Service horticulturist, (who) seems to use a combination of art and science to make his prediction, is equal to the task. Beginning in late February, when the small red buds begin to appear, he makes daily visits to observe the trees, watching for the change in the buds from a tight red to a puffy white. He also considers two factors, daylight and temperature, (which) affect the blooming time. In general, the length of daylight tells plants when to blossom, and there are some biologists (who) feel daylight is a more reliable factor than temperature. The horticulturist has learned, however, that local temperature plays a special role in regard to cherry trees. Warm days with no snow on the ground will bring an earlier bloom than the same temperature accompanied by snow on the ground. He suggests that the trees are, in effect, standing with their "feet" in ice water although the days are warm. In this way, he estimates the week of peak bloom quite accurately to the satisfaction of the festival personnel and a great many people (who) arrive from out of town.

B. After you have written your answers to the following questions, compare your answers and your sentences with those of several of your classmates. If you have any questions, consult your instructor.

1. Where are the cherry trees growing? Use a complex sentence with "that" or "which" as the subject of the subordinate clause. _____

    _____

2. Why is it important to predict the peak blooming period? Use a complex sentence with "that" or "which" as the subject of the subordinate clause.

    _____

    _____

3. Who forecasts the blooming time? Use a complex sentence with "who" as

the subject of the subordinate clause. _____

_____

4. What factors does he consider in making his prediction? In your answer include a clause with "that," "which," or "who" as the subject of the sub-

ordinate clause. _____

_____

C. Together with your group, write a paragraph discussing some other indication of the arrival of spring. If you prefer, write about one of the other three seasons instead of spring. Be sure to check your sentences carefully for subject-verb agreement before you exchange paragraphs with another group.

LESSON 4

Agreement of Pronoun and Antecedent

An **antecedent** (**A**) is the noun or pronoun to which a **pronoun** (**P**) refers. The pronoun agrees in number, person, and gender with the antecedent.

	A		P
EXAMPLE:	Christopher showed Erika his art collection.

The possessive pronoun "his" refers to the noun "Christopher."

You probably make few errors in pronoun-antecedent agreement in simple sentences, such as the example above. The following sentence patterns, however, may give you trouble.

Words That Separate Antecedent and Pronoun

Be sure that the pronoun agrees with the antecedent and not with another noun that may be placed closer to the pronoun than the antecedent is.

	A		P
EXAMPLE:	One of the players injured in the game sprained his ankle.

The singular antecedent of the pronoun "his," is "one," not the plural noun "players."

Compound Antecedents

Compound antecedents usually require plural pronouns.

                        A   A   P

EXAMPLE: Christopher and Erika exhibited their oil paintings in the student art show.

However, if the two antecedents are joined by or, neither . . . nor, or either . . . or, the pronoun agrees with the antecedent closer to the pronoun.

When one antecedent is plural and the other singular, place the plural antecedent second to avoid writing an awkward sentence.

EXAMPLE: **Awkward:**   Neither my parents nor my brother would admit that he couldn't solve my sister's algebra problems.

Rewritten: Neither my brother nor my parents would admit that they couldn't solve my sister's algebra problems.

EXERCISE 4A

Fill in the correct pronouns on the lines in these sentences. Write the word or words that are the antecedents on the lines at the right.

EXAMPLE: The student artist who sold me these paintings signed his name in the corner.   ___artist___

1. Both Matt and Richard are exhibiting _____ paintings in the student art show.   _____

2. Jaime, one of the students in our photography class, produced _____ pictures with the aid of a computer.   _____

3. Neither Jan nor Theresa has ever entered _____ photographs in a competition before today.   _____

4. Mr. and Mrs. Asano, who are local artists, have given us _____ help in judging the entries in the exhibition.   _____

5. Neither the photographer nor the journalism students have completed _____ work on the publicity for the show.   _____

Collective Nouns

The nouns below are usually singular if you refer to the group as a unit.

audience	crowd	company	team
jury	government	group	class
number	band	management	committee
society	college	school	family

EXAMPLE: Our school band has its own bus.

In this example, you are referring to the band as a unit. If you are unsure whether to use a singular or plural pronoun, rewrite the sentence to make it less awkward.

EXERCISE 4B

Write its or their on the lines in the following sentences.

1. The committee made _____ recommendation yesterday.

2. The senior class will vote for _____ officers tomorrow.

3. Will the jury ever reach _____ decision on this case?

4. The audience sat quietly in _____ seats.

5. Last year the company that my father works for gave _____ employees a bonus in December.

Singular Words

The words below are singular. Pronouns that refer to these words should also be singular.

all	each	neither	one
any	either	nobody	some
anybody	everybody	none	somebody
anyone	everyone	no one	someone
anything	everything	nothing	something

                A   P

EXAMPLE: Has everyone finished his or her test? (not, their test)

The use of their with words like everyone and everybody is gaining acceptance. Many people would agree that it is acceptable to write: Has everyone finished their test?

When writing assignments for academic purposes, try rewriting the sentence to leave out the pronoun.

Rewrite: Has everyone finished the test?

This solution also avoids the problem of sexist language and the awkward alternative of writing sentences like the one in the example above.

EXERCISE 4C

Complete the following sentences with appropriate pronouns or rewrite the sentences to avoid problems of awkwardness.

1. Someone left _____ books on the desk.

2. Has anyone brought _____ camera?

3. Each of the girls has paid _____ dues to the club treasurer.

4. Nobody has received _____ grades in the mail yet.

5. Everyone must show _____ employee badge to the guard at the gate.

> ### GRAMMAR TIP
>
> The repeated use of his/her in a paragraph or an essay can become monotonous or sound forced. You usually can avoid this problem by using a plural noun antecedent and substituting their or by using a noun marker (a, an, or the).

Agreement of *Who, Whom, Which,* and *That* with Antecedents

Who, whom, which, and that should agree not only in gender, person, and number with their antecedents, but they should also agree with them in a special way.

Who and whom refer only to people.

    A   P
Marilyn, who lives next door, wants to be a model.

Which refers only to animals or things.

        A   P
Roy's car, which is twenty years old, is still running.

That may refer to animals or things, but not usually to people. The use of the word that to refer to people, however, is gaining wider acceptance, especially in conversation. Nevertheless, when you are writing assignments for school, it is a good idea to use who and whom in reference to people.

The car that I bought six months ago is falling apart.

The two dogs that belong to my neighbor like to dig.

EXERCISE 4D

Underline the pronoun that best completes each sentence.

1. The people (who, that) live on my street belong to a neighborhood-watch group.

2. I joined the group (who, that) was formed last year.

3. The neighborhood is watched by the people (who, that) live there.

4. There are signs in the windows of the members' houses (who, that) warn criminals to stay away.

5. I like living in a neighborhood (who, that) is safe.

┌───┐

GRAMMAR TIP

If you have difficulty knowing whether to use <u>who</u> or <u>whom</u> to introduce a subordinate clause, study the following explanations.

Use <u>who</u> to introduce a subordinate clause when it is the subject of the verb in that clause.

EXAMPLE: Mark did not know <u>who</u> had given the money to Alan.

(<u>Who</u> is the subject of the verb <u>had given</u>.)

Use <u>whom</u> to introduce a subordinate clause when it is the object of a verb or a preposition <u>in</u> that clause.

EXAMPLE: Mark did not know <u>whom</u> Alan had invited to the party.

(<u>Whom</u> is the object of the verb <u>had invited</u>.)

└───┘

Unclear Pronoun Reference

You will confuse your reader if there are two or more nouns the pronoun can refer to or if there is no antecedent at all for the pronoun. Learn to provide one specific antecedent for each pronoun by studying this section.

More Than One Possible Antecedent

EXAMPLE: Carol dropped the glass on the plate and broke <u>it</u>.

The antecedent is not clear. Did the glass break? Or was it the plate?

REVISED: When Carol dropped the glass on the plate, the glass broke.

The plate broke when Carol dropped a glass on it.

EXAMPLE: Damon told Marcus that Rita had found his wallet.

The antecedent of <u>his</u> is not clear. Who lost the wallet? Damon or Marcus?

REVISED: Damon said to Marcus, "Rita found your wallet." (Or "Rita found my wallet.")

No Specific Antecedent

EXAMPLE: I liked camp because <u>they</u> were so friendly.

The pronoun <u>they</u> cannot refer to the singular noun <u>camp</u>. Substitute a specific noun for the pronoun <u>they</u>.

REVISED: I liked camp because the counselors were so friendly.

GRAMMAR TIP

When you use a pronoun such as <u>it</u>, <u>that</u>, <u>they</u>, <u>this</u>, or <u>which</u>, be sure that the pronoun points clearly to one specific antecedent.

EXERCISE 4E

The antecedents of the underlined pronouns in these sentences are unclear. Give the pronouns specific antecedents or replace the pronouns with nouns. If necessary, rewrite the sentence entirely.

1. Jacquie told Tess that <u>she</u> had lost <u>her</u> pen.

   _____

2. There are so many automobile accidents because <u>they</u> are so careless.

   _____

3. Charles Brocard is a marine archaeologist. <u>This</u> is a new and challenging profession.

   _____

4. Juan told Bob that <u>his</u> car needed repainting.

   _____

5. In some parts of Canada <u>they</u> speak French.

   _____

LESSON 5
Sentence Combining

Lesson 5 will give you additional practice in subject/verb agreement and pronoun/antecedent agreement, which you have been studying in Chapter 7.

EXAMPLE: Combine these five sentences into one sentence. Use that as the subject of a subordinate clause. In this combined sentence, is the verb in the subordinate clause singular or plural? What is the subject of the verb? What is the antecedent of the subject?

1. Canadian geese return to the arctic in the spring.
2. The geese start digging beneath the soil.
3. Food is under the surface.
4. They want to find something for their baby goslings to eat.
5. The goslings were born during the winter in the United States.

Combined Sentence: When Canadian geese return to the arctic in the spring, they start digging beneath the soil to find food under the surface for their goslings that were born during the winter in the United States.

A. Combine these four sentences into one sentence. Use that to change the second sentence into a subordinate clause.

1. The Canadian geese population has increased so rapidly.
2. The marsh land where they normally find food has been destroyed.
3. It has been destroyed by their digging beneath the surface of the soil.
4. They dig through the surface of the soil to find food.

B. Combine these six sentences into one sentence. Change sentence 1 to an introductory subordinate clause. Change sentence 6 to a verbal phrase.

1. I was walking down an unpaved road in Alaska.
2. It was late afternoon.
3. It was summer.
4. I whistled a tune.
5. The tune was cheerful.
6. I whistled to frighten away any hungry bears.

C. Combine these five sentences into one sentence. Change sentence 5 to a subordinate clause beginning with which and place the clause between the subject and verb of the main clause.

1. The lighthouse of Pharos stands on an island in a harbor.
2. The island is Pharos.

3. The harbor is in Alexandria, Egypt.
4. The lighthouse is like a sentinel.
5. It is one of the Seven Wonders of the Ancient World.

D. Combine sentences 1 and 2 into a subordinate clause introduced by <u>who</u>. Place this clause between the subject and the verb of the main clause. Change sentence 4 to a verbal phrase.

1. Marian Anderson experienced racial prejudice.
2. She experienced it during her early years.
3. She became the first African-American singer to join the Metropolitan Opera.
4. She received the Presidential Medal of Freedom.

Chapter 7 Summary

plural	pronoun	subject	precedes
antecedents	singular	follows	

Choose words from the box above to complete these sentences.

Note: Some words may be used more than once.

1. A subject and a verb agree if you use the correct form of the verb with the

    _____.

2. To be sure that the verb agrees with the subject, mentally change the

    noun subject into a _____.

3. If the sentence begins with *here, there,* or *where,* the subject _____

    the verb.

4. Compound subjects usually take a _____ verb.

5. Pronouns such as *someone* or *anyone* refer to _____ antecedents.

6. Collective nouns such as *class* and *government* take _____ verbs if the subject acts as a single unit.

7. The words *mathematics, physics,* and *economics* used as subjects take _____ verbs.

8. Pronouns must agree with their _____.

Writing Assignment

Topic

Read the paragraph in Exercise 3B again. Using the answers that you gave to the questions at the end of the paragraph, write about how you protect and preserve your family photographs. If you do not keep family pictures, or if the responsibility is not yours, do you have some other favorite family heirloom that you want to preserve for future generations? Maybe it is a quilt, a collection of books, a journal, or a diary of your daily life. Explain how you plan to store these valuable items and how you will tell future generations why these things were so valuable to you.

Step 1. Begin by jotting down a few ideas before you write your paper.

Step 2. Then, look back over your notes and write a topic sentence.

Step 3. Assume that your reader is someone who has not read the paragraph. Tell that reader how you currently keep these photographs and how you may have to change the way you safeguard these family treasures. What information should you provide your reader? Refer to the section, *Considering Your Readers* in Chapter 10.

Step 4. Support your topic sentence with specific and concrete details.

Step 5. Exchange rough drafts with a classmate. Check the draft for subject-verb and pronoun-antecedent agreement errors. Discuss any comments your classmate may have made before you write the final draft. Proofread your final draft before you submit it to your instructor.

Alternative Writing Assignment

Topic

Toys obviously have changed quite a bit in the last twenty years. Electronic toys have replaced many of the old favorites. Are electronic toys more fun or more satisfying than non-electronic toys? If you believe that toys were more fun before the age of computers, describe some of the popular toys from your childhood.

Step 1. Whether you are writing about a new electronic toy or about a favorite childhood toy, begin by describing the toy. Make a list of the features that would appeal to a child.

Step 2. Explain how the child plays with the toy. For example, as a child, did you play with the toy alone or did you share it with a friend? In the case of many electronic toys, the child plays the game alone.

Step 3. Begin by jotting down a few ideas before you write your paper. Then look back over your notes and write a topic sentence.

Step 4. Assume that your reader is not familiar with the toy you have chosen. What information should you provide your reader? Refer to the section in Chapter 10, *Considering Your Readers*.

Step 5. Having taken your reader into consideration, choose specific and concrete details or examples to support your topic sentence.

Step 6. Exchange rough drafts with a classmate. Check the draft for subject-verb and pronoun-antecedent agreement errors. Discuss any comments your classmate may have made before you write the final draft. Proofread your final draft before you submit it to your instructor.

━━▶ CHAPTER 7

PRACTICE TEST: Agreement

Name _____

Date _____ Class Time _____

Instructor _____

I. Underline the correct verb in the sentences below.

1. According to a survey, a group of listeners (object, objects) to the program's talk-show format.

2. On the last page of the report (was, were) listed the preferences of these listeners.

3. There (has, have) been some changes made in the original program.

4. This past week, news and music (has, have) replaced the talk-show format.

5. The new format, according to the station manager, (seem, seems) to please the audience.

II. Underline the correct verb in the sentences below.

1. Economics (is, are) not a difficult subject for Alan.

2. The audience (were, was) delighted by the speaker's sense of humor.

3. Each of the students (learn, learns) at a different rate.

4. These new scissors never (need, needs) sharpening.

5. Neither of the players (seem, seems) to be worried about the outcome of the game.

III. Underline the correct pronoun in the following sentences.

1. Both Allison and Meredith said (she, they) would come to the study session.

CHAPTER 7   PRACTICE TEST (Cont.)

2. Neither Allison nor Meredith remembered to bring (their, her) class notes to the study session.

3. Western Mills promoted (its, their) new cereal by passing out samples of the product in the markets.

4. The basketball team has won all (their, its) home games.

5. Many states, like Florida, allow some of (its, their) traffic violators to attend traffic schools instead of paying fines.

IV. Rewrite these sentences by giving unclear pronouns specific antecedents or by replacing the underlined pronouns with nouns.

1. Marsha called her mother once a week when <u>she</u> was out of town.

   _____

2. The doctor returned his patient's call before <u>he</u> went to lunch.

   _____

3. <u>They</u> should make pedestrians and roller skaters stay off the bike path.

   _____

4. Jared is studying marine biology. <u>This</u> is a rewarding profession.

   _____

5. Daniel turned in a late research paper <u>which</u> annoyed his history instructor.

   _____

V. Write your own sentences according to the instructions given.

1. Write a sentence beginning with <u>Here is</u>.

   _____

2. Write a sentence using the words <u>either</u> George <u>or</u> Laura as the subject. Use a verb in the present tense.

_____

3. Write a sentence with the word <u>news</u> as the subject. Use a verb in the present tense.

_____

4. Write a sentence using the word <u>anyone</u> as the subject. Use a verb in the present tense.

_____

5. Write a sentence using <u>who</u>, <u>which</u>, or <u>that</u> as the subject of a subordinate clause.

_____

VI. Insert commas where needed in the following sentences.

1. Hal Prince who won a Tony award last year will direct the new musical.

2. The director who was pleased with the actors' performances that day called for one more rehearsal.

3. When the actors heard the announcement they all cheered.

4. The musicians were also happy when they heard the announcement.

5. The new play which was opening in New York in a week was sure to be a hit.

Editing
Practice

Underline the nine errors in the agreement of subjects and verbs or of pronouns and antecedents in the following paragraph. Then write the correct forms on the lines provided.

EXAMPLE: The work of dedicated scientists and new techniques

of exploration <u>makes</u> these discoveries possible.   _____ make _____

For centuries Alexandria, one of Egypt's coastal cities, has sheltered in their harbor a treasure waiting to be discovered by archaeologists. Here is the ruins of the ancient city of Alexandria, lying approximately 30 feet below the modern city. Each of the archaeologists, who trained as scuba divers, have exchanged his tools for underwater cameras, computers, and scuba gear to make the search. There was 3,500 dives made before maps could be drawn to guide the team in its exploration of the site. A small paved island, believed to have been the site of the palace where both Julius Caesar and Marc Antony paid his respects to Cleopatra, has been located. Despite their wealth and power, neither Cleopatra nor Marc Antony were destined to enjoy a long and peaceful life in this sophisticated cultural center of the ancient world. Now with this discovery of Cleopatra's sunken city comes some major decisions. Should scientists bring the objects out of the sea or leave them where they have been resting for all these centuries? Some of the scientists who made these discoveries favors leaving the objects in the sea. A group of Egyptian citizens, however, propose making an archaeological diving park in the harbor, thereby using the old Alexandria to attract tourists to the modern Alexandria.

1. _____ 2. _____ 3. _____ 4. _____

5. _____ 6. _____ 7. _____ 8. _____

9. _____

Answer the following questions in complete sentences.

1. What discovery has been made, and where was it made?

   _____

   _____

2. How does marine archaeology differ from land archaeology?

   _____

   _____

3. Why did the team of scientists have to make a map of the site?

   _____

   _____

4. Did either Cleopatra or Marc Antony live to old age? Which sentence in the paragraph explains your answer?

   _____

   _____

5. What decision do the scientists have to make as a result of their discovery?

   _____

   _____

Commas

Rules for Using Commas

1. Use a comma between two main clauses connected by a coordinating connective.
2. Use a comma to separate three or more items in a series.
3. Use a comma after introductory words and phrases.
4. Use a comma after introductory subordinate clauses.
5. Use commas to separate two or more adjectives before a noun.
6. Use commas to enclose words that interrupt.
7. Use commas to set off words in direct address.
8. Use commas to set off nonessential words, phrases, and clauses.
9. Use commas to set off direct quotations.
10. Use a comma after each item in dates, geographical names, and addresses.

Many writers are confused about when to use commas. Perhaps someone told you to read the sentence aloud and put a comma in wherever you pause. Although it is true that commas generally do mark a break or a pause, it is not a good idea to rely on your ear in this way. It is much better to learn the uses of commas. Studying the lessons in this chapter should help you understand the use of commas.

Use a Comma Between Two Main Clauses Connected by a Coordinating Connective

LESSON 1

Place a comma before a coordinating connective (<u>and</u>, <u>but</u>, <u>for</u>, <u>or</u>, <u>nor</u>, <u>so</u>, and <u>yet</u>) when it joins two main clauses.

EXAMPLE: The outfielder <u>dropped</u> the fly ball, and the runner on third base <u>scored</u>.

Unnecessary Commas: The following sentence does not have a comma before the connective. In this sentence, and connects the two parts of a compound verb, not two main clauses.

EXAMPLE: The outfielder <u><u>caught</u></u> the ball <u>and</u> <u><u>threw</u></u> it to third base.

EXERCISE 1A

Insert commas between main clauses where necessary.

It is not true that flamingos are pink only because they eat pink shellfish. The pinkness of flamingos is determined by food but it is not determined by pink shellfish. The factors in the flamingo's diet that ensure pinkness are carotenoid pigments and these pigments are found in plankton, diatoms, and blue-green algae. The flamingos eat the plankton and algae. Then they process the yellow carotene into a red compound and that substance is stored in their legs and their feathers. Flamingos must get enough of the right pigment or they will lose their color when they molt. The pink color is very important as flamingos do not seem to breed successfully without it. In captivity they were once fed ground-up carrots and red pepper to keep them in the pink but now the zoo keepers try to reproduce their natural diet.

Underline the unnecessary commas. Do not underline the commas that separate main clauses.

The government has spent billions of dollars to protect our shorelines from the destruction of storms, but coastal geologists maintain that these efforts only accelerate the damage. Engineers build structures such as jetties, or breakwaters, yet they fail to stop the erosion. Geologists say that this policy is based on a misunderstanding, for all the engineers' good intentions. Beaches do not need these barriers, and actually provide protection for the continent. Sand builds up in sand dunes when the ocean is calm, and waves move this sand out to the sea bottom during a storm. Beaches then become flatter, so waves break earlier, and cause less erosion. Beaches that have neither seawalls, nor bulkheads to interrupt the natural cycle rebuild their defenses as calmer waters carry the sand back to the shore. Miles of east-coast beaches have disappeared after 70 years of engineered beach construction, and the loss can only continue if the advice of geologists is ignored.

LESSON	# Use a Comma to Separate Items in a Series
2	

Use a comma to separate *three or more items* in a series. The items may be single words, phrases, or clauses. A comma before the last item is optional if there are exactly three items in the series. In the following examples, you may omit the comma before <u>and</u> in sentence 1 if you wish.

EXAMPLES: 1. Aaron is taking courses in marketing, accounting, and statistics this semester. (words)

2. I went to the bank, did some shopping, bought a newspaper, and returned home by noon. (phrases)

3. Leroy cut the grass, Cathy pulled the weeds in the flower beds, and Pat trimmed the hedges. (main clauses)

Unnecessary Commas: No comma is necessary in the following sentence because there are only two items in the series.

EXAMPLE: Juanita is taking courses in drafting and mathematics this semester.

EXERCISE 2A

Write a sentence using each of the following series or pairs. Use commas where needed.

1. LaToya   Ali   Stacy   Dwayne

_____

2. listened attentively   took notes   reviewed chapter summaries

_____

3. watched TV   listened to CDs

_____

4. writing   telephoning   faxing

_____

5. made a list   drew a cluster   prepared an outline

_____

EXERCISE 2B

Insert commas where necessary. In some sentences the comma is optional.

1. Gordon Parks is a noted photographer, poet, author, filmmaker and composer.

2. He once attributed his early determination to become a photographer to three influences: some 1930s Farm Security Administration photographs an art show in a Chicago museum, and a newsreel of a World War II Japanese bombing raid.

3. He began his career on the Seattle waterfront with an excellent inexpensive secondhand camera.

4. The young Midwesterner, who spent his early years in Kansas Minnesota, and Washington, had his first photo exhibit in the storefront window of the Eastman Kodak Company in Minneapolis.

5. He was a staff photographer at *Life* magazine for 20 years where he developed an expertise in photojournalism documentaries and fashion photography.

6. Parks achieved an international reputation as one of several African-American photographers whose pictures of African Americans revealed the close family ties and rich community life in the midst of a segregated restrictive society.

7. His photographs, such as his famous "American Gothic," recorded the black experience, but he actually had a broader interest in the poverty prejudice and injustices suffered by the defenseless everywhere.

Use a Comma After Introductory Words and Phrases

At the beginning of a sentence, use a comma after a long phrase.

EXAMPLES: 1. *By the end of the second week of school,* Ken began making plans for Thanksgiving weekend.

2. *Looking at his calendar,* Ken realized that he had weeks to wait for the holiday.

The comma after a single introductory word or a short introductory phrase is optional. Although many writers use the comma after these expressions, others do not.

EXAMPLES: 1. *During the recent heat wave,* we hoped a rainstorm would bring relief. Finally, one arrived, but the humidity only increased.

2. *In that heat,* no one could work outdoors comfortably.

3. *After work,* we went to a movie to cool off before eating dinner.

COMMA TIP

If there is any question about the meaning of the sentence, use a comma after a single word or a short phrase of introduction.

1. Inside, the theater was cool and dark.

2. While ordering, my friends and I drank iced tea at the restaurant.

Try reading these two sentences without commas, and you will see why the comma in each case is essential to understanding the meaning.

EXERCISE 3A

Insert commas where necessary. In some sentences the comma is optional.

1. Among the staples of southwestern cooking the chile is probably the most essential.

2. By the way New Mexicans spell "chile" with a final "e" not an "i."

3. In addition the chile is not actually a pepper as Columbus believed when he "discovered" it on one of his voyages.

4. In fact the capsicum (chile) is a distant cousin of the tomato and is classified by botanists as a fruit.

5. Ranging from mild to incredibly hot the chile's color depends on when it is harvested.

6. Produced by the same plant green chilies are picked early and red chilies late in the season after they have matured.

7. Moreover color is no guide to pungency; red or green sauce can be mild or hot depending on each specific batch.

8. While eating a food flavored with the chile you may suddenly need to put out the fire, but eat something sweet or creamy instead of reaching for a glass of ice water.

EXERCISE 3B

Insert commas where necessary. In some sentences the comma is optional.

1. As a matter of fact few people would say that telling a lie is okay.

2. But they would have to admit that they tell lies sometimes.

3. At work they often say to another employee, "What a fine report you produced!"

4. In their own minds they are probably thinking, "I could have done it better."

5. Lying for all its possible social value, is almost never called by its real name.

6. For example some politicians would only admit they told a lie by saying, "Mistakes were made."

LESSON 4
Use a Comma After Introductory Subordinate Clauses

Use a comma after a subordinate clause at the beginning of a sentence.

EXAMPLE: *When you move to your new office,* send us your address.

Editing
Practice

Insert commas following introductory phrases and subordinate clauses where necessary. Some sentences do not need commas added. Do not remove any commas from the paragraph.

Although a comet looks very beautiful as it sails across the sky it is not much more than a dirty snowball. A comet consists of chunks of rocky or metallic material dust and ice. While the ice is mainly frozen water it also contains a mixture of methane, ammonia, and carbon dioxide molecules. When a comet passes close to the sun it loses some of its matter. Some of its ice turns to a gas form as a comet nears the sun. The gases spread out around the nucleus, forming a large, thin atmosphere called a "coma," which glows in the sunlight. If the supply of gases from the nucleus changes a comet can brighten and fade noticeably. As a comet approaches the sun a solar wind sweeps a comet's gases away from the sun. So a second tail consisting of dust particles may also appear. Although this dust tail is shorter than the gas tail it may also be visible from Earth. In fact some comets have been observed to have as many as nine tails.

EXERCISE 4A

If the sentence is punctuated correctly, write "Yes" on the line at the right. If the sentence is incorrectly punctuated, write "No" on the line. Insert or remove commas in the sentences as needed.

1. Country music began several hundred years ago, when Scotch-Irish settlers came to the Appalachian region bringing their folk music with them.   _____

2. Although the newcomers still played the "old" music, it began to change with their use of "new" homemade instruments such as the banjo, the guitar, and the zither. _____

3. This "fiddle music" or "Old Time Music" gained a wider audience during the 1920s after Victor Records arrived in the South to record these rural musicians. _____

4. In 1926 when Jimmie Rodgers, recognized today as the "Father of Country Music," and his hillbilly band moved to Asheville they began attracting enthusiastic audiences. _____

5. Since the music has borrowed extensively from spirituals, blues, jazz, and honky-tonk and has added instruments such as drums and the electric guitar, it has evolved into a distinctively American music. _____

6. The lyrics tell stories about ordinary people and their continual struggle with the harsh facts of their lives. _____

7. Because "country" music has now become the music of our towns and cities it has been called the "folk music" of working people and a "native American art form." _____

Group ACTIVITY

In the following paragraph, insert commas as needed between two main clauses joined by coordinating connectives, between items in a series, and following introductory phrases and subordinate clauses. Do not remove commas. Then answer the questions below the paragraph.

Geothermal heat may be a new source of energy for us but it is an ancient means of providing power by tapping a natural resource. Subsidized by federal grants and tax advantages developers have tripled the use of geothermal power. In many western states today communities are hoping to reduce their dependence on fossil fuels by utilizing this alternative energy source where it is available. Since geothermal heat is a fairly economical source of power it has a growing number of supporters. Boise, Idaho, has become well-known among proponents of this form of energy because this city has taken advantage of the hot wells underneath it. Boise has laid pipes beneath its streets to heat restaurants shops business offices and the state office buildings. This old-new source of power can supply only a small part of the nation's energy needs but it can provide a substantial savings to those regions possessing this natural advantage.

Together with a group check each other's insertion of commas in the paragraph. Then write sentences as directed below, and exchange your work with that of another group. Check each other's sentences for the correct use of commas.

1. What is meant by geothermal heat? (Your answer should have at least two main clauses joined by a comma and a coordinating connective.)
2. Why has Boise, Idaho, chosen to use this method to heat businesses? (Your answer should have an introductory phrase followed by a comma.)
3. What changes has Boise made in its street design? (Your answer should have items in a series separated by commas.)
4. Why have developers shown an interest in using geothermal heat? (Your answer should have an introductory subordinate clause followed by a comma.)

LESSON 5   Use Commas to Separate Adjectives Before a Noun

Use commas to separate two or more adjectives that modify the same noun if a coordinating connective such as <u>and</u> or <u>but</u> can be inserted between the adjectives. You can use two tests to tell whether or not to put a comma between modifiers before a noun.

1. Use a comma if <u>and</u> or <u>but</u> can be inserted between the adjectives.
2. Use a comma if <u>you can</u> reverse the order of the adjectives.

EXAMPLE: Bob was the most aggressive, skillful player on the court.

Use a comma because you could say:

1. Bob was the most aggressive and skillful player on the court.
or
2. Bob was the most skillful, aggressive player on the court.

Unnecessary Commas: Do not put a comma between adjectives if <u>and</u> or <u>but</u> cannot be placed between them or if you cannot reverse their order.

> **EXAMPLE:**   He was the most aggressive, skillful basketball player on the court.

You would not write <u>skillful and basketball player</u>.

You cannot reverse the words—<u>basketball skillful player</u>.

Therefore, do not put a comma between <u>skillful</u> and <u>basketball</u>.

The adjectives placed before <u>basketball player</u> modify both words. Commas should not be inserted between a modifier and a noun.

EXERCISE 5A

Insert additional commas as needed in the following sentences to separate adjectives before a noun. Do not remove any of the commas.

1. In the early morning, the joggers run effortlessly along the deserted shell-strewn beach.

2. Even on gray foggy chilly mornings, they wear only tank tops and brief running shorts.

3. Bicycle riders on the nearby winding concrete bike path must be alert as jogging parents push their small children in vehicles especially constructed for this purpose.

4. Some cyclists are also accompanied by their youngsters riding in low plastic-curtained trailers attached to the backs of their bikes.

5. When the morning overcast begins to burn off, the second shift appears: volleyball players head for the courts, and bikini-clad sun seekers lie down on their brightly colored beach towels for a serious tanning session.

EXERCISE 5B

If the sentence is punctuated correctly, write "Yes" on the line at the right. If the sentence is punctuated incorrectly, write "No" on the line. Insert or remove commas in the sentences as needed.

1. Woodchucks are plump, low-slung animals.   _____

2. They are not the largest, North American rodents; beavers are.   _____

3. Most slow fat woodchucks hibernate in winter.   _____

4. Woodchucks are found in rural and suburban areas in the eastern United States.   _____

5. Woodchucks will eat any growing, green plants.   _____

LESSON 6

Use Commas to Enclose Words That Interrupt

Use commas on both sides of a word (or a group of words) that interrupts the flow of thought in a sentence.

EXAMPLES: 1. Airline pilots, <u>by the way</u>, are often cautious automobile drivers.

2. The guests, <u>it seems</u>, are enjoying the party.

3. Several changes in the enrollment procedure, <u>however</u>, are planned for the coming semester.

Do not use just one comma; enclose the interrupting word or words between two commas.

Unnecessary Commas: Do not use commas to enclose prepositional phrases that do not interrupt the flow of thought in a sentence.

EXAMPLE: The dwarf lemon tree <u>in the tub</u> <u>on the patio</u> grew rapidly and produced fruit <u>in no time at all</u>. This sentence does not require any commas.

EXERCISE 6A

Insert commas around words that interrupt the sentences.

Most experts agree despite conclusive evidence that the lemon tree

probably originated in southeast Asia in the vicinity of Burma thousands of years ago. Although this evergreen tree is sensitive to freezing weather, the fruit does best as a matter of fact exposed to the occasional cold snap that a hot, humid climate lacks. California growers as a result use wind machines and heaters in their groves to regulate temperature. Lemon trees under ideal conditions can bear buds, flowers, developing fruit, and mature fruit all at the same time. Citrus trees moreover require a fair amount of water; rain however can damage the fruit. Every part of the fruit we are told from seed to peel has a use from food preparation and general household use to medicinal and commercial applications. Most of us without a doubt use lemons most frequently as flavor intensifiers. In some cultures people indeed know the meaning of using the entire fruit: they eat the lemon as we would an apple, peel and all.

EXERCISE 6B

If the sentence is punctuated correctly, write "Yes" on the line at the right. If the sentence is punctuated incorrectly, write "No" on the line. Insert or remove commas in the sentences as needed.

1. Mr. Toshida, arrived in San Francisco with his family, from a small town in Japan. _____

2. Dr. Okada, however, came to San Francisco from Tokyo. _____

3. Both men it would appear, had little trouble adjusting to life in America. _____

4. Mr. Toshida made his fortune, I believe, by manufacturing computer chips. _____

5. Dr. Okada in no time at all was successful as a dentist. _____

Use Commas to Set Off Words in Direct Address

Use commas to set off the names and titles of people spoken to directly.

EXAMPLES: 1. "Pat, will you please call Dr. Hodge for me?" Paul said.

2. "I called you, Dr. Hodge, to ask for some information," said Pat.

3. "How often should Paul take the medicine, Doctor?" asked Pat.

These three examples show words in direct address at the beginning, in the middle, and at the end of sentences. Notice the use of commas.

EXERCISE 7A

Insert commas for words of direct address where necessary.

1. "I don't entirely agree Jim with your position," said Ella.

2. "Ella you never agree with me," said Jim.

3. "I agree with you most of the time Jim," said Ella.

4. "Well then Ella why don't you agree with me now?" said Jim.

5. "Jim I cannot agree with you because you are wrong," said Ella.

6. "Ella tell me that you love me anyway," said Jim.

EXERCISE 7B

If the sentence is punctuated correctly, write "Yes" on the line at the right. If the sentence is punctuated incorrectly, write "No" on the line. Insert commas as needed in the sentences that are punctuated incorrectly.

1. Scott do you have time to review this proposal with me this afternoon?   _____

2. It is a pleasure to recommend you for promotion to office manager Mrs. Vasquez.   _____

3. We are sending the information that you requested sir by second-day air letter.   _____

4. Your request for a month's leave of absence, Alice, has been approved. _____

5. Thank you one and all for your work on this important project. _____

Use Commas to Set Off Nonessential Words, Phrases, and Clauses

LESSON 8

Insert commas to enclose words, phrases, and clauses containing nonessential material. The information in these words may add some details, but the reader could understand the main idea of the sentence if the words were left out.

EXAMPLES:
1. Lorena Harris, <u>who is our pitcher</u>, will be a sportscaster next fall.

2. *The Cider House Rules,* <u>a novel by John Irving</u>, has been made into a movie.

Omit the words enclosed by commas, and the sentences above read:

1. Lorena Harris will be a sportscaster next fall.
2. *The Cider House Rules* has been made into a movie.

As you can see, the main ideas of both sentences are unchanged by omitting the nonessential words.

Unnecessary Commas: Do not use commas to enclose words, phrases, and clauses that are essential to the meaning of the sentence.

EXAMPLE: Will the person <u>who parked in the loading zone</u> move his car?

If the subordinate clause <u>who parked in the loading zone</u> is omitted, the main idea of the sentence is lost. The person cannot be identified; you do not know who should move his car.

EXAMPLE: The novel *The Cider House Rules* has been made into a movie.

In this sentence the title is necessary to identify the book; therefore, you do not use commas.

EXERCISE 8A

Insert commas where necessary. Some sentences may not need commas.

1. My friend Carla Caraway went to New York to get a job as a dancer.

2. A young woman alone in a strange city must learn how to take care of herself.

3. She auditioned for Judith Jamison the famous choreographer of the Alvin Ailey company.

4. Carla breathless and exhausted waited after the audition to hear the choreographer's opinion.

5. Carla joined the Alvin Ailey company one of the best dance companies in the world.

EXERCISE 8B

In the following sentences, insert commas where required to set off nonessential words, phrases, and clauses.

1. The talented American contralto Marian Anderson who had sung at the White House was barred from singing in Constitution Hall in Washington.

2. Instead Ms. Anderson sang at the Lincoln Memorial before 75,000 people who had gathered in support of her.

3. Three Aaron Copland ballets drawing upon American themes are *Billy the Kid, Rodeo,* and *Appalachian Spring.*

4. Copland wrote *Appalachian Spring* for Martha Graham choreographer and dancer.

5. Ernest Hemingway an American author began his first job as a newspaper reporter at the age of eighteen.

6. The novel *A Farewell to Arms* was based on Hemingway's experiences as an ambulance driver during World War I.

7. American heroes who had been neglected by standard history books were portrayed by Jacob Lawrence in his paintings.

8. Gilbert Stuart an early American painter is best known for his portraits of George Washington.

9. Frank Lloyd Wright one of the first architects to use glass and metal walls for office buildings achieved early recognition outside the United States.

10. The hotel that Wright designed in Tokyo after World War I showed inventiveness in its earthquake-resistant construction.

<table>
<tr><td>LESSON
9</td><td># Use Commas to Set Off
Direct Quotations</td></tr>
</table>

Use commas to set off direct quotations from the rest of the sentence.

EXAMPLES: 1. "Perhaps," my brother said to me, "you should study once in a while."
2. She asked, "Won't anybody help me?"
3. "I don't want to watch television tonight," Jan said.
4. "I'll be back in an hour," Jim answered, "so don't leave without me."

In sentence 3, although "I don't want to watch television tonight," is a main clause, do not use a period until the end of the complete statement. Note that commas are placed inside the quotation marks.

EXERCISE 9A

Insert commas where necessary in the sentences below.

1. "I can never do these homework assignments" Gary complained.

2. "Well" said his mother "you haven't even tried."

3. "I never learn anything in that class" he said "so what's the point?"

4. "Besides" he said to her "I have a date tonight."

5. "Gary, you should do your assignment before you go out" his mother advised.

6. "I have to leave in one hour" he told his mother.

7. "If you begin to work right now" she said "you will have plenty of time."

8. "I'll do it when I come home" he said as he left the house.

9. "Gary, come right back here" she called "and finish your homework."

10. "You might as well relax, Mom" said Gary's sister. "He has already gone."

Insert commas where required to set off:

a. direct quotations
b. words of direct address
c. nonessential words or phrases

1. "Greg did you hear about the recent triathalon competition in Hawaii?" Diane asked.

2. "I hadn't realized" she continued "how popular the sport has become."

3. "The athlete who attempts the Ironman competition must be in top physical condition Diane" Greg replied.

4. "Most other triathalon competitions as a matter of fact are not as demanding as the Ironman" he pointed out.

5. "If your goal Greg is just to complete the triathalon" Diane said "you don't need to worry about speed."

6. The doctor said "Hypothermia can be a threat to the swimmers if the water is especially cold."

7. "One of the greatest dangers to the athletes during the marathon run" he added "is dehydration."

8. "For most triathalons, competitors are required to sign waivers releasing the promoters from responsibility for the athletes' safety" Greg said.

9. Diane remarked "The most successful athletes as I might have expected train under conditions similar to those of the competition."

10. "Competitors should train for at least three months" the doctor advised "in each of the three sports: swimming, running, and cycling."

Use Commas in Dates, Geographical Names, and Addresses

LESSON 10

Use commas after every item in dates, geographical names, and addresses as shown in the following examples:

Dates: Maria started a new job on Monday, June 6, 2005.

Unnecessary Commas: Commas may be omitted when the day of the month is not given.

> **EXAMPLE:** Maria started a new job in June 2005.

Also, commas are omitted when the day of the month precedes the month.

> **EXAMPLE:** Maria started a new job on 6 June 2005.

Geographical Names: Miami, Florida, is the site of the Orange Bowl.

Addresses: James Webb's address is 2208 N. McKnight Road, Philadelphia, PA 19103. (The zip code is not separated by a comma from the name of the state.)

EXERCISE 10A

Insert commas where necessary in the following sentences.

1. George will move to Las Vegas Nevada in January.

2. His address has been The Stanford Arms Hotel 536 W. 18th Street Rittman Indiana 46206 for the last six years.

3. We will forward his mail to his new address: The Luxor Hotel Las Vegas Nevada 89501.

4. Bill Wilson is a salesperson for Fashion Clothing Co. 2473 White Plains Road Bronx New York 10111.

5. On 15 April 2005 Bill traveled from New York to Dallas Texas to attend a fashion show.

6. The fashion show was held at the Plaza Hotel 8 Fifth Street Dallas Texas.

If the sentence is punctuated correctly, write "Yes" on the line at the right. If the sentence is punctuated incorrectly, write "No" on the line. Insert commas in sentences as necessary.

1. Send Lynn's mail in care of Mrs. R.B. Singer, 1532 Stone Canyon Drive Santa Maria Arizona 85321 starting Tuesday July 19, 2005.   _____

2. Elvis Presley was born on January 8, 1935, in Tupelo, Mississippi, according to the records.   _____

3. Circle March 15 on your calendar as a reminder to file your income tax.   _____

4. Return this form to the Department of Motor Vehicles, 128 S. Cadillac Ave., Newbury, Montana 59711, by Monday, March 7, 2005, to avoid paying a penalty.   _____

5. Nat wrote to the American Association of Community Colleges at One Dupont Circle, Washington, D.C. 20036 for a list of colleges in Texas and Arizona.   _____

6. Charles Lindbergh, flying the "Spirit of Saint Louis," left Mineola New York on May 20 1927 and arrived in Paris France on May 21, 1927.   _____

Group
ACTIVITY

As a group, plan a trip that you might take. Make an outline of the places you would like to go. Then read the Editing Practice following the Practice Test at the end of this chapter. Using the Romero family's experience as a guide, write a paragraph describing the things you expect to see and do. Try to include the following items punctuated with the appropriate commas in your sentences.

1. Adjectives before a noun
2. Words that interrupt
3. Words of direct address
4. Nonessential words, phrases, or clauses
5. Direct quotations
6. Dates, geographical names, and addresses

 LESSON
11

Sentence Combining

In this exercise you will be combining words, phrases, and clauses into sentences and correctly punctuating them. In the example that follows, the combined sentence opens with an introductory subordinate clause and two prepositional phrases. Notice the placement of the commas. Why are there no commas after <u>several</u> and <u>dozen</u>? Are the commas after <u>mountainside</u> and <u>lights</u> optional?

1. Astronomers meet on the darkest nights.
2. The nights are darkest during the week after the new moon.
3. These are amateur astronomers.
4. There are several dozen of them.
5. They meet once a month.
6. They meet on a mountainside.
7. They are far above the city lights.
8. They look through telescopes.
9. They look at the mysteries of the sky.

Combined Sentence: When the nights are the darkest, during the week after the new moon, several dozen amateur astronomers meet once a month on a mountainside, far above the city lights, to look through their telescopes at the mysteries of the sky.

A. Combine these four sentences into one sentence. Use commas to enclose the nonessential phrase. Change sentence 4 into a verbal phrase and punctuate it correctly.

1. The 100-inch Hooker telescope is at Mount Wilson, California.
2. It was built in 1917.
3. It helped produce some of the triumphs of twentieth-century astronomy.
4. The triumphs of twentieth-century astronomy include the Big Bang Theory.

B. Combine these four sentences into one sentence. Begin your sentence with a subordinate clause introduced by the subordinator *although*.

1. The 100-inch telescope was considered obsolete in 1985.
2. But new inventions and a determined effort saved the Hooker.
3. The effort was made by rich private benefactors.
4. The historic telescope reopened in 1994.

C. Combine these five sentences into one sentence. Change sentence 1 into an introductory subordinate clause. Use a compound verb in the main clause. Change sentences 3, 4, and 5 into a series of prepositional phrases.

1. Tree-ripened lemons have more flavor.
2. Most lemons are picked green.
3. They are put into storage.

4. Lemons are later shipped to supermarkets.
5. They are shipped across the country.

D. Combine these six sentences into one sentence. Change the first sentence into a subordinate clause introduced by the pronoun *who*. Change sentences 5 and 6 into a final subordinate clause with a compound verb.

1. Roller bladers start at the art museum.
2. They head north along the east bank of the river.
3. They skate on the pavement.
4. It is flat and level and smooth.
5. It runs for miles.
6. The pavement is ideal for both beginning and speed skaters.

Note: There is more than one way to combine each group of sentences into one sentence. The instructions are suggestions intended to help you. You, of course, may combine them in your own way.

Chapter 8 Summary

direct	subordinate	nonessential
interrupts	series	direct
main	three	two
item	set off	phrase

Choose words from the box to complete the sentences below. The answers are the ten uses for commas, which should serve as a guide to comma placement.

1. Use commas between two _____ clauses connected by coordinating connectives.

2. Use commas to separate words, phrases, or clauses in a _____ .

   There should be more than _____ items listed.

3. Place a comma after a long introductory _____ .

4. Place a comma after a _____ clause at the beginning of a sentence.

5. Use commas to separate _____ or more adjectives that modify the same noun.

6. Use commas on both sides of a word (or group of words) that _____ the flow of thought in a sentence.

7. Use commas to _____ the names and titles of people spoken to directly.

8. Use commas to enclose words, phrases, and clauses containing _____ material.

9. Use commas to set off _____ quotations from the rest of the sentence.

10. Use commas after every _____ in addresses or dates.

Writing Assignment

Topic

Our lives are often complicated by having to make difficult decisions. Recall a time in your life when you had to make a decision that affected the course your life would take. Explain the events leading up to the decision you made. Analyze how you came to the decision and what effects your choices had on you and those near to you. If you have not made any life-changing decisions, you could write about a decision that was important but not life changing. You might prefer to write about a decision that was made by someone you know.

Step 1. A cluster diagram might be a useful way to get started on this topic. Put your name in the middle, or the name of the person who made the decision you are writing about. Then draw lines to circles that contain the decision (or other possible decisions), and lines to additional circles that contain the results, both real and imagined, of that decision. See Chapter 10 for an explanation of cluster diagram.

Step 2. Now you are ready to write down which path you followed toward your decision and to formulate a topic sentence. Turn to Chapter 10 for help in organizing your paragraph. Will you state the topic sentence near the beginning and develop it with supporting ideas throughout the paragraph? Or do you want to offer the path you or someone you know followed to the decision and then provide the topic sentence?

Step 3. Read the paragraphs in the section, *Organizing with Transitional Words and Phrases* in Chapter 10, Lesson 4. This is a good time to focus your attention on those useful transitional words a writer can include to move smoothly from one idea to another. Read your rough draft aloud to hear if you need to add any of these expressions. Sometimes your ear is more reliable than your eye in this case.

Step 4. Turn to the list of rules for using commas at the beginning of this chapter for a quick review. Then check your rough draft carefully to see if you need to add any commas or eliminate any unnecessary ones.

Alternative Writing Assignment

Topic

Read the sentences in Exercise 3B again. The subject of "social lying" is one that is familiar to almost everyone. Many philosophical and religious traditions condemn all lies and deceit. But where do you draw the line? Explain your personal reaction to telling little white lies.

Step 1. Here are some questions you might consider as you plan your response:

a. Do you ever lie to be socially tactful? "Yes, I think your dress is very attractive, just right for you." Actually, you think she should return it to the store.
b. Do you ever lie as a matter of personal convenience? "I'm sorry I couldn't attend the meeting, but a personal problem came up unexpectedly." Your problem: You just didn't want to go to the meeting.
c. When you know that someone is telling you a white lie, how do you react, how do you feel?
d. What do you think of a parent who asks a child to tell a white lie? "If that's Mrs. Taylor on the phone, tell her that I'm not home."
e. Sometimes a person even masquerades as someone else to achieve a goal. Think, for example, of police who assume false identities to infiltrate drug rings, of civil rights advocates who pose as apartment applicants, or news reporters who investigate possible fraud? Do you find this kind of deceit acceptable?

Step 2. Jot down your ideas and decide on a topic sentence expressing your position on the subject. See Chapter 10, Lesson 4 for help in organizing your paragraph. Will you state the topic sentence near the beginning and develop it with specific support throughout the paragraph? Or do you want to make your case by offering examples first, and build up to the topic sentence at the end of the paragraph? Perhaps you may want to place the topic sentence close to the opening of the paragraph and restate it using different words at the end.

Step 3. Read the paragraphs on *Organizing with Transitional Words and Phrases* in Chapter 10. This is a good time to focus your attention on those useful transitional words a writer can include to move smoothly from one idea to another. Read your rough draft aloud to hear if you need to add any of these expressions. Sometimes your ear is more reliable than your eye in this case.

Step 4. Turn to the list of rules for using commas at the beginning of this chapter for a quick review. Then check your rough draft carefully to see if you need to add any commas or delete any unnecessary ones.

CHAPTER 8

PRACTICE TEST: Commas

Name _____

Date _____ Class Time _____

Instructor _____

I. Insert commas where they are necessary. Some sentences may not require commas.

1. The senator in the meantime had difficulty raising money for a reelection campaign.

2. Orrin likes to watch movies that were directed by Alfred Hitchcock.

3. No one in our tour group but Mr. Froloff spoke Russian.

4. Rachel wears a safety helmet a warm jacket blue jeans and cowboy boots when she goes horseback riding each week.

5. While painting the women talked about how to clean paintbrushes.

6. My new travel bag which fits under an airline seat carries all I need for a weeklong stay.

7. Spring officially began on March 21 at 4:19 P.M.

8. Cheri tried out for the soccer team but she wasn't chosen.

9. Wall Street a narrow street in lower Manhattan is one of the world's great financial districts.

10. Readers would you like to learn how to make $85,000 a year in the real estate market?

11. Everyone who has seen that film seems to think it will win an Oscar.

12. We sat on the pier and watched the surfers while we ate our picnic lunch.

13. "Housing affordability" Senator Bidwell asserted "is a national issue."

14. When the crew began to knock the building down people gathered at a safe distance to watch.

CHAPTER 8   PRACTICE TEST (Cont.)

15. Jesse couldn't decide whether to buy a bicycle a surfboard a camera or a radio with his prize money.

16. Mr. Suarez mailed his application for membership to The Nature Conservancy 4245 N. Fairfax Drive Suite 100 Arlington VA 22203-1606 last week.

17. To protect her photographs Chiara encloses them in plastic sleeves and mounts them on acid-free paper.

18. Most cats don't like to exercise and can gain weight quickly when they are overfed.

19. The Atlantic Computer Center at 1852 Kingsdale Avenue has computers for sale at reasonable prices.

20. Children crowded in front of the aquarium tank to watch the gentle wavy motions of the jellyfish.

II. Following the directions, write sentences of your own.

1. Write a sentence containing two main clauses joined by a coordinating connective. Punctuate the sentence correctly.

   _____

2. Write a sentence containing three or more adjectives that modify the same noun. Punctuate the sentence correctly.

   _____

3. Write a sentence that contains an introductory phrase or an introductory subordinate clause. Punctuate the sentence correctly.

   _____

4. Write a sentence that contains a complete address, including the city, the state, and the zip code. Punctuate the sentence correctly.

   _____

Editing
Practice

Insert commas where necessary.

Last summer Juan Romero a schoolteacher and his family drove across the country from Pueblo Colorado to Washington D.C. They left Pueblo on July 2 in their new brown tightly-packed minivan and they planned to return on August 31. Since they were going to be away a long time Mr. Romero had asked the post office to forward their mail to them at their friends' house 22654 Constitution Drive Washington D.C. After leaving Pueblo Mr. Romero and his wife Julia and their four children Alfredo Maria Pedro and Juan Jr. drove south to Santa Fe New Mexico. As the Romeros drove east along Route 40 they passed an Indian trading post. "Let's stop here" Alfredo shouted. When the car rolled to a stop Mr. and Mrs. Romero gave each child some money to spend in the trading post. In a short while they returned to the car carrying Indian arrowheads peace pipes pottery and a feather headdress. The family who were now even more crowded together in the minivan drove through Texas Arkansas and Tennessee. Mrs. Romero could tell that the children were bored so she persuaded her husband to stop in Memphis at Graceland. In a flash the four youngsters escaped from the backseat to buy autographed records a large plastic guitar a harmonica and a white cowboy hat. Once back on the road Mr. Romero said that he would not stop again until they had reached their destination. However before they had traveled much farther they had made several stops at parrot jungles alligator farms and other roadside tourist attractions even stopping at the beach in Norfolk Virginia. "On our trip back to Colorado" said Mrs. Romero "we'll have no room to sit if we stop at one more place." From then on therefore they just bought food which filled their stomachs but not the car. After seeing the sights in Washington D.C. they returned to Pueblo and the whole family agreed that they had had a memorable vacation.

Usage, Punctuation, and Sentence Mechanics

9

USAGE

Words that sound alike or look alike can cause many problems in spelling. Study the following words and refer to these pages when you are writing your paragraphs.

LESSON 1

A/An/And

1. Use <u>a</u> before words beginning with consonants or consonant sounds.

   EXAMPLES: <u>a</u> chair, <u>a</u> boy, <u>a</u> tree, <u>a</u> picture, <u>a</u> year

2. Use <u>an</u> before words beginning with vowels (a, e, i, o, u) or a silent *h*.

   EXAMPLES: <u>an</u> apple, <u>an</u> egg, <u>an</u> idea, <u>an</u> honor, <u>an</u> opal

3. <u>And</u> connects words, phrases, and clauses. It is a coordinating connective.

   EXAMPLE: Dan plays both the guitar <u>and</u> the piano.

EXERCISE 1A

Use these words in sentences of your own.

1. (a)_____

2. (an)_____

3. (and)_____

Accept/Except

1. <u>Accept</u> is a verb. It means to receive gladly; to agree to.

EXAMPLE: Will Julie <u>accept</u> the job offer in Alaska?

2. <u>Except</u> is a preposition. It means excluding, but.

EXAMPLE: None of us has been to Alaska <u>except</u> Ward.

EXERCISE 1B

Fill in the blanks with the correct words.

1. Stan will _____ the award for our division at the luncheon.

2. Everyone attended the luncheon _____ Jerry.

Use these words in sentences of your own.

1. (accept) _____

2. (except) _____

Advice/Advise

1. Advice is a noun. It means an opinion about what could or should be done about a problem.

   EXAMPLE: We all depend on Sally for advice.

2. Advise is a verb. It means to offer advice; to counsel. *Note:* Pronounce the s like a z.

   EXAMPLE: She advised me to petition for graduation soon.

EXERCISE 1C

Fill in the blanks with the correct words.

1. Can the counselor_____ me what courses to take next semester?

2. Will you follow her _____?

Use these words in sentences of your own.

1. (advice) _____

2. (advise) _____

Affect/Effect

1. Affect is usually used as a verb. It means to have an influence on; to touch or move the emotions of someone.

   EXAMPLE: The drop in sales may affect the company's future plans.

2. Effect is usually used as a noun. It means the final result; the outcome.

   EXAMPLE: All employees felt the effect of the budget cut.

EXERCISE 1D

Fill in the blanks with the correct words.

1. The recent cold weather may _____ the fruit crop.

2. The _____ of the freeze became quickly apparent in the rising price of produce.

Use these words in sentences of your own.

1. (affect) _____

2. (effect) _____

Already/All Ready

1. Already is an adverb. It means by this time; before; previously.

   EXAMPLE: They had already bought their tickets.

2. All ready is an adjective. It is used to express complete readiness.

   EXAMPLE: The tourists were all ready to board the plane.

EXERCISE 1E

Fill in the blanks with the correct words.

1. Is everyone _____ to go to the beach?

2. We have _____ packed a lunch to take with us.

Use these words in sentences of your own.

1. (already)_____

2. (all ready)_____

Mini Review 1

Underline the correct form of the word in parentheses.

1. The (affect, effect) of his (advice, advise) was greater than he had expected.
2. We were (all ready, already) to go (accept, except) for Denise.
3. The drive was pleasant (except, accept) for (an, a) unexpected detour.
4. The new ruling has (already, all ready) (affected, effected) office morale.
5. Would you (advice, advise) me to (accept, except) the position?

LESSON
2

Dessert/Desert

1. <u>Dessert</u> is a noun. It means the last course of a lunch or a dinner.

   EXAMPLE: His favorite <u>dessert</u> is apple pie.

2. <u>Desert</u> is used as a noun to mean barren land, an area of little rainfall.

   EXAMPLE: The Sahara <u>Desert</u> is in Africa.

3. <u>Desert</u> is used as a verb to mean to leave or abandon.

   EXAMPLE: The soldier <u>deserted</u> his post during the battle.

EXERCISE 2A

Fill in the blanks with the correct words.

1. Maria prepared fried bananas for _____.

2. Many flowers bloom in the _____ in the spring.

3. Brian's father _____ his family.

Use these words in sentences of your own.

1. (dessert) _____

2. (desert, noun) _____

3. (desert, verb) _____

Its/It's

1. <u>It's</u> is the contraction of <u>it is</u> or <u>it has</u>.

   EXAMPLE: It's time to feed the cat.

2. <u>Its</u> is the possessive form of the pronoun it.

   EXAMPLE: The cat doesn't like <u>its</u> food.

EXERCISE 2B

Fill in the blanks with the correct words.

1. _____ been raining all day.

2. The bear stayed in _____ cave during the storm.

Use these words in sentences of your own.

1. (its) _____

2. (it's) _____

Know/No

1. <u>Know</u> is a verb. It means to understand; to be familiar with; to be certain of.

   EXAMPLE: Who <u>knows</u> the way to the museum?

2. <u>No</u> is a negative. It means not any; not one.

   EXAMPLE: We have <u>no</u> map.

EXERCISE 2C

Fill in the blanks with the correct words.

1. Kathy _____ longer lives in Denver.

2. Dave _____ her new address in Portland.

Use these words in sentences of your own.

1. (know) _____

2. (no) _____

Lead/Led

1. <u>Lead</u> is a noun. It is pronounced "led." It means a soft, bluish-white element used in pencils. If it is used as a verb, it is pronounced "leed." It means to show the way by going in advance; to conduct.

   EXAMPLES: <u>Lead</u> is a dense metal.
   The conductor will <u>lead</u> the orchestra.

2. <u>Led</u> is the past tense and the past participle of the verb <u>lead</u>.

   EXAMPLE: The guide <u>led</u> us through the forest.

EXERCISE 2D

Fill in the blanks with the correct words.

1. Early alchemists tried to make gold out of _____.

2. The sergeant _____ his men into battle.

Use these words in sentences of your own.

1. (lead, noun) _____

2. (lead, verb) _____

3. (led) _____

Loose/Lose

1. <u>Loose</u> is an adjective. It means not tight fitting; too large; not fastened.

   EXAMPLE: The string on that package was too <u>loose</u>.

2. <u>Lose</u> is a verb. Pronounce the <u>s</u> like a <u>z</u>. It means to misplace; to fail to win.

   EXAMPLE: I hope the package won't <u>lose</u> its wrappings.

EXERCISE 2E

Fill in the blanks with the correct words.

1. I will _____ these keys if I don't buy a new key ring.

2. The key ring broke, and the _____ keys fell to the pavement.

Use these words in sentences of your own.

1. (loose) _____

2. (lose) _____

Mini Review 2

Underline the correct form of the word in parentheses.

1. The guide (lead, led) the hikers through the (desert, dessert).
2. We (no, know) a restaurant that serves the best (desserts, deserts) in town.
3. There is (no, know) (lead, led) in a pencil.
4. The dog (lead, led) (its, it's) puppies to the food.
5. Tighten that screw; (its, it's) (lose, loose) again.
6. I (no, know) that Bob will (lose, loose) our respect if he (desserts, deserts) the group now.

LESSON
3

Past/Passed

1. <u>Past</u> is a noun. It means the time before the present. It can be used as an adjective to describe that which has already occurred.

   EXAMPLE: Try not to think about the <u>past</u>.

2. <u>Passed</u> is the past tense and the past participle form of the verb <u>pass</u>. It means succeeded in, handed in, or went by.

   EXAMPLES: Andrea waved and smiled as she <u>passed</u> by us.

   Larry <u>passed</u> in his term paper on time.

EXERCISE 3A

Fill in the blanks with the correct words.

1. Henry liked to tell us about his _____ experiences.

2. Tom _____ by our house last night about this time.

Use these words in sentences of your own.

1. (past) _____

2. (passed) _____

Personal/Personnel

1. <u>Personal</u> is an adjective. It means something private or one's own. Pronounce this word with the accent on the first syllable.

   EXAMPLE: My diary is my <u>personal</u> property.

2. Personnel is a noun. It means the group of people employed by a business or a service. Pronounce this word with the accent on the last syllable. It may take either a singular or a plural verb.

EXAMPLE:　The president of the company sent a memo to all of the personnel.

EXERCISE 3B

Fill in the blanks with the correct words.

1. Please don't ask so many _____ questions.

2. She was vice-president in charge of _____ in our company.

Use these words in sentences of your own.

1. (personal) _____

2. (personnel) _____

Principal/Principle

1. Principal is usually used as a noun. It means a person who is a leader, someone who is in charge. When it is used as an adjective, it means leading or chief.

EXAMPLE:　The principal of the high school spoke at the assembly.

2. Principle is a noun. It refers to basic truths, rules of human conduct, and fundamental laws.

EXAMPLE:　Our constitution is based on the principles of democracy.

EXERCISE 3C

Fill in the blank with the correct words.

1. I know him to be a man of high _____.

2. The _____ partner in the law firm signed the contract.

Use these words in sentences of your own.

1. (principal, noun) _____

2. (principal, adjective) _____

3. (principle) _____

Quiet/Quite

1. <u>Quiet</u> means silent, free of noise.

   EXAMPLE: I need a <u>quiet</u> place to study.

2. <u>Quite</u> means entirely, really, rather.

   EXAMPLE: You have been <u>quite</u> busy all day.

EXERCISE 3D

Fill in the blanks with the correct words.

1. The Smith family lives on a very _____ street.

2. The street is not _____ as _____ as it used to be.

Use these words in sentences of your own.

1. (quiet) _____

2. (quite) _____

Suppose/Supposed

<u>Suppose</u> is a verb. It means to assume to be true; to guess; to think.

   EXAMPLE: Do you <u>suppose</u> it will rain today?

Note: The verb <u>suppose</u> is often used in the passive and is followed by <u>to</u>. Do not forget to add the **d** to the verb: <u>supposed</u>.

Supposed to, in this sense, means to expect or require.

> **EXAMPLE:** He is supposed to clean his room.

The example means that he is expected to clean his room.

EXERCISE 3E

Fill in the blanks with the correct words.

1. This is _____ to be one of the best restaurants in town.

2. I _____ we will arrive home by noon.

Use these words in sentences of your own.

1. (suppose) _____

2. (supposed) _____

Then/Than

1. Then is an adverb. It means at that time; next in time, space, or order.

> **EXAMPLE:** Tom and Rhonda had dinner, and then Rhonda watched TV.

2. Than is used in comparative statements to introduce the second item.

> **EXAMPLE:** Tom said he would rather wash the dinner dishes than watch TV.

EXERCISE 3F

Fill in the blanks with the correct words.

1. Mike gets up earlier _____ Jay does.

2. He prepares breakfast, and _____ he takes a shower.

Use these words in sentences of your own.

1. (then) _____

2. (than) _____

There/Their/They're

1. <u>There</u> shows direction. It means at that place. It is often used to introduce a thought, as in <u>there</u> is or <u>there</u> are.

   EXAMPLE: <u>There</u> are no tickets left for the World Series games.

2. <u>Their</u> is the possessive form of the pronoun <u>they</u>. It means belonging to them.

   EXAMPLE: Some of the fans have already received <u>their</u> tickets in the mail.

3. <u>They're</u> is a contraction of the two words <u>they are</u>.

   EXAMPLE: <u>They're</u> going to the game.

EXERCISE 3G

Fill in the blanks with the correct words.

1. _____ is going to be a parade on St. Patrick's Day.

2. I hear that _____ giving a party in _____ home to celebrate the holiday.

Use these words in sentences of your own.

1. (there) _____

2. (their) _____

3. (they're) _____

Mini Review 3

Underline the correct forms of the words in parentheses.

1. Hal's (principals, principles) would not let him charge (personnel, personal) expenses to his expense account.
2. I had (suppose, supposed) that he would rather fly (then, than) drive to the conference.
3. We were (quiet, quite) surprised by the changes in the company (personal, personnel).
4. Based on (passed, past) experience, the organizers were (supposed, suppose) to reserve a bigger ballroom for the meeting.
5. (They're, their, there) expecting a larger crowd (then, than) they had last year.

LESSON
4

Through/Though/Thought

1. Through means finished. It also means to go in one side and out the other.

   EXAMPLES: He was through with his work.

   He walked through the parking lot.

2. Though means the same as although; despite the fact that.

   EXAMPLE: Though Jim had left home early, he arrived at work late.

3. Thought is the past tense and the past participle of think. It can also be used as a noun, and it means an idea.

   EXAMPLE: He thought he could get to work on time.

EXERCISE 4A

Fill in the blanks with the correct words.

1. _____ Jim set his alarm clock, he overslept.

2. He _____ that he could get _____ morning traffic quickly.

Use these words in sentences of your own.

1. (through) _____

2. (though) _____

3. (thought) _____

To/Two/Too

1. <u>To</u> means in the direction of, when it is used as a preposition.

EXAMPLE: Pierre is going <u>to</u> Atlanta this month.

Sometimes the word <u>to</u> is the first word in a verbal phrase.

EXAMPLE: He is going <u>to move</u> to a new apartment next month.

2. <u>Two</u> is the same as the number 2.

EXAMPLE: He will have <u>two</u> roommates in his new apartment.

3. <u>Too</u> means also; in addition to; very; overly so.

EXAMPLE: The rent is <u>too</u> high for him to live there alone.

EXERCISE 4B

Fill in the blanks with the correct words.

1. At 5:10 P.M. _____ women approached the bank teller.

2. The teller told them that it was _____ late _____ withdraw money from the bank.

Use these words in sentences of your own.

1. (to) _____

2. (two) _____

3. (too) _____

Use/Used

1. <u>Use</u> is a verb. It means to employ; to make use of. Pronounce the <u>s</u> like <u>z</u>.

   EXAMPLE: Selena <u>used</u> a broom to sweep the floor.

2. <u>Used</u> is often followed by the word <u>to</u>. It means accustomed to; familiar with; was in the habit of.

   EXAMPLE: She <u>used to</u> play tennis every weekend.

EXERCISE 4C

Fill in the blanks with the correct words.

1. Accountants have always _____ adding machines.

2. Accountants are _____ to adding long columns of numbers on the machines.

Use these words in sentences of your own.

1. (use) _____

2. (used) _____

Weather/Whether

1. <u>Weather</u> is a noun. It refers to the state of the atmosphere at a given time or place.

   EXAMPLE: The <u>weather</u> in Boston is usually cold in December.

2. <u>Whether</u> is a conjunction. It means if it is so that; if it is the case that; in case; either.

   EXAMPLE: We should find out <u>whether</u> it will snow tomorrow.

EXERCISE 4D

Fill in the blanks with the correct words.

1. Airline pilots frequently check the _____ conditions before landing in Boston.

2. Derek did not know _____ to fly to Boston or to take the train.

Use these words in sentences of your own.

1. (weather) _____

2. (whether) _____

Whose/Who's

1. Whose is the possessive form of the pronoun who. It means belonging to whom.

   EXAMPLE: Whose tennis shoes are these?

2. Who's is a contraction of the two words who is.

   EXAMPLE: Who's going to put them in the closet?

EXERCISE 4E

Fill in the blanks with the correct words.

1. _____ calling, please?

2. I don't know _____ number I have called.

Use these words in sentences of your own.

1. (whose) _____

2. (who's) _____

Your/You're

1. <u>Your</u> is the possessive form of the pronoun <u>you</u>. It means belonging to you.

   EXAMPLE: <u>Your</u> car is in the parking lot.

1. <u>You're</u> is the contraction of the two words <u>you are</u>.

   EXAMPLE: <u>You're</u> going to drive home with Lorraine.

EXERCISE 4F

Fill in the blanks with the correct words.

1. John told Mary, "_____ going to the concert with us tomorrow."

2. Mary said, "I'm glad you bought _____ tickets a few weeks ago."

Use these words in sentences of your own.

1. (your) _____

2. (you're) _____

Mini Review 4

Underline the correct forms of the words in parentheses.

1. (Whose, Who's) (you're, your) favorite singer?
2. I (though, thought, through) you (use, used) to work at the art museum.
3. We wondered (weather, whether) you would postpone (your, you're) trip because of the (weather, whether).
4. (Whose, Who's) idea was it to sign up for those (to, too, two) courses?
5. It's not (two, too, to) clear (whose, who's) to blame.

Group ACTIVITY

Underline the correct forms of the words in parentheses; then get together with two or three classmates and check each other's work. As a group, write a paragraph defining an ideal restaurant. Use some of the words explained in the usage lessons you have just completed. Place those words in parentheses as shown in the paragraph below. Check the spelling and usage of the words carefully before exchanging your work with that of another group. Then go over the paragraph of the other group and select the correctly used words in it.

Did you (know, no) that (their, there) are about sixty robot makers in the U.S.? Most of those companies are (loosing, losing) money right now. (It's, Its) a difficult business because (to, too, two) many companies offer similar products. The (principle, principal) reason for buying robots is to enable (a, an) factory to slash costs and cut (personnel, personal). However, (quiet, quite) a few of the robot makers admit that human beings still must do a lot of the work. (Their, They're, There) especially popular in the automobile industry (where, were, wear) robots have created (a, an) increased output in welding and spray painting. Chrysler and Ford Motor Co. have (lead, led) the way in converting from human workers to robotic workers. Now factories other (than, then) auto manufacturers are (excepting, accepting) robots as a viable tool, like the hammer or screwdriver. The (affect, effect) of robotics can be noticed in industries that build everything from disk drives to helicopters. Robot makers (advise, advice) purchasers not to buy robots without buying computers. Robots are (suppose, supposed) to be pretty dumb without computers guiding (there, they're, their) movements.

PUNCTUATION

Punctuation at the End of a Sentence

In addition to commas, writers use several other marks of punctuation to make their meaning clear to readers. When you write, you should be able to guide your readers by punctuating your sentences accurately.

Period (.)

Use a period at the end of a sentence.

> **EXAMPLE:**   The Nguyen family planned their trip carefully. They studied maps and travel books.

Question Mark (?)

Use a question mark at the end of a direct question.

> **EXAMPLE:**   When did the Native Americans make the pictographs?

Do not use a question mark after an indirect question, a sentence in which the question is part of the statement.

> **EXAMPLE:**   We wondered when the Native Americans made the pictographs.

Do not use a question mark after a polite request.

> **EXAMPLE:**   Would you please return the enclosed form in the envelope provided.

Exclamation Point (!)

Use an exclamation point after words, phrases, or clauses that express shock or excitement.

> **EXAMPLE:**   Look at this magnificent painting!

Do not overuse the exclamation point. Save it for genuine expressions of emotion.

Add periods or question marks to the following sentences.

Pictographs, ancient paintings on rock surfaces, have fascinated people for many years _____ Who created these paintings _____ Why did they paint on the surfaces of rocks and caves _____ It is generally believed that the ancestors of modern Native American tribes produced these paintings as answers for spiritual needs _____ Indian artists used two methods of drawing on stone _____ The first involved engraving the surface of rocks, resulting in designs known as petroglyphs _____ The second and more common method involved painting with colored minerals on the surface of the rocks _____ These are pictographs _____ Does anyone know exactly how long ago these rock paintings were made _____

LESSON 2   Semicolon and Colon

Semicolon (;)

1. The semicolon is used as a connector.
   a. The semicolon joins two main clauses with closely related ideas to form a compound sentence.

EXAMPLE: Since her arrival in the United States, Ann Nguyen has been too busy earning a living to travel in this country; now she and her husband are planning their first trip.

b. The semicolon is used before adverbial connectives such as
    however, nevertheless, consequently, therefore, and then to join
    two main clauses.

> **EXAMPLE:**   They want to travel through several states in a short time;
> therefore, they will join a tour group for this trip.

2. The semicolon is used as a separator. The semicolon is used between
    words or word groups in a series if the items in the series contain one or
    more commas.

> **EXAMPLE:**   Their travel plans include Philadelphia, Pennsylvania;
> Boston, Massachusetts; and Washington, D.C.

Colon (:)

1. The colon is used at the end of a main clause to introduce a list.

> **EXAMPLE:**   On their next trip, they would like to visit four other
> states: Arizona, Utah, Wyoming, and South Dakota.

2. The colon often comes after words like the following or as follows.

> **EXAMPLE:**   On this tour they plan to see the following places: the
> Grand Canyon, Bryce Canyon National Park, Yellowstone
> National Park, and Mount Rushmore.

3. The colon is used after a salutation in a business letter.

> **EXAMPLE:**   Dear Mr. Wilkins:
> Please consider me for the position of junior accountant
> in your firm.

4. The colon separates hours and minutes when you are writing the time.

> **EXAMPLE:**   Our class meets daily at 10:30 A.M.

Do not use a colon if no minutes are given.

> **EXAMPLE:**   Our class meets daily at 10 A.M.

GRAMMAR TIP

Remember that the colon introduces a list following a main clause. If you are uncertain about using a colon before a series of words, bracket those words to see if they are necessary to complete a main clause.

EXAMPLES:

1. They will visit four other states: [Arizona, Utah, Wyoming, and South Dakota]. If you put a period after "states," you have written a complete sentence. Therefore, a colon may be used between "states" and "Arizona."

2. They will visit [Arizona, Utah, Wyoming, and South Dakota]. If you put a period after "visit," you have written an incomplete sentence. Therefore, a colon may not be used between "visit" and "Arizona." These words are direct objects that should not be separated from the verb.

3. In Washington, D.C., Ann especially enjoyed three places: [Mt.Vernon, the Lincoln Memorial, and the Smithsonian]. If you put a period after "places," you have written a complete sentence. Therefore, a colon may be used between "places" and "Mt. Vernon."

4. In Washington, D.C. the three places that Ann especially enjoyed were [Mt.Vernon, the Lincoln Memorial, and the Smithsonian]. If you put a period after "were," you have written an incomplete sentence. Therefore, a colon may not be used between "were" and "Mt. Vernon." These words are noun completers linked by the verb to the subject.

EXERCISE 2A

Insert semicolons or colons where they are needed in the following sentences.

1. Men of the Native American Hopi tribe don masks and costumes in their religious ceremonies to impersonate supernatural beings called *kachinas* these kachinas can represent both good and evil spirits.

2. Hopi children believe in kachinas in much the same way other children believe in Santa Claus in fact, male relatives in their guise as kachinas sometimes bring gifts to the children.

3. Hopi kachina dolls are small dolls made to resemble the kachinas they are carved from dried cottonwood roots and painted with poster paints.

4. The names of many of these dolls are descriptive, such as cross-legged kachina, and they are often named for the following birds and mammals rooster, bear, eagle, and badger.

5. Since Hopis are a farming people and rain is vital to their crops, dolls often show these symbols for rain and water lightning bolts on the head, a fore-

head band symbolizing a rainbow, feathers on the head standing for clouds, and the fringe of a sash representing rain.

6. The dolls are not religious objects they hang upon the walls or from the rafters of the house where they serve the important educational purpose of familiarizing the child with the many different kachinas of the Hopi people.

Group
ACTIVITY

Add colons, semicolons, periods, or question marks as needed in the following letter.

Mrs Stephanie Culp
Priority Management Systems, Inc
1379 Heather Lane
Baltimore, MD 21203

Dear Mrs Culp

I recently read an article that explained how your company, Priority Management Systems, Inc , helps make business offices more efficient I would like your advice about the following problems I have a messy desk, an overflowing file cabinet, and a drawer full of unpaid bills

The article stated that you advise executives as follows set up a system of baskets on the desk to sort out the papers however I can never find the time to stop and rearrange my papers

Would you be willing to visit my office to help me get organized I would be very appreciative furthermore I would be willing to pay you well for your time Please send me a copy of your book, How to Get Organized When You Don't Have the Time, as soon as possible.

Sincerely yours,

Annette Harris

After completing the exercise above, get together with two or three classmates to check each other's work. Cut out an article that describes a service or an advertisement that offers a service from a newspaper or magazine and bring it to class. Choose one of the articles that your group has brought to class and respond to it in a letter as the writer of the letter above did. Use the patterns below as a guide for your sentences.

1. Letter salutation: _____

2. Main clause: list. _____

3. Main clause; however, main clause. _____

4. Main clause; main clause. _____

LESSON 3   Quotation Marks

Direct Quotations

Quotation marks are used primarily in direct quotations. Put quotation marks around the exact words of the speaker. Use a comma before the direct quotation. Use a capital letter for the first word of the direct quotation.

EXAMPLES: 1. Pete called, "Anyone for tennis?"

2. "I would rather play golf," replied Tiger.

Split Quotations

EXAMPLES: 1. "Come on, Lindsay, turn off the television," Venus said. "Let's play tennis instead of watching TV."

2. "But, Venus," Lindsay asked, "don't you want to see if Tiger wins this match on TV?"

> ## Split Quotations
>
> Note the punctuation for split quotations:
>
> In Example 1, there are two sentences. The first sentence begins with <u>Come</u> and ends with <u>said</u>. Therefore, the <u>L</u> of <u>Let's</u> is capitalized as the first word of the <u>second</u> sentence.
>
> In Example 2, the word <u>don't</u> <u>begins</u> with a small letter because the words on either side of <u>Lindsay asked</u> are <u>the</u> two parts of a single sentence.

Punctuation at the End of a Quotation

Periods and commas are always placed <u>inside</u> quotation marks.

EXAMPLES: 1. "Let's go shoot a few baskets, Michael."

2. "I'm playing in a golf tournament today," Michael answered.

Semicolons and colons are placed <u>outside</u> quotation marks.

EXAMPLE: We groaned when we read the headline: "Lakers lose to the Pacers 120–87"; the Lakers had been favored to win.

Question marks and exclamation points are placed <u>outside</u> quotation marks except when the quotation itself is a question or an <u>exclamation</u>.

EXAMPLE: Did Andre say, "I want to play tennis"?

EXCEPTIONS: 1. Pete called, "Anyone for tennis?" (The quotation is a question.)

2. The fans shouted, "Touchdown! Touchdown!" (The quotation is an exclamation.)

Unnecessary Quotation Marks: Do not enclose an indirect quotation in quotation marks. It is a report in different words of what a speaker or writer said. The word "that" usually indicates the following words are an indirect quotation.

EXAMPLES: Marcus said, "I'll never eat at Joe's Pizza Palace again." (direct quotation)

Marcus said <u>that</u> he would never eat at Joe's Pizza Palace again. (<u>Indirect</u> quotation, do not use quotation marks.)

EXERCISE 3A

Use quotation marks as needed in the following sentences.

1. Have you ever watched *TV Mystery Theater*? he asked.

2. Mr. Marquez said that we are having a quiz today.

3. Did Steve actually say, I'll pay for lunch tomorrow if we win tonight ?

4. When I was three years old, Rose said, my favorite poem was *The Owl and the Pussycat.*

5. We were all disappointed when Darin announced, I am resigning at the end of this month; we had counted on him to finish the project.

EXERCISE 3B

Write your own sentences including the items in parentheses.

1. (a split quotation) _____

2. (a direct quotation that is a question) _____

3. (an indirect quotation) _____

SENTENCE MECHANICS

LESSON 1   # Capital Letters

EXERCISE 1A

Answer the following questions to see how many uses of capital letters you already know. Refer to an almanac or an encyclopedia if necessary.

1. Write the title and the first and last names of the sixteenth U.S. president.

   _____

2. In what state was he born?

   _____

3. Write the season of the year and the name of the month in which he was born.

   _____

4. What is the name of the holiday we observe in his honor?

   _____

5. What political party did he belong to?

   _____

6. What war was fought during his administration?

   _____

7. Give the title of a famous speech that he made honoring U.S. soldiers who fell in battle. Near what town and in what state did he make it?

   _____

   _____

8. What is the name of the proclamation he made?

   _____

9. Write the full name of the person who assassinated him.

   _____

10. In what building did the assassination take place?

    _____

11. In what city and state is he buried?

    _____

12. What is the name of the river near his memorial?

    _____

13. Write the title of a college course in which you might learn more about this president.

_____

14. Write the address of the present residence of U.S. presidents. Include the name of the street.

_____

_____

Rules of Capitalization

Always capitalize:

1.	The first word of a sentence and the first word of a direct quotation.	**H**e suggested, "**L**et's go for a walk now."
2.	The name of a person.	**A**lbert **E**instein
3.	The personal pronoun <u>I</u>.	**I** **I**'m
4.	The names of continents, countries, nationalities, states, cities, bodies of water, places, and streets.	**A**sia **J**apan **A**tlantic **O**cean **A**merican **D**allas, **T**exas **G**riffith **P**ark **E**lm **S**treet
5.	The names of the days of the week, months, and holidays (but not the seasons).	**T**hursday **N**ovember (fall) **V**eterans **D**ay
6.	The names of commercial products (but not the type of product).	**A**rrowhead water **P**illsbury flour **I**vory soap
7.	The names of companies, organizations, and government agencies and offices.	**B**oeing **C**o. **D**emocratic **P**arty **D**epartment of **M**otor **V**ehicles **D**epartment of **S**tate
8.	The titles of people, books, magazines, newspapers, articles, stories, poems, films, television shows, songs, and papers that you write. _Note:_ Do not capitalize small words like <u>the</u>, <u>in</u>, or <u>a</u> within titles.	**C**hief **J**ustice **H**ughes **M**r. **D**r. **P**resident **A**dams "**D**ream **D**eferred" _The **W**izard of **O**z_ _**M**asterpiece **T**heater_
9.	The names of schools, colleges and universities, academic departments, degrees, and specific courses.	**M**adison **C**ollege **D**epartment of **M**usic **A**ssociate of **A**rts **H**istory 101

EXERCISE 1B

Capitalize letters where necessary in the sentences below.

1. ann nguyen has become an american citizen.

2. i'm passing english 1, but i'm failing history 21.

3. when mary went to new york, she visited the metropolitan museum of art.

4. i have already seen the play, *phantom of the opera.*

5. sue's favorite lunch consists of ritz crackers, kraft cheese, and coca-cola.

6. when darlene went to sears, she bought wamsutta sheets for her new bed.

7. are you going to watch the sugar bowl game on new year's day?

8. in the spring i usually spend saturdays working in my garden.

9. yellowstone national park is the largest national park in the united states.

10. my instructor told me to read a novel by hemingway this weekend, but i watched television.

EXERCISE 1C

Cross out the errors in capitalization in each sentence. Write the corrections on the lines.

1. my Son brushes with crest Toothpaste every Morning.

   _____

   _____

   _____

   _____

   _____

2. We visited the liberty bell in philadelphia last august.

    _____

    _____

    _____

    _____

3. i don't think that the senator should have traveled at government expense to the french riviera, Do you?

    _____

    _____

    _____

    _____

4. Paul likes to watch *good morning america* every morning before going to work at boeing aircraft co.

    _____

    _____

    _____

    _____

    _____

    _____

5. Chuck said, "let's go to a Rock Concert next saturday."

    _____

    _____

    _____

LESSON 2   Abbreviations

Use only standard abbreviations that your reader can easily understand. Consult a dictionary or spell out the words if you are unsure about the abbreviation.

A. Abbreviate titles used before or after proper names. Use a period after abbreviations and after initials.

Nathan B. Marx, Jr.	Dr. Juan Diaz	P.M.
Sen. Patrick Leahy	Audrey Krall, M.D.	B.A.
Ms. Barbara Santoro	Curtis Kam, Ph.D.	etc.

B. Use standard abbreviations for the names of organizations, corporations, and countries. It is not necessary to use a period in these abbreviations when more than two words are abbreviated.

UCLA	NAACP
USA	NASA
GTE	FBI

Nor is it necessary to use a period with postal abbreviations of states: FL (Florida), OH (Ohio).

C. Abbreviate specific times and numbers: You may use the dollar sign with specific amounts.

EXAMPLES: 1. The plane landed at 10:20 A.M. (or a.m.)

2. My ticket cost $299.95.

3. Trisha was no. (or NO.) 9 on the waiting list.

D. Before using an abbreviation unfamiliar to your reader, first write the complete name followed by the abbreviation in parentheses. Then use the abbreviation whenever you refer to it.

EXAMPLE: For the past fourteen years, the Center for Marine Conservation (CMC), a nonprofit environmental group, has sponsored an international coastal cleanup. Last year the CMC collected 3.36 million pounds of debris in the United States.

Correct the abbreviation errors in the following sentences. Write the corrections on the lines at the right.

1. Two members of the C.I.A. testified before a congressional committee in Washington, D.C. last week.   _____

2. Harrison gained four pounds after he joined the US Navy.   _____

3. Dr Alvin Poussaint is a professor of psychiatry at Harvard Medical School.   _____

4. The O.S.U. students are studying for finals this week.   _____

5. Derryk B Jones, Jr was a reporter who covered the bombing in Germany during World War II.   _____

6. Ms Albertson will deliver the commencement address at 11 AM on Friday.   _____

LESSON 3

Numbers

When you are using numbers in your writing, follow these rules:

1. Spell out any number that can be written in one or two words.

EXAMPLES: When I turn thirty-nine, I hope to be living in my own home.

There were 18,134 fans in the stadium by game time.

2. Spell out any number that begins a sentence.

EXAMPLE: Eighteen thousand, one hundred and thirty-four fans were in the stadium by game time.

However, you could always rewrite the sentence as in the first example above.

3. If one or more numbers in a series need to be written as numerals, write all the numbers as numerals.

> **EXAMPLE:**   The movie theater sold 138 tickets to the horror movie, 24 to a comedy, and 50 to an animated feature.

4. Use numerals to write the following:
   a. Dates: Franklin D. Roosevelt was born on January 30, 1882.
   b. Times of the day: My next class starts at 10:50 A.M.
   c. Addresses: My sister lives at 348 West 97th Street.
   d. Percentages: Only 10 percent of the voters turned out last November.
   e. Pages and sections of a book: Refer to page 103 in Chapter 3 for further information.
   f. Exact amounts of money: My new shoes cost $35.79.
   g. Scores: The Pacers won the NBA Eastern Conference championship by defeating the Knicks 93 to 80.

EXERCISE 3A

If you find a number error in a sentence, underline the error and write the correction on the line at the right. If the sentence does not contain an error, write C on the line at the right.

1. 48 books in the first shipment were damaged and had to be returned.   _____

2. The check for our lunch totaled $24.72 including the eight percent sales tax.   _____

3. One cup of green pea soup contains 165 calories, nine grams of protein, and 3 grams of fat.   _____

4. Nearly 2,500 athletes participated in the XVIII Winter Olympics, which opened on February 7,1998, in Nagano, Japan.   _____

5. Oprah Winfrey was 50 years old on January 29, 2004.   _____

6. Clarice's last garage sale brought in a grand total of $49.65.   _____

7. The final score was Phoenix, seventy-two, and San Antonio, seventy.   _____

8. The British Prime Minister lives at Ten Downing Street.   _____

9. Devon set his alarm clock for 6:15 A.M.   _____

10. The Golden Gate Bridge has a span of four thousand two-hundred feet.   _____

Sentence Combining

Lesson 4 will further develop your skills in writing complex sentences and punctuating them by using subordinate clauses, verbal phrases, and nonessential phrases.

EXAMPLE:

1. The state of Alaska has placed advertisements.
2. The advertisements are in newspapers.
3. These newspapers are in other states.
4. The advertisements are intended to discourage people.
5. They tell people not to come to Alaska.
6. The advertisements say that only people with definite job offers should come.
7. Many people come anyway.

Combined Sentence: The state of Alaska has placed advertisements in the newspapers of other states discouraging people from coming to Alaska unless they have definite job offers, but many people come anyway.

Before you begin to work on the following sentences, see if you can identify the two main clauses, the verbal phrase, and the subordinate clause that the writer used to combine the seven sentences in the example into one compound-complex sentence.

A. Combine these five sentences into one complex sentence. Sentences 3, 4, and 5 can be combined into a subordinate clause beginning with the word who.

1. Mr. Furutani is a translator.
2. He enjoys working from his home.
3. He translates foreign languages.
4. He works for a translating company.
5. It is a worldwide company.

B. Combine these four sentences into one sentence. Change sentence 2 into a subordinate clause beginning with <u>whose</u>. Change sentence 4 into a subordinate clause beginning with the word <u>that</u>.

    1. The Native American artists made paintings.
    2. The paintings have been found in caves.
    3. The artists used abstract symbols.
    4. The symbols may represent the dreams or visions of the artists.

C. Combine these five sentences into one sentence. Change sentence 4 into a nonessential phrase enclosed by commas.

    1. Lightweight radios entertain joggers and automobile drivers.
    2. Tape units entertain joggers and automobile drivers.
    3. These radios and tape units are equipped with tiny headphones.
    4. These radios and tape units are the nation's latest fad.
    5. This is an electronic fad.

D. Combine these five sentences into one. Change sentences 2 and 3 to nonessential phrases enclosed by commas. Change sentence 4 to a verbal phrase. Change sentence 5 to a phrase introduced by the preposition <u>by</u>.

    1. The Argentine Gaucho uses the bola.
    2. He is a cowboy of the pampas.
    3. The bola is a rope with weights attached.
    4. It is used to catch cattle or game.
    5. The bola entangles their legs.

Chapter 9 Summary

period	semicolon	capital
quotation marks	colon	
comma	question mark	

Choose words from the box above to complete these sentences.

    1. Use a _____ at the end of a sentence.

2. Use a _____ at the end of a direct question but not after an indirect question.

3. Use a _____ between two main clauses to form a compound sentence.

4. Use a _____ at the end of the main clause to introduce a list.

5. Use _____ around the exact words of a speaker.

6. Use a _____ to separate three or more items in a series.

7. Use _____ letters to begin the first word in a sentence, the name of a person or place, and the names of the days of the week.

Writing Assignment

Topic A

In a recent newspaper article, one woman complained about her husband's devotion to his new home computer. You, yourself, may have heard the golf widow lamenting about the amount of time her husband spends on the golf course. Women, of course, are not immune to this disease; ask the man whose wife has become an exercise enthusiast and lives at the gym and the tennis court.

Do you know someone who has a hobby or a leisure-time activity that occupies most of his or her spare time and/or money? Write a composition about the effects of such an activity upon the person, the family, and the person's friends.

Topic B

On the other hand, you may regard enthusiasm for a hobby as commendable. Perhaps, as a result of this activity, the person makes a contribution to family and community as well as becoming an interesting friend. Learning a great deal about a subject through a hobby may even influence a career choice.

Write a composition showing the benefits of becoming an expert in some hobby or activity.

Step 1. Jot down your ideas on the subject by listing, using a cluster, or free writing.

Topic A

In regard to the drawbacks of such an activity, you might consider these questions: Does the activity consume virtually all of the person's spare time? Does money spent on the hobby seem excessive; for example, buying even nonessential items related to the hobby just because they are available? Do family and friends take second place to the hobby? Has this neglect strained personal relationships?

Topic B

In regard to benefits, consider the following: Does the activity relieve everyday stresses? Does it provide a break in the evening or on weekends from a dull, routine job? Does it provide a social outlet or a sense of belonging to a group? Does it encourage the person to exercise outdoors instead of sitting in front of the television? Has it helped to develop individual strength and a sense of purpose? Do the family, friends, and/or community benefit from this activity?

Step 2. From your jottings, develop a topic sentence that expresses your view of the drawbacks or the benefits of leisure-time activities. Turn to Chapter 10 for help in using both general and specific support for your topic sentence. Making an outline before you begin to write the entire paragraph may help focus your ideas.

Step 3. After you have written your paragraph, consult the section on *Revision* in Chapter 10 and use it as a guide to editing your paragraph. When you have answered "yes" to all the questions in Lesson 5, you are ready to proofread your paper. Look carefully at your revised paragraph for punctuation and spelling errors. Recheck the use of apostrophes in possessives. Does each sentence contain at least one subject and one complete verb? Review the information in Chapter 9 about sentence mechanics to help you proofread your paper. Now you are ready to write a final draft and submit your work to your instructor.

Alternative Writing Assignment

Topic

Our country has a number of different cultural groups such as Native Americans, African Americans, Asians, and Latinos. Although all cultures hold certain behavior patterns and institutions in common, each group has its own distinguishing features. Select a culture that is familiar to you and write about the characteristics that set it apart.

Step 1. List several aspects of this culture and give specific examples from your own experience. You might consider such cultural aspects as dating rituals, marriage customs, or the role of men or women in the family. Another area you might write about is the responsibilities of children to their parents or the responsibilities of parents to their children.

Step 2. Select from your list a few ways in which your culture may differ from the mainstream culture of the country. Jot down a few sentences about the differences. How do you fit into these patterns?

Step 3. From your jottings, develop a topic sentence that expresses your view on the differences you know about in one particular culture. Do not try to discuss more than one culture in this assignment. Turn to Chapter 10 for help in using both general and specific support for your topic sentence. Making an outline before you begin to write the entire paragraph may help you focus your ideas.

Step 4. From your outline, write a paragraph about the cultural traits that interest you. Consult the section on *Revision* in Chapter 10 and try to answer the questions given there about your paragraph. When you have answered "yes" to all the questions in Lesson 5, you are ready to proofread your paper.

Step 5. Look carefully at your revised paragraph for punctuation and spelling errors. Recheck the use of apostrophes in possessives. Does each sentence contain at least one subject and one complete verb? Review the information in Chapter 9 about mechanics to help you proofread your paper. Now you are ready to write a final draft and submit your work to your instructor.

CHAPTER 9

PRACTICE TEST: Usage, Punctuation, and Sentence Mechanics

Name _____

Date _____ Class Time _____

Instructor _____

I. Add periods, question marks, or exclamation points to the ends of the following sentences.

   1. Mr. Sullivan asked himself why no one had answered his advertisement

   2. Andrew B. Easton is a special consultant on our staff

   3. When will the FAA complete its investigation of the airplane crash

   4. Hooray That's the best news I ever heard

   5. The conference in St. Louis begins on September 30

II. Insert semicolons and colons where they are needed in the following sentences. Do not remove commas.

   1. Chicago has a $175 million municipal library however many of the nation's libraries suffer, unfortunately, from a lack of funds.

   2. The company has stores in four locations Rochester, New York San Antonio, Texas Salem, Oregon and Springfield, Massachusetts.

   3. Bring the following items for Saturday's hike walking shoes, a hat or cap, a warm sweater, a waterproof jacket, and a sack lunch.

   4. At 11 30 Sunday night Nina stared at the blank sheet of paper the essay was due at 8 00 the next morning.

   5. Molly couldn't believe her eyes the grade on her physics midterm was an "A."

CHAPTER 9   PRACTICE TEST (Cont.)

III. Capitalize where necessary.

1. the jordans have season tickets for the dallas cowboys.

2. last spring i drove through the south from texas to florida.

3. dale is studying spanish and chemistry at adams community college.

4. my aunt sophie's favorite corn chips are fritos.

5. on tuesday night the president will address the nation from the oval office.

IV. Correct the errors in abbreviations in the following sentences.

1. Sondra Zabar, M D is the name of my children's pediatrician.

2. Brian received a refund from the I.R.S. this year.

3. The package was sent to 15 State Street, Minneapolis, M.N. last week.

4. Marva was contestant no 4 in the competition.

5. Tracy earned an MA degree in 2004 from N.Y.U.

V. In the following sentences, correct the errors in numbers.

1. 4 of my friends drove to Florida during spring break.

2. Girl Scout Troop 88 sold 115 boxes of chocolate chip cookies, forty boxes of sandwich cookies, and fifteen boxes of sugar cookies.

3. On Monday after her flight from China, Kai-Y spent 3 hours trying to locate her 2 suitcases.

4. The assignment for Friday's test includes the material on pages fifteen through twenty-one in Chapter Eight.

5. The catalog price of seventy-nine fifty for the windbreaker does not include the shipping charge of four twenty-five.

VI. For each word listed below, write a sentence of your own using that word correctly.

1. use _____

2. loose _____

3. whose _____

4. effect _____

5. suppose _____

Editing
Practice

In the following paragraph, underline the errors in capitalization, abbreviations, and numbers. Write the correct forms in the space between the lines.

A remarkable Museum has opened its doors in NYC. It is the Rose Center for Earth and Space at the american museum of natural history. $210-million was spent to make this building the world's most advanced Planetarium. Visitors can learn about star clusters, gas clouds, and galaxies, with all the information coming from N.A.S.A. The visitors stand atop an 8-foot deep bowl to view light and laser effects. after the show, visitors exit onto a long runway that circles the sphere's exterior. "The Rose Space Center will bring in visitors from asia, europe, and africa to learn about their universe," Dr Ellen V Futter, the museum's president, claims. Dr. Futter had been President at Barnard College in Manhattan for 13 years before coming to the museum. She is delighted that the Rose Space Center will draw visitors with varying educational backgrounds, unlike a College with strict admission standards.

Writing a Paragraph

Planning a Paragraph

How can you learn to write clear, interesting paragraphs? Let's assume that you have an assignment in front of you on the subject of protecting the environment, but so far you haven't written a word. Your first question is, "How do I start?" You can continue to stare at the blank sheet of paper while waiting for inspiration; you can dash off whatever comes to mind and hope for the best; or you can begin by planning your paragraph before you write it.

Getting Started

Frequently the assigned topic will be broad enough to give each student an opportunity to draw on previous knowledge of the subject. For example, in the exercises that follow, you will be asked to discuss what you can do to protect the environment. Hardly a day goes by that you don't read or hear about the threat to life on our planet by the destruction of the environment, but what can you do about it? You have some general ideas about the problem, but what do you know specifically about it? Where do you find the information to write an entire paragraph on the subject?

First, look for ideas by exploring these six common sources of information:

1. Your own observation and experience
2. The observation and experience of people you know
3. Your college classes
4. Your reading

5. Radio and television programs
6. Internet links

A journal can help you to record and organize information from these sources.

Keeping a Journal

Some professional writers keep a journal to record their observations of people, scenes, and events as well as their responses to reading, including quotations and reactions to other writers' ideas. As a beginning writer, you may find that you enjoy writing in a journal for your own satisfaction instead of limiting your writing to class assignments. Some students say that after writing regularly in a journal, writing in class becomes easier.

How to Keep a Journal

1. Use a small spiral notebook you can carry with you in your purse or pocket along with a pencil or pen.
2. Write regularly, at least three or four times a week.
3. Date each entry.
4. If you use readings from books, magazines, or newspapers, record the name of the author and the title of the material.
5. Vary your entries by experimenting with freewriting, firsthand observations of your surroundings, and reading notes.

You cannot make a mistake in your journal. The notes you enter may help you slow down and really look at the things around you. You might want to write about the first time you see a particular kind of flower each spring, or about the first snowfall each winter. You could even use colored pencils to add a drawing of what you have described in words.

How to Record Your Observations

Go outside. Walk around a parking lot, a patio, a porch. Find a brook or a pond, anything that is making a sound. If you live in the city, go to a neighborhood park and sit on a bench or under a tree. Ask yourself questions:

What's different today?
What sounds do I hear?
What smells do I detect?

If you have a camera, you might want to take photos and paste the photos into your journal. Pay attention to details, such as size and color. You will soon find that your writing improves as you become a better observer of the world around you.

You may find that your journal can help you develop ideas for writing assignments in this class as well as others you are taking. Get in the habit of writing regularly.

You probably have found enough material in these sources for ten paragraphs if you can just take the first step. Begin by using the following techniques to start the writing process.

Listing Ideas

Make a list of your ideas on the subject by jotting down words and phrases in any order that they occur to you. Do not be concerned about anything except getting your thoughts down on paper. Here is an example of a list of ideas on the subject of protecting the environment:

Keep my car in efficient operating condition.
Don't use products made from polystyrene foam.
Plant trees; landscape with shrubs that require little water.
Recycle bottles, papers, etc.
Carry cloth shopping bag to avoid using plastic bags at store.
Use microwave for cooking small portions of food.
Install a low-flow shower head.
Contribute money to organizations working to save environment.
Write letters to legislators on issues involving environment.
Write letters to manufacturers to protest "overpackaging" of products.
Join local groups that are working to save the environment.
Conserve energy in my home.
Drive my car as little as possible; use bike, walk to do errands.
Use cloth napkins instead of paper; don't use paper plates, etc.

You have completed a list of ideas; now you need to focus on one of them for your paragraph. Organize the material by grouping similar items. For example, from the list above, grouping the suggestions about cars could lead to the topic, acting responsibly as a car owner. You may want to start another list expanding on that idea. Your revised list might look something like this:

Avoid making unnecessary sudden stops and starts.
Keep engine tuned properly for efficient operation.
Reduce speed.
Join car pool or use public transportation when possible.
Bike or walk when doing errands.
Drive a small or medium-sized fuel-efficient car.
Keep tires properly inflated; check for wear periodically.

Make a list of your ideas on the topic "What Can I Do to Protect the Environment?" Discuss them with other students if you are working with a group in class.

_____

_____

_____

_____

_____

_____

_____

_____

Freewriting

Instead of making a list, you may want to write in longer phrases and sentences in your search for material. Although your instructor has already provided the topic for your writing, you still have plenty of opportunity to develop your own response. Here is an example of freewriting:

What can be done to save energy besides turning off the lights? In the kitchen, for instance, both microwave ovens and stove-top cooking use less energy heating up a small meal than a conventional oven does. If you have a refrigerator over ten years old and can afford to, buy an energy-efficient one to save power. Use reusable plastic containers to pack lunches instead of using plastic bags that fill up landfills. Turn down the thermostat ten degrees on the water heater, or put a jacket around it to save energy. In the bathroom, limit shower time to five minutes instead of almost draining the tank of hot water. Can also put a water regulator on the shower head to save water. Turn off tap while brushing teeth or shaving. If you have an air conditioner, keep thermostat at 78 in the summer to cut down on use. In winter set thermostat between 65 and 68 and wear a sweater. Use biodegradable dishwashing liquid and laundry detergent. Don't buy products made of foam; choose cardboard instead of foam egg cartons, for example. Buying in bulk will cut down on packaging materials. Take plastics, aluminum cans, newspapers, glass to recycling centers.

EXERCISE 1B

Give yourself 15 or 20 minutes to practice freewriting on the topic, "What Can I Do to Protect the Environment?"

_____

_____

_____

_____

_____

_____

_____

_____

_____

After you have completed the exercise above, analyze what you have written to see if you have material for a paragraph by asking yourself some questions. How many possible topics do you have that you could develop? List them. What point is most important to you? If you choose the topic of greatest interest to you, you may find it easier to write your paragraph.

In addition to **listing ideas** and **freewriting**, **clustering** is another technique you might try in your search for a topic.

Clustering

Clustering should have a special appeal to those who like to sketch a diagram or make a map to explain a point. This technique will not only help you to put words on paper, but when you have finished, you may also discover connections among your thoughts that listing might not reveal. In the center of a blank sheet of paper, write the main word of your assignment and circle it. As you think of ideas, write them down, drawing lines to show the connections among them. Circle each word for easy reading. An example is shown on the next page.

The writer of the cluster has a number of ideas that could be used as topics for a paragraph. "Protect the environment" is obviously too broad and complicated a subject for a single paragraph, but "recycling" and "reduce use of paper and plastics" are possibilities. Notice the connection the writer makes between "reduce the need for landfills" and "work on local problems." Some of the topics the writer thought of during the process of drawing the cluster, such as "save energy," led to ideas that would require some research and further limitation of the subject. However, the writer's interest in a local problem might be strong motivation for writing.

EXERCISE 1C

In the box below, make your own cluster on how you can protect the environment, and analyze it for possible topics.

Example of Clustering

Ask yourself which ideas interest you the most, which ones would require research, and which ones you already have material for. Making the cluster diagram may make it easier for you to determine which points you want to exclude and which ones you want to emphasize. You can clearly see which direction to take with the available information.

Considering Your Readers

After you have chosen your topic and are ready to begin the first draft of your paragraph, consider another important point: "Who will your readers be?" If you can decide on a reader, real or imagined, you will sharpen the focus of the paragraph and generate additional ideas. Words may flow a little more easily as you gain a purpose other than writing to complete an assignment for class.

Having decided on your readers, ask yourself what you might need to add to your material to attract, hold, and inform them. With your topic in mind, write down your answers to the following questions:

Who exactly are your readers? What are their occupations?
What are their educational backgrounds?
What are their values? Their prejudices?
Why is this subject important to them?
What information can you expect them to know about the subject?
What information must you supply?
Do you want to persuade them to take action?

By the time you have answered these questions and any others you might think of, you should have added some important details to your notes and have a better sense of what you want to do.

Group ACTIVITY

Suppose you have decided that the best place for an individual to begin protecting the environment is at home. You know that some communities require their citizens to separate trash. You have been separating yours and placing bottles, cans, and papers in separate recycling containers. Include some other activities you have begun to do at home, referring to the list you made in Exercise 1A, the freewriting you did in Exercise 1B, or the cluster you drew in Exercise 1C. Don't forget to answer the questions about your intended readers before you begin to write.

At your next class meeting, be prepared to share the ideas you generated for a paragraph through the listing, freewriting, or clustering exercises and your list of answers to the questions about your readers. Get together with a few classmates. Working together, you can help each other plan a paragraph on the subject of protecting the environment. Concentrate on narrowing your focus to reach the best topic for your paragraph.

Outlining

Sometimes you will have a strong opinion about the topic before you begin making a list.

A student named Cathy wrote the paragraph, "The Effects of the Oil-Drilling Project," that follows. She knew who her intended readers were and what her opinion was, but she needed to get the reasons for her opinion down on paper before deciding on the exact wording of her topic sentence.

Cathy had read that an oil company was planning to drill for oil on a vacant lot near her house. On further investigation, she discovered that the company intended to erect a 135-foot derrick to begin with and then planned to drill up to 30 wells. Horrified, Cathy decided to write a letter to the city council members to dissuade them from approving the drilling project. She thought she knew what she wanted to say to her readers, so she drew up the following list as she sorted out her ideas in preparation for her letter:

Pollution of the air
Pollution of the ground water
Increased noise
Possible spills
Possible accidents
Waste disposal problems
Smells
Carcinogens
Loss of property values
Increased truck traffic

Making the list helped Cathy see that she had a lot of material to cover. She realized that making an outline would help her organize her material into a more manageable shape. She looked at the list and noticed that it could be broken down into three sections—the three major effects the oil project would have on her neighborhood:

1. Pollution
2. Increased noise
3. Increased traffic

Now, she needed to fit in the other items on her list under these three major subjects:

1. Pollution
    a. Air
    b. Ground
    c. Water

2. Increased noise
    a. Babies sleeping
    b. People working at home
    c. Interrupted conversations

3. Increased traffic
    a. Trucks bringing in equipment
    b. Trucks carrying away the oil
    c. Workers arriving and leaving

Cathy could now clearly see what her subject would cover and how she could develop her ideas. She began by writing her topic sentence:

> Increased noise, air pollution, and traffic will make life unpleasant for those of us who live near the oil-drilling project.

By "gathering up" her three major points from her outline, she was able to construct her topic sentence and to give shape to her paragraph.

Here is Cathy's paragraph as it looked when she was finished with the prewriting and writing stages:

The Effects of the Oil-Drilling Project

Increased noise, air pollution, and traffic will make life unpleasant for people in the vicinity of the oil-drilling project. Drilling operations will be conducted from 8 A.M. to 7 P.M. Although many people are at work between those hours, many more are at home. Small children and babies nap during the day, as do elderly people who often do not sleep well at night. Most people leave their windows open to let in the breezes, and conducting conversations at a normal level will be impossible. And those people who earn their living by working at home will have a hard time concentrating because of the drilling noise. Furthermore, increased truck traffic will make the streets more noisy and dangerous. Pedestrians and drivers will have to be extra cautious to avoid encounters with large trucks bringing in equipment or hauling away oil and other products. The oil workers' cars and trucks will also contribute to the increased traffic in our quiet neighborhood. Finally, the problem of pollution will affect all those who live in the area surrounding the project. Site preparation, drilling, and production operations will pollute the air by emitting dust, odors, and hydrocarbons. Oil spills may contaminate the ground water. For all of these reasons, I urge the members of the City Council not to approve the oil-drilling project.

You probably noticed that Cathy decided to write about pollution last instead of first as indicated in her outline. Why do you think she decided to do it that way?

Remember, the list and the outline are there to guide you in developing your paragraph. They should serve as an organizing method to put your ideas together coherently. It is not necessary to follow them exactly or to include everything in your paragraph. You are free to rearrange the order, omit certain ideas, or add other ideas as you are writing.

Group
ACTIVITY

By now you should have an outline and at least one rough draft. Bring your outline and rough draft to class. Form a group with several of your classmates to go over each other's work. You can help each other decide how the paragraph you are planning to write relates to your outline and which major points to stress. You may decide to change the order or leave out some parts of the outline altogether. Also, you can help each other to formulate a good topic sentence.

LESSON 2
The Topic Sentence

Composing the Topic Sentence

The topic sentence gives the writer's opinion about the topic, and it contains the main idea of the paragraph. Although a writer can place the topic sentence anywhere in the paragraph, it most commonly appears near the beginning. When you are writing a topic sentence, begin by looking at your list of ideas to determine how you can sum them up into one main point that will guide your discussion throughout the paragraph.

EXAMPLE: Here is a list of Duke Ellington's contributions to jazz.

1. As a bandleader, Ellington was unique, creating his own jazz classification.
2. As a pianist, he was an original solo player and an imaginative accompanist.
3. He composed more than one thousand tunes.
4. He made over 2,000 arrangements, suiting them to individual players.
5. By the late 1970s, Ellington had recorded more than 150 albums.
6. He has had an important, lasting influence on musicians, composers, and arrangers.

Topic Sentence: Duke Ellington remains an outstanding figure in jazz.

OR

No one has made more contributions to jazz than Duke Ellington.

Judging the Topic Sentence

1. The topic sentence contains a controlling idea. It makes a judgment and gives an opinion about the topic.

    EXAMPLES: The Florida Keys have coral reefs. (No opinion is expressed about the subject.)
    The coral reefs near the Florida Keys offer hiding places for beautiful and unusual fish. (The controlling idea gives the writer's opinion about the subject.)

2. The topic sentence narrows and limits the subject.

    EXAMPLES: The grasses and other plants are dying. (too broad)
    As the turtle grasses have died off, large quantities of algae have formed and killed the sponges and corals. (limited)

3. The topic sentence is precise.

    EXAMPLES: Florida Bay water is polluted. (too general)
    The water in Florida Bay is becoming too salty because it is not getting enough fresh water. (specific)

4. The topic sentence is clear.

    EXAMPLES: The fish that used to live in the Florida Bay have disappeared. (vague)
    Fish such as the tarpon and the bonefish have left because they have nothing to feed on. (clear)

WRITING TIP

You can write better topic sentences if you follow these three suggestions:

1. Avoid dead-end sentences or statements of fact or of intent.

   This paragraph will deal with the problems of the Florida Bay.

2. Avoid wild guesses.

   When the scientists can figure out why the algae bloom in the bay, they will be able to solve the problem of the dying reefs.

3. Avoid questions.

   What is the significance of the increased salinity of the Florida Bay?

EXERCISE 2A

For each group of sentences, write a topic sentence that could be used to develop a paragraph on the topic.

A.

1. The college bookstore was jammed with people.

2. It took me about 75 minutes to select and purchase books.

3. I could barely move through the aisles.

4. There were long lines at all the registers.

5. It was difficult to reach the books I needed on the shelves because of the huge crowd.

6. My feet were stepped on, and I was pushed and jostled rudely.

7. Furthermore, it was stuffy inside, about 85 to 90 degrees.

8. But the worst part was that the books were so expensive; I spent $268.20.

Topic Sentence: _____

B.

1. Some fish make high-frequency sounds that are audible to other fish.

2. Fish use sound to keep schools of fish together.

3. Sounds give messages about mating, spawning, and fighting.

4. Changes in color and pattern tell a competitor that the fish will defend its territory and food.

5. Chemical signals probably involve taste and smell in mating rituals.

6. Ritualized movements are another means of relaying information.

7. Fish with electrical organs can give shocks as a warning to other fish.

Topic Sentence: _____

C.

1. Gold miners of the 1850s faced a long, demanding journey to reach the gold fields.

2. They lived in primitive camps where tents or crude shelters provided minimum cover from the weather.

3. Miners spent hours working in the hot sun, mud, or icy water.

4. Health conditions were poor, and medicine was often nonexistent.

5. Saloon keepers, dance-hall women, gamblers, and merchants ultimately kept more of the gold than the miners did.

6. Within a few years, businessmen with capital to invest forced most of the individual miners from the gold fields.

Topic Sentence: _____

D.

1. Albert Einstein was born in Germany in 1879.

2. He became a professor of physics in Berlin in 1914.

3. The Nazi government revoked his citizenship in 1934 because he was Jewish, and he fled to America where he worked at Princeton University until his death in 1955.

4. His theory of relativity proposed new approaches to space and time that differed from those useful in everyday life.

5. For his work in theoretical physics, he received the Nobel Prize in physics in 1921.

Topic Sentence: _____

E.

1. Americans take 20,000 tons of aspirin a day.

2. We inhale the nicotine of 600 billion cigarettes a year.

3. We spend 10 billion dollars a year on alcoholic beverages.

4. Cola, cocoa, coffee, and tea that we drink daily contain caffeine and two other drugs.

5. Many people can't face the day without tranquilizers.

Topic Sentence: _____

EXERCISE 2B

Subject. Write to a friend recommending a book you have read or a film you have seen.

Step 1. Using Exercise 2A as a guide, list four to six reasons for your recommendation.

Step 2. Write a topic sentence on the subject.

Supporting the Topic Sentence

By grouping the items on your list and writing the topic sentence, you now have a plan for your paragraph. You will be able to write the first draft after you take the next step—developing specific support for the main idea of the topic sentence. This material will come from your personal experience, your firsthand observation, and your reading.

General/Specific: A writer uses both general statements and specific words to get a point across to the reader. A term is general or specific only in relation to another term. For example, in the student's paragraph about the effects of the oil-drilling project, you can see that "trucks bringing in equipment" is more specific than the general description of "increased traffic."

Specific words explain a writer's meaning by giving details and creating pictures in the reader's mind. In the following example, the general statements on the left are explained in detail by the addition of specific support on the right. This writer describes the grounds at Monticello, Thomas Jefferson's home in Virginia.

General	Specific
Monticello had numerous flower gardens.	Twenty oval-shaped flower beds were located at the four corners of the house while long flower borders, divided into 87 ten-foot compartments, were placed on either side of a walkway that circled the front lawn.
The beds contained a variety of flowers.	In addition to tulips, sweet William, and Maltese cross, imported from Europe, the garden included the cardinal flower native to the northeastern United States and the "Columbian Lily" discovered by Lewis and Clark on their expedition.
Some of Monticello's original trees remain.	Five trees date from Jefferson's time: two tulip poplars, a sugar maple, a European larch, and a red cedar.
A "kitchen" garden provided vegetables for the family.	The garden had over 250 kinds of vegetables and herbs, such as sesame grown for its oil, sea kale, tomatoes, and twenty varieties of peas.

Three Kinds of Support

The three kinds of specific support that you will use most frequently in your writing assignments are **descriptive details, facts,** and **examples.** Although you could develop a paragraph with only one kind of support, generally you will use a combination of different types.

Descriptive Details: When you describe a subject in specific terms, you are appealing to the reader's five senses (sight, sound, smell, taste, and touch). If you are successful, the reader can see, hear, and feel vicariously what you experienced firsthand.

In the following example, a student uses specific descriptive details to describe the atmosphere and the food that contributed to her dining pleasure.

General Statement and Topic Sentence: We recently had a pleasant time in a Mexican restaurant.

Specific Support

    We recently had a pleasant time in a Mexican restaurant. When we entered, the hostess seated us in a room with exposed brick walls and brightly painted murals of scenes in Mexico. The hostess also brought a basket of tortilla chips and a spicy salsa for dipping. The waitresses were dressed in white peasant blouses and colorful skirts with wide sashes wrapped around their waists to emphasize the festive mood. Knowing little about Mexican food, we followed the waitress's recommendations and ordered a combination plate of appetizers as a starter. It came with a chicken tamale, a ground beef chile relleno, a cheese enchilada, and a lobster taquito. We chose as the main course a shredded beef tostada served in a crisp tortilla shell. The tostada consisted of refried beans, rice mixed with corn and green peas, salsa Mexicana, and was topped with shreds of beef and a scoop of guacamole. It was very tempting and proved to be delicious. We wanted, of course, to leave room for the dessert, a flan, made of eggs and cream and covered with a syrup of brown sugar and honey. We enjoyed this delightful dinner and were especially pleased with the strolling guitarists who entertained our table with quietly performed songs from Mexico as we ate.

EXERCISE 2C

Underline the specific descriptive details in the paragraph describing the Mexican restaurant. Then write some specific descriptive details to support the following general statements.

General Statement

1. Robert was surprised by what he saw in the courtroom [or classroom]. (your choice)

_____

_____

General Statement

2. I have found the best place to study is the school library [or my bedroom]. (your choice)

_____

_____

Facts: Many times you will want to offer some evidence that can be verified. Facts provide exact details, for example, names, dates, places, and numbers. The following paragraph supports a general statement with factual details.

General Statement and Topic Sentence: Mrs. Pankhurst's activities, in fact, had an important influence on her American counterparts during those years.

Specific Support

      The Seneca Falls Convention of 1848 is usually given as the event marking the beginning of the women's rights movement in the United States. Elizabeth Cady Stanton, Lucretia Mott, Susan B. Anthony, Lucy Stone, and Sojourner Truth are familiar names to most of us. Less well-known to Americans is Emmeline Pankhurst, who was one of the leaders of the British movement from 1903 to 1914. Mrs. Pankhurst's activities, in fact, had an important influence on her American counterparts during those years. Unable to move legislators by words, she founded the Women's Social and Political Union, whose motto was "Deeds not Words," and drew lower-class women into the movement. These British women used militant action as a new weapon, publicly heckling politicians and embarrassing police by provoking them to take violent action against women. When Mrs. Pankhurst arrived in the United States in 1913 to lecture at Madison Square Garden, she was detained temporarily at Ellis Island as an undesirable alien. When she returned, she was also arrested by the English and imprisoned. By 1914 she had been arrested six times. The militancy of the British suffragettes gained international attention at a time when leaders of the American movement seemed to be marking time. Encouraged by Mrs. Pankhurst's success, the American movement took on new life as women sought public attention by parading, speaking at outdoor meetings, and picketing. This renewal of action would culminate after World War I in the passage of the Nineteenth Amendment in 1919, followed by its ratification in 1920 during the Wilson Administration.

EXERCISE 2D

Underline examples of factual details, such as names, dates, places, and numbers in the paragraph above. Then write some specific factual details to support the following general statements.

General Statement

   1. Jean planned her trip carefully.

     _____

     _____

General Statement

2. If I could buy a new car, I would buy a _____. (your choice)

_____

_____

Examples: Another way to clarify your meaning is by giving your reader a short illustration with an example or two. The student writer of the following paragraph uses examples (and details) to define people who like to save things.

General Statement and Topic Sentence: "Squirrel people" will save just about anything.

Specific Support

    <u>"Squirrel people" will save just about anything.</u> My aunt "squirrels" away clothes among other things. Her closets are packed with boxes and bags of mothballed clothes from the 1970s and the 1980s. Some women who are sentimental "to a fault" save all manner of romantic mementos. One friend has shoe boxes full of love letters and crackly dry, dusty old flowers. She saves matchbooks, napkins, ticket stubs, champagne corks, and even swizzle sticks from romantically memorable evenings. Another acquaintance keeps her souvenirs from the past ten years in marked files. She has a "Steve" file and a "Robert" file, among others. Parents are notoriously sentimental squirrel people. My parents' closet shelves have boxes with baby hair in envelopes, baby teeth in little boxes, bronzed baby shoes, bean and macaroni sculptures made in school, little plaster handprints, and, of course, mounds of photographs, report cards, and awards. My grandmother's files, drawers, and cupboards are full to the brim with string, coupons, business cards, glass jars, wine bottles, plastic containers, coffee tins, shopping bags with handles, empty egg cartons, buttons, rubber bands from newspapers, and scraps of material. She keeps small boxes to wrap presents in and gives me my presents in the same wrapping paper that I used to wrap her presents in. Don't laugh—every family has at least one squirrel.

EXERCISE 2E

Write some specific examples to support the following general statements.

General Statement

1. Some advertisements use humor to sell a product.

    _____

    _____

General Statement

2. Tim was obviously suffering from stage fright.

    _____

    _____

LESSON 3 **Unity**

The student who wrote a paragraph in Lesson 1 of this chapter on the effects of the oil-drilling project on the environment discarded three items from her list when she was planning her paragraph: waste disposal problems, carcinogens, and loss of property values. These items were of concern to her, but they did not support her topic—"the effect of increased noise, air pollution, and traffic on the quality of life." In fact, she might have developed these three items in separate paragraphs. The writer knew that *all* the sentences in a paragraph must support the main idea in a topic sentence if the paragraph is to have *unity*.

EXERCISE 3A

Draw a line through the sentences that do not support the main idea in the topic sentence. For each item that you cross out, write a sentence of support on the lines that follow.

A. *Topic Sentence:* A dictionary is an indispensable tool for a student in a writing class.

1. It gives the origin and development of words.

2. A good hardback dictionary costs very little, considering its many uses.

3. This book is a good source of biographical information.

4. It tells the meaning of a word.

5. A dictionary should be required for most classes.

6. It lists both synonyms and antonyms.

_____

_____

_____

B. *Topic Sentence:* You don't have to join an expensive health club to keep fit.

1. Walk whenever possible, rather than drive your car.

2. You will find it easier to lose weight when dieting if you exercise.

3. Most park and recreation departments offer free or low-cost exercise classes.

4. You will sleep better at night if you exercise daily.

5. Exercise daily at a specific time.

6. Many television channels present daily exercise programs for you to do at home.

_____

_____

_____

C. *Topic Sentence:* Success in taking an essay exam depends on careful preparation.

1. Ask the instructor if he or she is going to give a multiple-choice test in addition to the essay exam.

2. Study your class notes to see what the instructor has emphasized.

3. Start studying well in advance of the test date, rather than the night before the exam.

4. Take along a candy bar to eat for quick energy during the exam.

5. If the instructor gives the class study guides, use them as a source of possible topics for essays.

6. Try to anticipate possible topics for essays; then outline answers.

_____

_____

_____

D. *Topic Sentence:* Good teachers have well-defined instructional methods.

1. They lecture clearly and slowly enough for students to take notes.

2. They participate in school functions.

3. They encourage students to ask questions in class.

4. They do not allow one student to monopolize class discussions.

5. They grade the work fairly and consistently.

6. They often attend teachers' conferences.

_____

_____

_____

Cross out the sentences that break the unity of the following paragraph. On the lines below, write sentences of your own that will fit into the paragraph and replace those you removed.

I have enjoyed this English class. We not only reviewed the basics of English grammar, spelling, and punctuation, but we also learned to expand sentences with the use of words, phrases, and clauses and to write well-developed paragraphs. The course theme might have been "taking a second look at what we know" by reviewing the little things we take for granted but have forgotten. My physics class never reviewed any subject that we had already studied. The teacher expected us to know everything. The workbook that we used in this English class was well structured and clearly written. Our instructor gave us assignments from the workbook and explained any of the material that we had questions about. My math teacher ignored the textbook he had assigned and just lectured during class time. If we studied the practice tests ahead of time, the tests in this class were not difficult. My teachers in other classes made the tests too hard by not telling us what would be on them. I was discouraged by my low grades. The tests in this class were fun to take. As for the writing assignments, I found them interesting and helpful. All in all, I can honestly say that I learned a great deal in my English class this semester.

_____

_____

_____

_____

_____

LESSON 4

Organizing a Paragraph

When you write a topic sentence stating the main idea that you plan to develop in your paragraph, you begin organizing it. When you cross out all the ideas in your list or cluster that do not directly support the topic sentence, you take another important step in that direction. If you also make an outline, even though you may alter it while writing your paragraph, you arrange your notes into a pattern that you can use to guide your first draft. Some writers feel limited by an outline and prefer to start writing without one, moving ideas around as they expand on their material. Whether you use an outline or not, keep in mind that each sentence of your paragraph should lead to the next one as logically and clearly as possible. Writers, of course, use many different ways to organize their paragraphs. For many of the assignments in this course, you may find the following three methods of organization useful.

Three Ways to Organize a Paragraph

1. *General to Particular:* State the topic sentence near the beginning of the paragraph and then provide enough specific support to explain your idea to the reader.

> During the 1980s, basketball was transformed into a game that highlighted running, quickness, and physical agility. For years, slow, deliberate play was the style in basketball, and teams required big centers and well-coordinated team effort. Teams passed the ball frequently to work it inside for a relatively short, easy shot. Player height was, of course, a valued physical trait. In the 1980s height was still a distinct advantage, but tall players, like Magic Johnson of the Lakers and Larry Bird of the Celtics, added another dimension to the game by displaying the agility of six-foot athletes. The three-point basket contributed to the wide-open running game as teams quickly learned to push the ball up the court and take many shots, including the long three-pointer. Although team play was still important, the individual skills of running, dribbling, passing, and shooting attracted additional fans to the game. The popularity of this wide-open style resulted in increased revenues from both paid attendance and television. Subsequently, salaries rose for talented players with running-game skills. The Los Angeles Lakers, a winning team that captured nine NBA divisional titles and five world championships, typified that change.

2. *Particular to General:* Using this method, a reversal of the first one, get right down to specifics early in the paragraph. Lead up to the generalization contained in the topic sentence, which you place near the end of the paragraph.

The game of basketball has always placed a premium on the height of players. During the 1990s, the franchise stars in the National Basketball League (NBA) were the giants, notably Shaquille O'Neal of the Lakers, Hakeem Olajuwon of the Rockets, and David Robinson of the Spurs. These men towered over all the other players on the court, who themselves stood at heights between 6 and 7 feet. Any knowledgeable fan, however, recognized the skills of the talented, "smaller" men playing with the NBA's best teams. Topnotch point guards, for example, could dribble the length of the court, pass unerringly, shoot accurately from any range, and play aggressive and tenacious defense. Michael Jordan of the Bulls, rated by many experts as the greatest player of all time, John Stockton of the Jazz, and Gary Payton of the Trail Blazers were prime examples of the importance of these key players. They contributed as much to team success as did the taller players, who figured so prominently in sports news. They played, in fact, a considerable role in making professional basketball of the 90's a fast-paced, exciting sport enjoyed by an increasing number of fans everywhere.

3. *Giving Reasons to Persuade:* You have a strong opinion to express and want to persuade your readers to share your point of view. Develop several valid reasons to support your position. State your main point in a topic sentence near the beginning of the paragraph, and if you wish, restate it in different words at the end of the paragraph as the student writer of the following one did.

A TV dinner, the instant meal in a throwaway pan, is one answer to the question, "What's for dinner?" The preparation of these frozen dinners requires no skill or thought other than the ability to read and to turn on the oven. They save the cook plenty of time, but they may deprive children of more than the flavor and nutrition of a home-cooked meal. First, our ever-increasing dependency on instant foods in throwaway containers may rob our children of a vital lesson. Because throwaway pans mean no table to set and no dishes to wash, children do not learn the responsibility of sharing these household chores. To have duties in a family assures them of being an integral part of the family. In addition, instant dinners require little or no preparation, so children are denied the valuable experience of learning to fix a meal. Moreover, they miss the praise they love to receive for a casserole they helped prepare or the cookies they baked "all by themselves." Children lose an opportunity to learn the value of giving and receiving in a family setting. Finally, families are often deprived of the intimacy that develops at the dinner table. Since TV dinners encourage us to eat in front of the television, we often forfeit this time together to watch a TV program. Gathered around the dinner table, the family can talk about the day's activities. Children and parents need this time to eat and talk together. When we hurry to heat and eat the food, and throw away the pan after dinner, we may also throw away the opportunity to develop lasting relationships that cannot be replaced by any instant, disposable product.

Write a paragraph on <u>one</u> of the following topics, using <u>one</u> of the methods in this lesson: general to particular, particular to general, or giving reasons to persuade.

1. A product that has remained popular for years

2. An important change in an activity or occupation

3. An important change in family values or relationships

Organizing with Transitional Words and Phrases

Arranging materials in a special pattern, such as general to particular, benefits both you as a writer and your reader. You have come a long way from your first tentative list of ideas to the carefully organized paragraph you now have in front of you.

If you read your paragraph aloud, however, your ears may tell you something that your eyes have overlooked. Although your discussion follows a logical order and does not stray from the path, the road may seem bumpy and not clearly marked. Therefore, you need to provide some signposts to guide your reader—transitional words and phrases that will show the relationships among your ideas in the paragraph.

The following list contains the most commonly used transitional terms. Choose these useful expressions to fit the context of your sentences, or the result may be the opposite of what you intend. A careless choice can obscure what a writer is trying to make clear.

Transitional Words and Phrases

Addition—also, and, another, furthermore, moreover, too, in addition, in fact

Time—after, before, finally, first, second, meanwhile, next, then, while

Illustration—for example, for instance, such as, to illustrate

Contrast—but, however, instead, nevertheless, still, yet, in contrast, on the contrary, on the other hand

Conclusion—consequently, finally, thus, as a result, in conclusion, in general, in summary

Connect the following sentences by writing on each line an appropriate transitional word or phrase from the preceding box. Try to use a different word or phrase each time.

1. I am not against health foods in general. _____ I am opposed to the commercialization of certain foods known as "health foods."

2. Some T-shirt wearers have become walking billboards for a favorite product, while others display personal statements on their shirts. _____, many companies specialize in the personalization of T-shirts.

3. The ATM is a convenience that I have found very useful. _____, with the ATM, I never have to wait in line with more than two people. _____, the ATM is open twenty-four hours a day, on holidays, and weekends. _____, I don't have to deal with an unpleasant human bank teller or one who tries to rush me. _____, the ATM makes banking more convenient for me.

4. How often have you, as a student, taken a test you felt was unsuitable for the material being covered? Have you ever been asked on a test, _____, to fit complex, detailed information into a framework of true-or-false questions?

5. Some kinds of "squirreling" or saving are considered acceptable, _____, stamp or coin collecting. _____, there are those wise people who save articles for future use. A true "squirrel" person, _____, pushes saving to an extreme.

6. The night before my final exam, I could not fall asleep until 3 A.M. My dog, _____, woke me up at 5 A.M., and I couldn't go back to sleep. _____, when I sat down at 8 A.M. to take my exam, I was very tired.

7. In my tight-knit community in England, everything was within a short bus ride or walking distance. In my American city, _____, everything is so spread out that I need a car to get around.

Read the following article carefully. Some difficult words are numbered and defined at the end of the article. Use your dictionary for other unfamiliar words. Underline all the transitional words and phrases.

Pre-Columbian Art

Pre-Columbian[1] Mexican art was collected extensively by the famous artist Diego Rivera. His collection of ceramic figures resulted in the first exhibit of the art of Western Mexico in 1946 in Mexico City. Since then, many exhibitions of these figures have been organized all over the world. Now, we recognize that West Mexican art consists mainly of ceramic figure sculpture that was found in tombs in the present Mexican states of Nayarit, Jalisco, and Colima. However, today these three names are used to describe pottery based on style rather than geography. It is clear, for example, that typical Nayarit figures can occur in the same tombs with figures of the Jalisco type. These artists of West Mexico made both large hollow and small solid tomb figures. Both have been found in the same burial chamber. To illustrate, the figures of Nayarit are characterized by their active forms, with clearly defined fingers and toes. Arms were usually long thin ropes of clay. No attention was paid to anatomical[2] details of the arms. Moreover, in the Nayarit figures, great attention was paid to the hair, which was incised[3] in many straight lines. Figures of both sexes wore round earrings, nose ornaments, and facial markings that look like long slashes on the cheeks. Furthermore, these figures were usually painted red. On the other hand, Jalisco figures were usually gray or cream-colored. The heads of the Jalisco figures were elongated[4] and decorated with an ornament that crisscrosses the head. In addition, they had enlarged, staring eyes, hatchet-shaped noses, and large, open mouths, with the teeth clearly defined. In contrast, the Colima figures were usually bright orange to deep red with spots of black scattered over their surface. The human figures of the Colima group were posed in a stiff formal style. It looks as though they were posing for the artist. No carving or other decoration was used. The Colima figures were often animals, especially dogs. These dogs are thought to have been the gods that escorted the humans to the next world. In conclusion, these clay figures are only a small part of the artistic output of the ancient Mexican people. We can never know about their music, their oral literature, their wood sculpture, or their textiles. But the clay sculptures are beautiful works done by master artists.

Vocabulary
1. Pre-Columbian: The historical period before Columbus arrived in America
2. anatomical: structural
3. incised: carved, cut into
4. elongated: stretched out and narrowed

LESSON 5 Editing the Paragraph

Revision

At last you have a paragraph in response to your first assignment. All you have to do is make a neat copy to turn in to your instructor. Right? Not quite. Now that your paragraph has taken form, you need to look at it as objectively as possible. Put it aside for at least an hour or two, preferably overnight, and then read it aloud or have someone in your class read it to you. Try to see it as though you were reading it for the first time. Just reading the paragraph, however, is not enough; you must take an active role in revision. Begin by directing your attention to the topic sentence, development, unity, and organization of the paragraph. Here are a few questions you might consider:

1. Can you sum up the main point of the paragraph clearly and concisely in a few words? Does the topic sentence need rethinking and restating to clarify your meaning?

2. Does your ear catch any weak spots where the thought seems to falter? Is your discussion difficult to follow in places?

3. Was your voice strong and clear in the first supporting sentences only to become uncertain and fade away as you continued? Do you need to develop additional support or to clarify your ideas?

4. Did you stick to your subject? Does every sentence contribute an essential point or clarifying details?

5. Does it all hang together? Is there a plan, a logic in the order in which the supporting sentences are presented?

6. Does the thought flow smoothly? Should you arrange your sentences in a different sequence? Have you provided links between sentences? Underline the transitional words and phrases. Do you need to add or change any? Is each one the best choice in the context of the sentence?

7. Do you sound interested in your subject? Are you knowledgeable about it? Do you speak in a natural voice, or do you sound artificial and forced?

8. Have you been considerate of your readers and given them all the information they need to understand your ideas as clearly as possible?

Proofreading

After you have revised the paragraph to your satisfaction, you are ready to proofread it. Here is a checklist based on the exercises in this book to guide your proofreading.

1. Spelling
2. Punctuation and capitalization
3. Use of the apostrophe in possessives
4. Fragments
5. Comma splices and run-on sentences
6. Agreement of subject-verb and pronoun-antecedent
7. Pronoun reference
8. Faulty parallelism
9. Sentence structure: rewrite unclear, awkwardly constructed sentences
10. Diction: choose accurate, appropriate words
11. Dangling and misplaced modifiers
12. Wordiness

Guide to Revision of Writing Assignments

Your instructor may use the following symbols in marking your papers.

Symbol	Error	Symbol	Error
Pl	Plural	No Cap	No Capital
Pos	Possessive	Adj	Adjective
P Shift	Pronoun Shift in Person	Adv	Adverb
Case	Pronoun Case	S-V Agr	Agreement of Subject and Verb
Vb	Verb	P-A Agr	Agreement of Pronoun and Antecedent
V Shift	Sequence of Tenses		
V Tense	Incorrect Use of Tenses	Ref	Pronoun Reference
SS	Faulty Sentence Structure	RO	Run-On Sentence
VF	Incorrect Verbal Form	MM	Misplaced Modifier
CS	Comma Splice	Sp	Spelling
Frag	Fragment	W	Wordiness
C	Comma	WW	Wrong Word
P	Other Marks of Punctuation	^	Omission of Word
Cap	Capital	¶	Paragraph

Writing Assignment

Topic

Write a paragraph of approximately 200 words about the different roles that people play every day. Before you begin to write, review the steps for planning and writing a paragraph described in this chapter. If you do not want to write about yourself, write about the roles of a person you know very well.

Step 1. Think about the different roles we all play every day. For example, as a woman, you may play the roles of a sister, a daughter, a daughter-in-law, and a mother just within your family. As a woman or as a man, you may play one role in your neighborhood, one at a club you belong to, and still another at work as an employee. In school, you play the roles of a student and a friend. You undoubtedly can think of many other roles. After you have decided on the roles you will discuss, jot down your ideas by listing, using a cluster, or freewriting.

Step 2. As you write your rough draft, describe each role in detail. Is one role more difficult than another? Are these roles ever in conflict? As a man, for instance, do you have any problems playing the roles of husband and employee, or of son-in-law and father?

Step 3. After you have written your paragraph, follow the suggestions on editing, revision, and proofreading.

Alternative Writing Assignment

Revise the paragraphs you have written for assignments in this class during the past semester. Use the information in Chapter 10 to help you with your revisions.

Begin by checking through the eight questions listed under *Revision* in Lesson 5. Using them as a guide, refer back to specific lessons in the chapter. For example, question 1 concerns the topic sentence. Reread Lesson 2 (The Topic Sentence) and determine if your topic sentences state the main idea of the paragraphs clearly and precisely.

If your instructor approves, choose one paragraph that you have revised and resubmit it for a second evaluation.

Appendixes

Editing Practice

Sentences

Exercise 1

Underline the errors and write the corrections on the lines at the right.

1. The mens' caps are available in four sizes. _____

2. Alisha has never forgave Ron for the accident. _____

3. There's only ten students in our class. _____

4. Everyone plans to go hiking except Laurel and myself. _____

5. Set down on that couch. _____

6. While he is studying Ed listens to the radio. _____

7. Each of your papers show improvement. _____

8. The grocery list includes the following; rice, apples, and bananas. _____

9. Phil stopped working, and took a nap. _____

10. Nolan sometimes drives to work however he prefers to walk. _____

Exercise 2

Underline the errors and write the corrections on the lines at the right.

1. The presidential candidate announced that he will choose his running mate tomorrow. _____

2. As the crowd watched, the huge balloon rose more high than the trees. _____

3. My Aunt is a U.S. naval officer on a cruiser in the
   Pacific.   _____

4. This restaurant is always crowded at noon, we will
   have to wait for a table.   _____

5. If Rachel leads the group discussion. Everyone will
   want to attend the meeting.   _____

6. Mi Lee does not come to work as a rule until noon.   _____

7. The quarterback weighs one hundred eighty-six pounds.   _____

8. There is a difference of opinion between him and I.   _____

9. The sentences in this exercise looks easy.   _____

10. Denyce says that theres nothing worth watching on
    TV tonight.   _____

Exercise 3

Underline the errors and write the corrections on the lines at the right.

1. A Community College is located four blocks from
   my house.   _____

2. Are those pears ripe.   _____

3. These seats are more better than the ones we had
   before.   _____

4. Terry had three goals; to finish school, to find a job,
   and to buy a car.   _____

5. Adina dropped a glass on the plate and broke it.   _____

6. While you were sleeping. The storm started.   _____

7. Linda is an excellent teacher. This is a rewarding
   occupation.   _____

8. "Please lend me some CDs for the party tonight"
   Mario said.   _____

9. Who's tennis shoes are these?   _____

10. Dr. Shapiro however will do the surgery.   _____

Exercise 4

Underline the errors and write the corrections on the lines at the right.

1. We invited Ray to the party, but Sylvia and him had
   tickets to the basketball game.   _____

2. Everyone in our group found James to be resourceful,
   cooperative, and a hard worker.   _____

3. The bird flew out of it's cage.   _____

4. On June 17, 2001 our son was graduated from college.   _____

5. Dionne talks the most fastest of anyone I know.   _____

6. Everybody in our family seem to enjoy a barbecue at
   the park.   _____

7. The director has auditioned ten children for the part
   before she chose Renaldo.   _____

8. Toshio has lived on Catalina Ave for several years.   _____

9. The essay easy for Brad to write. He was glad that he
   had studied for the history test.   _____

10. There's protestors gathering in front of the city hall.   _____

Exercise 5

Underline the errors and write the corrections on the lines at the right.

1. Todd takes his dutys seriously.   _____

2. The referee's decision seemed fair to Pedro and I.   _____

3. Some office buildings have more faster elevators
   than others.   _____

4. While shopping, Mia lost her keys, her friend had an
   extra set.   _____

5. After the secretary had typed the letter she proofread it. _____

6. Toppers Pizza will deliver their pizzas to your home.   _____

7. Saul was excited, when the agency called with a job offer. _____

8. An oil spill closed the mississippi river for twenty-six miles. _____

9. Bike riding is a good way to meet people that is friendly. _____

10. All applicants must take a series of testses. _____

Exercise 6

Underline the errors and write the corrections on the lines at the right.

1. Mr. Turner had traveled four thousand miles by the time the plane lands in Hawaii. _____

2. Everyone laughs at my fathers jokes. _____

3. If you follow the directions on the map. You should have no difficulty locating the campgrounds. _____

4. The candidate found it difficult to except his defeat at the polls. _____

5. The class schedules for next semester are available in the Admissions Office but I don't have one yet. _____

6. She bought shoes made of the most softest leather she could find in the store. _____

7. Here's the three books you ordered last week. _____

8. Jessie wasn't enjoying the film nevertheless she stayed to the end. _____

9. Rudy told Alberto that he owed Martin fifty dollars. _____

10. Only Mr. Franklin and myself know the combination to the safe. _____

Exercise 7

Underline the errors and write the corrections on the lines at the right.

1. The nurse has gave first aid lessons to the counselors. _____

2. Laura and Phil met in May, and married just two
   months later in July.   _____

3. Lisa was the only cheerleader, who had dance training.   _____

4. Each of your papers show improvement.   _____

5. She addressed her letter to the President, the White
   House, Washington D.C. 20500.   _____

6. They was riding their bicycles from Oregon to Virginia.   _____

7. Swimming is my favorite sport. You enjoy a wonderful
   sense of freedom.   _____

8. Thomas received a AA degree last year.   _____

9. Latisha was to tired to continue.   _____

10. Those boxes contain old photoes.   _____

Exercise 8

Underline the errors and write the corrections on the lines at the right.

1. Kevin hasn't saved enough money for tuition, he has
   been working all summer.   _____

2. Roz walked by while we were washing the car with
   her collie.   _____

3. Francine use to eat at Café Piccolo every Friday.   _____

4. Following the instructions carefully Mario assembled
   the bicycle.   _____

5. Mathematics, of course, are required for engineering
   students.   _____

6. The cafeteria was crowded today. So many students
   drinking coffee between classes.   _____

7. The cat has been laying in the sun all morning.   _____

8. My uncle knows his business partner for over twenty-
   five years.   _____

9. Who's wet towel and sandy swimsuit are on the floor
   of the bathroom?   _____

10. Bargain Books will hold their semiannual sale next week. _____

Exercise 9

Underline the errors in the following sentences and write the corrections on the
lines at the right.

1. Whose going to win the prize?   _____

2. All the candidates have promise to lower taxes.   _____

3. My friend and me are looking for an apartment.   _____

4. Have you finished you're homework yet?   _____

5. Many corporations have opened day-care centers, they
   are open from nine to five.   _____

6. Tim's job; furthermore, gives him time to spend with
   his family.   _____

7. There's only three slices of cheese left.   _____

8. Kwan put two books, several pens, a calculator and a
   notebook in his backpack.   _____

9. The violence in the movie effected the audience a lot.   _____

10. The plastic pool is laying on the lawn.   _____

Exercise 10

Underline the errors and write the corrections on the lines at the right.

1. Sherman and Doreen play the lottery every week, but
   neither of them have ever won.   _____

2. We bought two loafs of cinnamon bread at the bakery.   _____

3. I've lost my book, but she's going to lend me her's.   _____

4. Writing hundreds of letters, public opinion was turned
   against the project.   _____

5. The daily noise of jack hammers and concrete trucks
   are annoying the nearby residents. _____

6. Either Lupe or Marcia left their books on the back
   seat of the car. _____

7. Thomas A. Edison who was a famous American inventor
   is often called the Wizard of Menlo Park. _____

8. Justin asking if I would meet him for lunch. I had
   promised to go shopping with Val. _____

9. The film won four awards, it is playing in a theater at
   the Cinema Center. _____

10. Andy said that "he always left the server at a restaurant
    a 15 percent tip." _____

Paragraphs

Underline the errors in the following paragraphs and write the corrections in the space between the lines.

I. The New York Botanical Garden

The New York Botanical Gardens forest stands in the Bronx. We usually associate the Bronx with the Yankees and urban blight but we would never think of a fifty-acre forest. The wooded land containing one of New Yorks treasures. "Most people dont even no about it" said Ken Lauby, the Botanical Garden's vice president. Most people who come to the Garden want to see the flower's. We would love for more people to see and appreciate the forest, he added. Its a tough time to be a tree, new york and other cities are struggling to find money for the forest's. Trees can't talk at City Council meetings, so if money have to be cut, it's usually the money for the Botanical Garden. But did you know that one hundred trees remove about a ton of pollution from the air each year. After a highway was built nearby some trees close to the roadway started to grow more slow. The forest faces other urban pressures. It's soil contains high concentrations of heavy metals, therefore, water penetrates at a slower rate then normal. Also, because visitors has tramped down the earth on some trails. New plants havent been able to grow but the woods has managed to thrive despite the stress.

II. Boomerang Throwers

Although there is now an association of devoted boomerang throwers the boomerang is not likely to have a noticeable affect on american sports. Companies who manufactures golf clubs and tennis rackets shouldnt be alarmed. The flat, curved wooden, boomerang served australian aborigine tribes as a battle weapon and to hunt small animals birds and fish. When this device is hurled it return to the hand of the thrower, however, the thrower must be an expert. Today its made of glass laminated birch polymer fiber and other materials. Called "the thinking mans Frisbee." It's appeal is mostly to men such as engineers and pilots. Theres approximately twenty US tournaments each year and a World Cup event every two years for enthusiasts A champion can throw a boomerang as far as the length of a football field and at the speed of over sixty miles an hour. Collectors range from the smithsonian institute in our nations capitol to a man in Canton Ohio with 15,000 boomerangs in his private collection.

III. Iguanas in Florida

Hungry ugly giant lizards has invaded some towns in southern florida. They are iguanas who had once been kept as pets but they are now rapidly, reproducing in the wild. The manager of a condominium said, Iguanas eat the flowers mess up the pools and dirty the sidewalks and lawns. Most of the time iguanas likes to lay in the grass in the warm sunshine and they hide in the treetops or in holes they have digged in the ground. A iguana can grow up to six feet in length and it's weight can be up to thirteen pounds, some iguanas are more large then any lizard found naturally in the US. They have more fiercer tempers then many of the ancient dinosaurs. In theory a good long cold snap should kill the iguanas but they have learned that if they stayed in water, they had a more better chance of keeping warm. Since iguanas are excellent swimmers they can stay submerged for fifteen minutes. At one point the residents of some towns in florida hired a trapper, but the lizards ran real fast and managed to escape her traps. One man said, "Its impossible to capture them, they are too smart for that." Theirs' little doubt that if you met an iguana in an alley or in your pool you would be pretty scared.

IV. Firefighters

Every summer wild fires in our forests burns millions of acres of trees. Posing a threat to everything in it's path. An elite group, known as the Arrowhead Hotshots, stand ready at two-hours' notice to take on one of the most riskiest assignments a firefighter can face. The Hotshots were sent to the most hazardous situations, they go where the terrain fire behavior and fuel made the fire most dangerous to fight. Founded in 1981 the organizations work center is located at an elevation of 6,240 feet in the general grant district of kings canyon national park in California. The candidates which arrives to enter the strenuous training program must be in top physical condition the highly structured exercises will call upon all their strength and endurance. When they are fighting a fire. A typical shift can last sixteen hours under conditions that is physically exhausting and emotionally draining. Living and working together as a unit for approximately six months, the program stresses compatibility and team spirit. Over the years tools and equipment has been real improved but the crew working on the ground are indispensable in finally putting out the flames.

V. Jazz in Chicago

In the Spring of 1915, a five-piece band of white musicians from New Orleans open in a café in a African-American neighborhood of Chicago. Jazz was beginning to find an audience among blacks but is unfamiliar to most white patrons. They was not an immediate success, but after lots of persuading, people started coming to dance at the café. By the time Louis Armstrong arrived in 1922; however, the scene had changed. Armstrong recalled, There was plenty of work, lots of dough flying around, all kinds of beautiful women at your service. He added that a musician at the time was treated like a god. By the end of the 20s over a million black people from the southern states had settled in Chicago. They work in the stockyards in the steel mills on the railroads and in heavy industry. There was clubs for blacks only but there was also those known as "black and tans" where both races mingled. The black musicians from the South felt at home in Chicago and white musicians were attracted to their music. Despite the alarmists which predicted that such crude sounds would corrupt the morals of young people. Jazz flourished in Chicago. This was still a segregated world but black and white musicians liked to get together and playing in clubs on the South Side after closing hours. By 1928 the scene change again many of the musicians who were no longer able to make a living in Chicago had went to New York. Nevertheless, those early years in Chicago brought a wider audience to jazz then the dancers which had swinged to the music at the begining of the decade.

VI. Hula Dancers

What picture comes to your minds eye when you hear the word "hula" If you are like most of us you see the following Hollywood stereotype a lovely young woman wearing a cellophane version of a grass skirt seductively rolling and swaying her hips to the strumming of a ukulele. The hula hoop used for exercising and to play has taken it's name from this popular image, they must move the hips in a gyrating motion to keep the hoop spinning. According to the many Hawaiians now living on the mainland. People in over thirty states was dancing the hula. Although many of these dancers are creating their own experimental versions of the dance they remains in touch with the ancient traditions. They want however to eliminate Hollywoods interpretation of the hula. The significance of the dance they maintain is not in the movement of hands and hips but in the chants who preserve the legends and history of the Hawaiian people. Past down from teacher to student. The hula survive a fifty-year ban by missionarys a long period of neglect and the glitz of the movies. Despite the innovations of todays dancers it seem likely that these ancient ceremonys will last for another century or too.

VII. Mustangs

The ranchers of frontier days admired the wild horses. Roaming the range lands of the West for its stamina and speed. They even captured some of the most fine mustangs to breed with their horses. But as farm machinery come into common use the horse no longer played a vital role on the ranch and farming Wild horses have began to be regarded as a nuisance, ranchers didn't want mustangs sharing the range with they're ever-increasing herds of cattle. Today the ranchers of the Southwest is divided by what some call "The Mustang Dilemma." People are debating the question of how many is too many. But are they talking about horses or people. Reno Nevada one of the most rapid growing cities of the West is a good example of people invading the mustangs range. The wild horses all ready now graze at the edges of the suburbs. Amidst power lines walls fences traffic and mile after mile of paved highways.

On one side of the controversy are those which wants fewer cattle on the range and more protection and room, for the mustang. On the other side in addition to the ranchers concerns some people want to protect the habitat of wild life in the area. They argue that herds must be thinned periodically they pose a threat not only to all wild life but to mustangs themselves as they compete for the range land that is left. Both sides make convincing arguments but on behalf of the mustang consider this fact it has gave it's name to a WWII aircraft a motorcycle seat a football team and a very popular car. Like those early ranchers we also admire the mustang.

VIII. Yoga

Yoga classes offers an unique opportunity to refine you're yoga practice threw repatterning mind-body functioning. By observing more closer what is going on in your body, your instructor tailor each session to you're individual needs. You will be well adviced to wear lose-fitting clothing and bring a sticky mat to lay on. With her hands-on guidance. You will learn healthful movement patterns relieve the stress in chronic pain areas and expand you range of motion while increasing strength and flexibility. Her one-on-one approach deepen your experience of the yoga pose's and provide a sequence of pose's that address your particular needs. Deep-tissue bodywork, assisted stretches, and adjustments while in the yoga poses.

The classes target the following conditions chronic back, neck, and shoulder pain, joint problems arthritic conditions traumatic injuries post-surgery rehabilitation illness recovery Your instructors year's of yoga, movement and bodywork experience provide a safe and more deeply careing environment. She be a Registered Movement Therapist, Registered Somatic Movement Educator and Certified Practitioner of Body-Mind Centering (BMC), based on the work of teacher, healer and Somatic Bodywork pioneer Bonnie Bainbridge-Cohen. Her dedication to yoga are shaped by her lifetime as a dancer, movement researcher, performance and visual artist. She have studied lots of therapeutic modalities including: Shiatsu, Rolfing, Feldenkrais and Pilates.

Additional Topics for Writing Assignments

1. Imagine that you are applying to participate in a student work-study program. If you are accepted, you will live in a foreign country for the summer. Describe yourself, your interests, your family, and your life in the United States. Explain why you want to go to that country to study. Do you have any special links to the country through your family? Are you interested in its language, art, history, geography, or neighboring countries? How would you benefit from the experience?

2. You will need a partner for this assignment. Choose a person in the class who is new to you rather than someone you already know. Interview that person so you can introduce your new friend to members of the class. Ask questions about family, schoolwork, goals, and ambitions. Take notes as you listen to the answers to your questions. Then write a paragraph introducing that person. When you have finished writing your paragraphs, form a group with two other students and take turns reading your paragraphs of introduction aloud.

3. Describe how you would spend a perfect day in the summer. Describe in detail the places you would go, what you would do there, what (or whom) you would take along, and what you especially like about summer. If you prefer another season, you might write about a perfect day in the spring, winter, or fall.

4. Explain what you liked or disliked about one of the following topics:
   a. A movie that you saw recently.
   b. A TV show that you watched recently.
   c. A book that you read recently.

5. Imagine that you are going to take a trip.
   a. Describe your destination, transportation, clothes, restaurants, nightclubs, souvenirs, parties, or anything else that you believe would contribute to an enjoyable vacation.
   b. Explain why you chose this particular place.
   c. What do you think are the benefits of taking a trip?

6. Tell about a past experience that you remember especially well. Perhaps it was the funniest, the most frightening, or the happiest experience you can remember.

   OR

   Describe some event that might be called the "big event" in your life.

7. Do you (or did you ever) belong to a group or an organization? Perhaps you work in a group on the job that functions as a team.
   a. Describe its purpose and its activities.
   b. Explain why you joined it. What do you contribute to it? To what do you attribute the high or low morale that may exist?
   c. Discuss your experiences as a member of a group. What do individual members of a group gain by their participation in it?

8. Let's assume that you now have your college degree and that you are applying for your first full-time job. Aside from salary, what working conditions and benefits are most important to you? Rank them in order of importance, and, in each instance, explain specifically its importance. *Remember:* do not write about salary. When your instructor returns your work, meet with three classmates and discuss your papers, comparing the points you listed. Choose the best paper from each group to read aloud to the class.

9. Discuss the advantages and disadvantages of going to school while holding a job.

OR

Write about how to succeed in school after being away for three years or more.

OR

Write about how you deal with pressure at work or at school.

10. Write about a profession or an occupation you would choose to enter if you could.
    a. Describe the kind of work you would be doing.
    b. Explain why this work appeals to you.
    c. Do you see any disadvantages in this profession or occupation?

11. Why did you decide to attend this college? Explain why and possibly how you chose this college. Describe your first impressions of the campus. How could the college be improved? You might discuss registration procedures, the cafeteria, counseling, class schedules, course offerings, or anything else you would like to see improved.

12. Go to a shopping mall or a park. Find a comfortable place to sit for a while in order to observe people carefully. Select one person and give a complete description of this person's appearance and behavior. If possible, take notes to refer to when you complete this assignment at home.

13. Recall the details of how you learned a specific skill such as swimming, skating, typing, driving a car, riding a bicycle or a surfboard, playing a musical instrument, or playing baseball or some other sport. Remember to describe the steps in your learning process.

14. Go to the campus career counseling center to inquire about a career that interests you. Who spoke with you? What information did you obtain that will be helpful to you? Tell why you felt encouraged or discouraged about seriously planning for that career. Explain why you do or do not feel that the center provides a worthwhile service. Do not copy from any written material you may receive at the center.

15. Write a letter to the editor of your campus newspaper, commenting on an article. Express your agreement or disagreement with the writer. Offer your own opinion based on your experience and observations on the subject. Support your point of view with specific examples. Don't just write in general terms. Attach a copy of the article that provoked your comments.

16. Many organizations operate nonprofit mentoring agencies that match adult volunteers with disadvantaged teenagers. Supporters of the programs believe that mentors are an effective way of helping these young people, and they have success stories that demonstrate this positive influence. Critics of the programs, however, say that mentor programs can create more problems than they solve, and they offer examples of disappointment and resentment. Several factors seem to be essential in determining the success or failure of this approach to a serious social problem: the screening and the training of the volunteers, the matching of mentor and teenager, and the dedication and responsibility of the mentors themselves. Explain whether you favor or oppose mentoring. Would you be willing to devote two years to being a mentor? What personal qualities do you think are most important for a successful mentor? Do you think that better ways exist within the family or the neighborhood to guide young people? Are there any risks in having an adult from "outside" attempt to guide a young person whose early years have been so difficult?

17. Explain why you are willing to try a new product. How does the manufacturer persuade you to buy something that you may not even need? Do you pay attention to advertisements in newspapers and magazines and on radio and television? If so, what kind of approach appeals to you? Do you respond favorably to coupons, to samples, and to store demonstrations? Do you ever buy a new product because a friend or an acquaintance recommends it? Write about specific products that you have actually used.

18. Many American college freshmen are having difficulty doing college work. In fact, a concerned faculty committee at one university has addressed a letter to the parents of all eighth graders in the state, warning them that it is not too soon to begin preparing these students for college. With this idea in mind, write a composition on one of the following topics:
    a. Assume that you are the parent of an eighth grader. What steps will you take to see that your child is prepared for college? What recommendations will you make to your child?
    b. Think back to your own years in junior high school and high school. Were you adequately prepared for college? What do you wish your parents, your teachers, and you had done differently? In what ways was your preparation good?

19. Women are often discouraged from entering certain occupations and professions. Do you think, for example, that women should be discouraged from becoming scientists, doctors, dentists, firefighters, police officers, heavy-equipment operators, or electricians? Are there any valid reasons for discrimination against women in these and other fields? If you believe that women should be encouraged to enter these fields, what, in your opinion, are the best ways to overcome the objections of others? Or do you

believe that there are some occupations that only men should pursue and some that only women should pursue?

Present the reasons for your point of view. Focus on one occupation or profession (for example, military service) to write about in specific detail instead of writing about several in general terms.

20. Evaluate this writing class. Explain why you like or dislike the workbook, tests, writing assignments, and classroom activities. Include any suggestions you may have to improve this course.

21. An activity like climbing Mt. Everest is expensive, dangerous, and physically and psychologically stressful. In your opinion, what are the benefits? Why do you think people subject themselves to such hardships? If you had your choice, would you go on such an expedition? Why or why not? If you did go, what steps would you take to prepare yourself for such an ordeal physically and psychologically? Use the questions as a guide to discuss your views about undertaking a difficult or dangerous adventure. Give specific reasons for attempting such a challenge and explain exactly how you would prepare yourself.

22. Disputes sometimes arise over the use of public lands or the allocation of public funds. Each side offers what appears to be a reasonable argument. Here are some samples of recent debates.

    a. Should funds from the federal gas tax (less than 1 percent) be spent on bicycle projects such as bike lanes, trails, and parking facilities? Opponents say we can't afford such luxuries because we don't have enough money to repair highways and bridges needed to ensure public safety. Cyclists say that riding a bike is not a luxury; streets must be safe for all those who bike to work, and thus reduce pollution, traffic, and wear on the roads.

    b. Environmentalists want to remove the automobile from Yosemite National Park to preserve the natural beauty by limiting the number of people in the park at a given time. Opponents counter that shuttles, day-use reservations, and higher fees will keep out ordinary American families to benefit a few hikers and backpackers.

    c. A similar argument has arisen in regard to the Grand Canyon. One group would ban or severely limit flights of small planes and helicopters over the park, charging that they contribute to the smog problem and disturb the tranquility of visitors who have come to enjoy the natural beauty. The defenders of these flights maintain that people should have the opportunity to enjoy the grandeur of the canyon in this unique way.

    Explain where you stand on one of these issues. You may not want to take either side, but, instead, propose a compromise. If you know of a similar debate in your area, you may, of course, write about that problem.

23. Every year a few top collegiate and professional athletes receive awards in recognition of their outstanding performances. What makes the "superstar" stand out from his or her extremely talented fellow athletes? Consider talent, coaching, discipline, motivation, and any other factors that may explain this athletic excellence. Or you may choose to write about the "superstar" in one of the performing arts.

24. Have you ever received a gift that you liked so much that you still remember how you felt when you opened the package? Describe the gift and explain what you particularly liked about it. When did you get it? Was the gift special, in part, because of your relationship with the giver? Was the gift a complete surprise, or was it something you had been wanting for a long time? Do you still have the gift? What is its condition today? If you no longer have it, what happened to it?

OR

Write about the pleasure you had planning and giving a gift to someone. Consider some of the questions above.

25. As you may already know, being sick can be expensive. If you have had to visit a doctor or an emergency room lately, you know how expensive it is. The situation is especially critical for those people who are at the poverty level, those who are called "the working poor." The "working poor" are those people who have an annual income below $15,000, and they frequently do not have the means to pay medical bills. In responding to the following questions, consider their problems." How do you think that medical bills should be paid? Should the patient have to pay all or part of the bill? Should either the state or the federal government pick up the bill? What should be the role of insurance companies? Discuss your opinions about the ways to pay for medical care by jotting down your ideas as they occur to you. Then select the two or three ideas you feel qualified to develop with specific support. You may want to inquire about the current methods of payment available in your state. Or, if you work, you may want to interview a person in the insurance department who can help answer some of these questions before you begin writing.

OR

If you prefer, write about one of the following subjects:
a. Your own situation
b. Uninsured children
c. Unemployed people
d. Elderly retired low-income people
Use the questions above as a guide in developing your paper.

26. Family lifestyles are changing. With the dramatic increase in single-parent and dual-career households, family life isn't as simple as it once was. Long commutes to and from work, community and school functions in the evenings, and involvement in health spa programs, social clubs, hobbies, and other leisure activities all occupy more family time. How have these factors affected family life today?

27. Many colleges have spent millions of dollars on wiring for "smart" classrooms (Internet-connected lecture halls) in the belief that technology will transform the way we learn. Some professors plan to change the way they teach their courses. For example, students can view film clips, hear speeches, and rearrange the material, write about it, and share it with someone in another location. If you have had an opportunity to access the Internet, do you agree or disagree with using this method to teach college courses? Give specific examples of how a student can benefit from access to the Internet.

If you disagree with using the Internet to teach courses, give specific reasons for your opinions.

28. **A possible topic for ESL students:** How would conducting business in your culture differ from doing business in the American culture? For example, in a "Japanese meeting, if you try to deviate from the prearranged agenda and force consideration of a new topic, you might make the business people very uncomfortable. The emphasis on conformity in the Japanese culture discourages individual initiative. Further, when Westerners speak, Japanese will often say, "Hai" (yes). This "hai" means, "Yes, I understand you," not "Yes, I agree with you." Because the Japanese person will attempt to tell a Westerner what he wants to hear, the American may think the other person is agreeing with him, when, in fact, they do not agree.

   If you identify with a different culture, explain how that culture's attitudes, speech patterns, and interpersonal behavior patterns would affect the way business is conducted. Compare and contrast those interactions with those in the United States.

29. Advertisers, as you know, use a variety of approaches to sell their products to us. Cut out an advertisement from a magazine or a newspaper and analyze the primary appeal it makes to the reader. As you study the ad, jot down your ideas in answer to the following questions. Include as many examples as you can find.

   a. If there is a picture, how is it part of the appeal? Did it attract you to the ad? How?
   b. Are the words persuasive?
   c. You have learned the importance of having the reader in mind when you write. Does the advertiser seem to be addressing a specific customer?
   d. Does the ad make any promises? Are there any facts?
   e. Does the ad appeal to any specific emotion or emotions?
   f. How successful is the advertisement? Would it persuade you to buy the product?

   Bring your advertisement and your notes to class. Form a group with three classmates to discuss your work in preparation for writing your rough draft. If your instructor approves, meet again to help each other with your rough drafts.

   You could meet with your group before you look for an ad and decide upon a single class of advertisements for all the members of your group to work on; for example, travel, cosmetics, pharmaceuticals, dental products, computers, insurance, or any number of others.

30. Do you exercise to keep fit as many other people do? Why do you believe it is important to exercise regularly? Describe the best way you have found to keep in shape. Supply specific details about the equipment needed, any problems you have encountered, successes you have had, or any other details to interest your reader in your experiences.

   Concentrate on one or two methods of keeping fit. Illustrate your successes or your failures by telling your reader exactly how you progressed at each step of training.

   If you do not exercise, write about the reasons for your choice.

31. Describe in detail a place on your college campus that has made an impression on you or has a strong attraction for you. When you write about this topic, you will be observing a scene firsthand.

     Step 1. Read the paragraph about the guitar store in Chapter 3 (Exercise 3D) as an example of observation and description.

     Step 2. Choose a place where you can sit comfortably and take notes as you observe what is going on around you. Look at the place as if you were seeing it for the first time. Describe the people you see. What activities are taking place? What do you hear? Imagine that your reader is a friend or a relative living in another state who has not seen your campus. What notes must you take to be able to write in detail about it?

     Step 3. After you have completed your notes, arrange the details. See if you can group some of the ideas together into three or four main points. Turn to Chapter 10 for instructions on how to make a simple outline.

     Step 4. As you plan your paragraph, decide what is most significant about your observation of the place. Focus on a single impression. For example, perhaps you enjoy the weekly campus concerts. You might say, "The design of our small campus theater added to my enjoyment of the noon concert last Wednesday."

     Step 5. Remember to develop each main supporting point with enough specific details to give your reader a clear picture of the place.

Glossary

Action verb   Tells what the subject does, did, or will do.

Adjective   Modifies a noun or pronoun. Answers one of the following questions: What kind? How many? Which one? Whose?

Adverb   Modifies a verb, adjective, or other adverb. Answers one of the following questions: When? Why? How? Where?

Adverbial connective   (for example, however, nevertheless, then) Used with a semicolon and a comma to join main clauses. Also called an adverbial conjunction or a conjunctive adverb.

Agreement   The matching in number, gender, and person between subjects and verbs or pronouns and antecedents.

Antecedent   The noun, pronoun, or noun phrase to which a pronoun refers.

Auxiliary verb   The helping verb used with a main verb to form a verb phrase.

Base form of the verb   The present form of the verb with no -s at the end.

Collective noun   (for example, family) Refers to a collection of persons, places, things, ideas, or activities.

Comma splice   Grammatical error made when main clauses are joined with only a comma and no connective.

Common noun   Names people, places, things, ideas, or activities in general.

Comparative   A form of the adjective or adverb used to compare two people, places, ideas, things, or actions.

Completer   Follows a linking verb to describe or rename the subject.

Complex sentence   Composed of a main clause and one or more subordinate clauses.

Compound antecedent   Two or more antecedents joined by a coordinating connective.

Compound object   Two or more objects joined by a coordinating connective.

Compound sentence   Two or more main clauses joined by a connective and appropriate punctuation.

Compound subject   Two or more subjects joined by a coordinating connective.

Compound verb   Two or more verbs joined by a coordinating connective.

Contraction   A word formed by combining two words with an apostrophe to substitute for the omission of letters.

Coordinating connective   (and, but, or, for, nor, so, yet) Used with a comma to join words, phrases, and main clauses. Also called a coordinating conjunction.

Dangling modifier   An adjective or adverb that does not modify any word in the sentence.

Gender   Refers to the masculine, feminine, or neuter forms of third person pronouns.

Indefinite pronoun   (for example, anyone or someone)   Refers to people, things, or ideas in general rather than to specific antecedents.

Irregular verb   Does not follow any spelling rules to form the past tense.

Linking verb   Shows a relationship between the subject and the completer.

Main clause   (independent clause)   A group of related words with a subject and a verb that can stand alone as a sentence if the first word is capitalized and the clause ends with a mark of punctuation such as a period or a question mark.

Misplaced modifier   An adjective or adverb that has been placed next to a word it does not modify.

Modifier   Describes, limits, or makes specific another word in the sentence.

Noun   Names a person, place, thing, idea, or activity.

Noun marker   (for example, a, an, the) An adjective that points to the noun that follows it.

Number   Indicates the singular and plural forms of pronouns. Singular means one person or thing. Plural means more than one person or thing.

Object   The noun or pronoun that answers the question "What?" or "Whom?" after an action verb. Objects also follow prepositions.

Parallel structure   The placing of similar items in similar grammatical form.

Participle   A verb form that may function as part of a verb phrase (was winning) or as an adjective (the winning team).

Past participle   Formed by adding -d or -ed to the base form of a regular verb.

Perfect tenses   Formed by using a form of the auxiliary verb have and the past participle of the main verb.

Person   Indicates the person speaking, the person spoken to, or the person or thing spoken about.

Phrase   Group of words without a subject and a verb. Examples are noun phrases, verbal phrases, verb phrases, and prepositional phrases.

Possessive noun   Changes spelling to indicate a belonging-to relationship.

Preposition   Used to show position, direction, or relationship.

Present participle   Formed by adding -ing to the base form of a verb.

Pronoun   Takes the place of a noun or refers to a noun. A personal pronoun shows person, number, and gender.

Proper noun   Names a specific person, place, thing, idea, or activity.

Regular verb   Adds -d or -ed to form the past tense.

Run-on sentence   A grammatical error made when main clauses are joined with no punctuation or connective between them.

Sentence   Has at least one subject and one verb and expresses a complete thought.

Sentence fragment   Begins with a capital letter and ends with a period, but does not express a complete thought or contain a main clause.

Simple sentence   Composed of one main clause.

Subject   The person or thing the verb is asking or telling about.

Subject of a command   Understood to be "you."

Subordinate clause   (dependent clause) A group of related words with a subject and a verb introduced by a subordinator. Makes an incomplete statement, so it must be attached to a main clause to be a complete sentence.

Subordinator   (for example, because, that, although)   Used to introduce a subordinate clause.

Superlative   A form of the adjective or adverb used to compare three or more items.

Tense   The change of verb form to indicate when the action occurred.

Verb   A word or group of words indicating action or a state of being.

Verb phrase   The combination of an auxiliary verb and one of the principal forms of a verb.

Verbal   Formed from a verb but cannot function as a main verb. Used as a noun, adjective, or adverb.

Verbal phrase   A group of words that includes a verbal, a noun, and/or a prepositional phrase.

Index